Rand McNally and Company

Unrivaled Chicago

Containing an Historical Narrative of the Great City's Development....

Rand McNally and Company

Unrivaled Chicago

Containing an Historical Narrative of the Great City's Development....

ISBN/EAN: 9783337030827

Printed in Europe, USA, Canada, Australia, Japan

Cover: Foto ©Andreas Hilbeck / pixelio.de

More available books at **www.hansebooks.com**

All About the Baby

and....
Preparations for its Advent; also Instruction as to the use of

Homeopathic Remedies

For the Treatment of Ordinary Ailments.

Many a serious disease might be averted by timely treatment, and the object of this volume is to instruct the mother on the proper care of her child, and to give this information in as plain and simple a manner as possible.

··· SOLD BY SUBSCRIPTION ONLY ···

Illustrated and Handsomely Bound in Polished Silk Cloth, Octavo, with Embossed Design in Gold and Colors   **$2.50**

Rand, McNally & Co., Publishers,

AGENTS WANTED.   166 Adams Street, Chicago.

THE LATEST ACKNOWLEDGED

Standard Manual

FOR

Presidents, Secretaries, Directors, Chairmen, Presiding Officers,

AND EVERYONE IN ANY WAY CONNECTED WITH PUBLIC LIFE OR CORPORATE BODIES, IS

Reed's Rules

BY

HON. THOMAS B. REED,
Speaker of the House of Representatives.

"Reasonable, right, as I read."
    J. STERLING MORTON, Secretary of Agriculture.
"I commend the book most highly."
    W. McKINLEY, Governor of Ohio.

IN HANDY POCKET FORM.
    CLOTH, 75 CENTS; LEATHER, $1.25.

RAND, McNALLY & CO., CHICAGO.

Maps and Guides

TO ALL OF THE

Principal Cities

AND

EVERY COUNTRY
...IN THE WORLD

Globes, Map Racks, Spring Map Rollers, German Maps, Wall and Pocket Maps, Historical Maps, Classical, Biblical, Historical, Anatomical, Astronomical, Physical, and General Atlases of all kinds kept in stock. Address

RAND, McNALLY & CO.,
Map Publishers and Engravers.
162 to 172 Adams Street, CHICAGO.

there is no establishment so remarkable as our

"STORE OF ALL THE PEOPLE,'

no production so unique, so wonderful in its effect upon the affairs of the People (we mean the thrifty, wide awake ones), as our new . . . .

General Catalogue and
♦ ♦ ♦ ♦ ♦ Buyers' Guide......

GET IT—GET OTHERS TO GET IT.

"It" is a book of 700 pages, containing 13,000 illustrations, and more than 40,000 dependable descriptions, including almost everything that's used in life.

"It" tells you what you ought to pay, no matter what you buy, or where you buy it.

"It" should be in the house of every bright buyer, the true and trusty guide to the value of all that's bought, showing how and where the most and best for the money may be had.

"It" is sent to any address for 15 cents, in coin or stamps. The book itself is free —the 15 cents is to pay part of the actual postage or expressage.

WE SAY AGAIN: GET IT—GET OTHERS TO GET IT,

for the CO-OPERATION of the People is what enables us to make and maintain prices in their favor, saving them the always high, and often exorbitant, charges of "middlemen."

THE STORE OF ALL THE PEOPLE.
MONARCHS OF THE MAIL ORDER BUSINESS.

Call and look through our great 10-acre store when in the city. We have uniformed guides, who will show you all points of interest; and, our word for it, you'll enjoy and never forget the visit.

111 to 116 Michigan Avenue, CHICAGO.

UNRIVALED CHICAGO

CONTAINING

AN HISTORICAL NARRATIVE

OF

THE GREAT CITY'S DEVELOPMENT

AND

DESCRIPTIONS OF POINTS OF INTEREST, SUCH AS
PARKS, BOULEVARDS, PROMINENT BUILDINGS, PUBLIC INSTITUTIONS,
COLLEGES, RAILROAD DEPOTS, HOTELS, ETC.

WITH

BIOGRAPHICAL SKETCHES OF REPRESENTATIVE MEN
IN THEIR SEVERAL LINES.

PROFUSELY ILLUSTRATED

AND

ACCOMPANIED BY TWO ACCURATE MAPS OF THE CITY.

CHICAGO AND NEW YORK:
RAND, McNALLY & COMPANY, PUBLISHERS.
1897.

Kimball Pianos

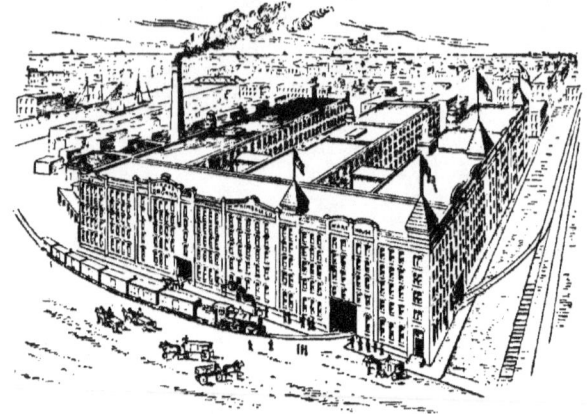

PIANO AND ORGAN FACTORIES OF W. W. KIMBALL CO., CHICAGO, U. S. A.

Output thirty Pianos and sixty Organs a day.
Floor space eleven acres.

Kimball Pianos were accorded Highest Honors at the World's Fair.

The following is a partial list of the many eminent musicians who use and recommend these instruments:

Adelina Patti.	Emma Eames.	Lillian Nordica.	Katherina Klafsky.
Emma Calvé.	Jean de Reszke.	Max Alvary.	Victor Maurel.
Lilli Lehmann.	Édouard de Reszke.	Francesco Tamagno.	G. Campanari.
Sophia Scalchi.	A. De Novellis.	Giuseppe Del Puente.	Francisco Vignas.
Minnie Hauk.	Jean Lassalle.	Fernando De Lucia.	Mario Ancona.
Emma Albani.	L. Mancinelli.	Conrad Behrens.	Paul Kalisch.
Rosa Sucher.	E. Bevignani.	Emil Fischer.	Luigi Arditi.
E. Fursch-Madi.	Pol. Plancon.	Pablo De Sarasate.	Durward Lely.
Guirrina Fabbri.	Emil Liebling.	Ovide Musin.	A. Mascheroni.
Clementine De Vere.	Chas. Kunkel.	Luigi Ravelli.	E. Remenyi.
Olimpia Guercia.	C. M. Ziehrer.	Julius Perotti.	Theodor Salmon.
Marie Tavary.	John Phillip Sousa.	Antonio Galassi.	E. Ruschweyh.
Pauline L'Allemand.	Robert Goldbeck.	Zelie de Lussan.	Henri Marteau.
Marguerite Samuel.	W. E. Heimendahl.	P. S. Gilmore.	César Thomson.

The Piano thus indorsed by the collective genius and authorities of the world may be found in large variety, together with the KIMBALL REED ORGANS and KIMBALL PIPE ORGANS, at the salesrooms of

W. W. Kimball Company,

Kimball Hall, Wabash Ave., near Jackson Street, ————Chicago.

Copyright, 1896, by Rand, McNally & Co.

GENERAL INDEX.

SUBJECTS.

Subject	Page
American Biscuit Co.	60
Armour Institute of Technology	96
Art Institute	95
Auditorium, The	84
Board of Trade	52
Board of Trade Building	51
Booth A. Packing Co.	62
Business Interests	51
Central Boulevard	17
Chamber of Commerce Building	51
Chicago Academy of Sciences	95
Chicago Astronomical Society	95
Chicago Athenaeum	96
Chicago College of Dental Surgery	123
Chicago College of Law	89
Chicago Edison Co.	59
Chicago Historical Society	96
Chicago Homeopathic Medical College	93
Chicago Opera House	86
Chicago Policlinic	93
Chicago Public Library	97
Chicago Telephone Co.	58
Chicago Varnish Co.	63
Chicago Veterinary College	95
Churches	98
City Parks	25
College of Physicians and Surgeons	93
College of Liberal Arts	88
Columbia Theater	85
Common Schools, The	88
Criminal Court and County Jail	31
Dental School, N. W. University	124
Dentists	
Depots	32
Douglas Boulevard	20
Douglas Park	20
Drainage System, The	28
Drexel Boulevard	23
Dunham Medical College	93
Early History	6
Fire Department	29
Fire of July, 1874	13
First National Bank	53
Gage Park	20
Garfield Park	17
Garfield Boulevard	20
Government Building	33
Graceland Cemetery	77
Grand Boulevard	24
Grand Opera House	86
Great Educational Center	88
Great Fire, The	13
Greatest Medical Center	102
Great Northern Theater	86
Hahnemann Hospital, The	116
Harbor	30
Haymarket Square	75
Henrici, Philip	61
Higher Institutions	88
Hooley's Theater	85
Hotels	82
Humboldt Boulevard	16
Humboldt Park	16
Illinois Art Association	95
Illinois Training School	95
Introduction	1
Jackson Park	23
Kaestner, Chas. & Co.	66
Lake Forest College	90
Lake Forest University	90
Lake Shore Drive	16
Lamson Bros. & Co.	54
Law Institute	98
Law School, N. W. University	88
Lawyers	35
Lincoln Park	16
McVicker's Theater	85
Marion-Sims Training School	95
Medical Libraries	98
Medical School, N. W. University	88
Michigan ave. Boulevard	25
Midway Plaisance	23
Military	34
Milwaukee Avenue	77
New City, The	14
Newberry Library	98
Northwestern University, The	88
Oakwood Boulevard	24
Orchestral Association, The	84
Park System, The	16
Physicians	100
Physio-Medical College	93
Places of Amusement	82
Police	29
Post-Graduate Medical College	117
Presbyterian Hospital	112
Public Buildings	34
Relic House	77
Rush Medical College	90
Schiller Theater	86
School of Pharmacy, N. W. University	88
Schwarz, Dupee & Co.	53
Southwest Boulevard	20
South Bend, Ind.	77
Studebaker Building, Michigan ave.	66
Studebaker Building, Wabash ave.	67
Thirty-fifth Street Boulevard	24
Track Elevation	28
Union Park	20
Union Stock Yards	51
University of Chicago	92
University of Ills. School of Pharmacy	92
Washington Boulevard	21
Washington Park	21
Water Supply, The	27
Western Bank Note & Eng. Co.	61
Woman's College	88
Woman's Medical School	89

BIOGRAPHY.

Name	Page
Adams, George E.	36
Aldrich, Chas. H.	36
Bancroft, Edgar A.	36
Barnum, Wm. H.	37
Belfield, Dr. W. T.	101
Bevan, Dr. A. D.	100
Bisbee, Lewis H.	37
Bishop, Dr. S. S.	102
Bond, Lester I.	38
Brewster, E. L.	54
Brophy, Dr. T. W.	124
Brown, Geo.	39
Brown, Dr. Sanger	101
Bucklin, H. E.	58
Bunker, Chas. H.	61
Byford, Dr. Henry T.	104
Camp, Isaac N.	70
Coe, Albert L.	77
Colburn, Dr. J. E.	104
Coleman, Dr. W. Franklin	103
Collins, L. C. Jr.	47
Counselman, Charles	55
Cowperthwait, Dr. A. C.	106
Crofts, Clayton E.	38
Cudahy, John	57
Davis, Dr. Chas. G.	105
Davis, Jr. Dr. N. S.	105
Dunn, John	79
Dunning, Andrew	74
Eberhart, John F.	80
Elliott, Edward S.	46
Elliott, William S., Jr.	41
Etheridge, Dr. J. H.	107
Forsyth, Jacob	65
Fowler, Frank T.	65
Gage, Lyman J.	53
Gilman, Dr. John E.	108
Goldspohn, Dr. A.	109
Gray, W. H.	74
Gridley, Nelson C.	40
Grosvenor, Dr. L. C.	109
Harper, Dr. John E.	101
Harper, William H.	56
Harvey, George M.	66
Hedges, Dr. S. P.	110
Hill, Lysander	41
Hirschl, Andrew J.	46
Hurd, Harvey B.	44
Hyde, Dr. James N.	111
Ingals, Dr. E. Fletcher	111
Isham, Dr. R. N.	113
Ives & David, Drs.	112
Jacobs, B. F.	70
Jay, Dr. Milton	113
Jones, J. M. W.	71
Jones, Dr. Samuel J.	112
Karpen, Adolph	66
Keeney, James F.	75
Kent, Sidney A.	55
Kimball, Wm. W.	74
Kimbark, S. D.	79
King, Dr. Oscar A.	114
Knight, Clarence A.	42
Kretzinger, Geo. W.	40
Kurz, Adolph	45
Law, Robert	63
Lawrence, Edward F.	53
Learning, Jeremiah	42
Low, Dr. James E.	124
Lowden, Frank G.	43
Ludlam, Dr. Reuben	116
Madden, Martin B.	64
Manierre, Dr. Chas. E.	115
Mann, James B.	43
Martin, Dr. Franklin H.	115
Mason, Wm. E.	44
McArthur, Dr. L. L.	100
McFatrich, Drs. Jas. B. and Geo. W.	114
Miller, John S.	38
Miller, Dr. Truman W.	118
Monroe, H. S.	45
Montgomery, Dr. J. H.	115
Newman, Dr. Henry P.	118
Owens, Dr. John E.	119
Parker, J. Grafton	78
Parker, John R.	47
Pratt, Dr. Edwin H.	121
Quincey, T. S.	72
Robinson, Daniel B.	65
Rosenthal, James	45
Rosenthal, Kurz & Hirschl	45
Sattley, W. N.	71
Scanlan, Kickham	48
Schneider, George	63
Schoeninger, Adolph	60
Sherman, E. B.	45
Smith, Abner	37
Smith, Dunlap	78
Smith, Lloyd J.	79
Spalding, Dr. Homan	120
Stearns, Dr. W. M.	121
Stensland, P. O.	30
Streeter, Dr. J. W.	119
Studebaker, Peter E.	66
Sudduth, Dr. Wm. X.	121
Tatge, William H.	46
Thornton, Charles S.	49
Torrence, J. T.	72
Trainor, John C.	40
Vocke, William	48
Wacker, Charles H.	68
Wait, Horatio L.	50
Wheeler, Harris A.	57
Winston, Frederick S.	51

GENERAL INDEX.

ILLUSTRATIONS.

Name	Page
Adams, George E.	36
Aldrich, Chas. H.	26
Armour Institute	95
Auditorium Hotel, entrance to Michigan ave.	83
Bancroft, Edgar A.	37
Barnum, Wm. H.	37
Belfield, Dr. Wm. T.	101
Bevan, Dr. A. D.	100
Bisbee, Lewis H.	37
Bishop, Dr. S. S.	102
Board of Trade Building	53
Bond, L. L.	38
Booth, A., Packing Co.'s Building	62
Brewster, E. L.	54
Brooks, Dr. Almon, Residence	103
Brophy, Dr. T. W.	124
Brown, George W.	39
Brown, Dr. Sanger	102
Bucklin, H. E., Building	58
Bucklin, H. E.	59
Bunker, Chas. H.	62
Byford, Dr. Henry T.	104
Camp, Isaac N.	71
Chicago Athletic Association	22
Chicago College of Dental Surgery	123
Chicago University, The	91
Chicago Varnish Co.'s Building	53
Coe, Albert L.	77
Colburn, Dr. Joseph E.	104
Coleman, Dr. W. F.	104
College of Physicians and Surgeons	93
Collins, L. C., Jr.	47
Columbus Memorial Building	25
Corner State and Monroe Streets	1
Counselman, Chas.	55
Cowperthwait, Dr. A. C.	106
Crafts, Clayton E.	38
Cudahy, John	57
Davis, Dr. Charles G.	105
Davis, Jr., Dr. N. S.	105
Dunn, John	80
Dynamo Room, Edison Co.	6
Eberhart, John F.	80
Elk in Lincoln Park	19
Elliott, Edward B.	40
Elliott, Wm. B., Jr.	71
Etheridge, Dr. John F.	102
Field, M. & Co.'s Building	85
First National Bank Building	54
Fourth Baptist Church	98
Fowler, Frank T.	65
Gage, Lyman J.	55
Gilman, Dr. John F.	108
Goldspohn, Dr. A.	109
Graceland Cemetery, Scene in	78
Grand Pacific Hotel	5
Grant Monument	3
Gray, Wm. H.	74
Gridley, N. C.	40
Grosvenor, Dr. L. C.	110
Harper, Wm. H.	57
Haymarket Square	76
Hedges, Dr. S. P.	111
Herald Building	12
Hirschl, Andrew J.	46
Hurd, Harvey B.	44
Hyde, Dr. James N.	111
Ingals, Dr. E. Fletcher	111
Insurance Exchange Building	27
Isham, Dr. R. N.	113
Jay, Dr. Milton	113
Jones, Dr. S. J.	113
Jones, J. M. W.	71
Kaestner, Chas. & Co.'s Building	66
Karpen, Adolph	65
Keeney, James F.	75
Kent, S. A.	56
Kimbark, S. D.	79
Kimball, W. W.	75
King, Dr. Oscar A.	114
Knight, Clarence A.	42
Knights Templar and Masons' Life Indemnity Co.	84
Kreizinger, Geo. W.	40
Kurz, Adolph	46
Lawrence, Edward F.	54
Leaming, Jeremiah	42
Lily Pond, Lincoln Park	90
Lily Pond, Washington Park	21
Lincoln Monument	32
Lincoln Park	18
Lincoln Park	15
Linne, Statue of	24
Low, Dr. James F.	124
Lowden, Frank O.	43
Ludlam, Dr. Reuben	116
Madden, M. B.	64
Manierre, Dr. Chas. E.	115
Mann, James R.	43
Map, Mouth of River	8
Marlin, Dr. Franklin H.	115
Mason, Wm. E.	44
Masonic Temple, The	100
McArthur, Dr. L. L.	100
McCormick Seminary	94
McFatrick, Dr. Geo. W.	114
McFatrick, Dr. James B.	114
Medical Center, View of	103
Miller, Dr. Truman W.	118
Milwaukee Ave.	77
Monadnock Block	14
Monroe, H. S.	45
Newberry Library	96
Newman, Dr. H. P.	118
New England Congregational Ch'ch.	99
Ottawa Indian Monument	9
Owens, Dr. John E.	119
Parker, J. Grafton	78
Parker, John R.	47
Post-Graduate Medical School	117
Pratt, Dr. Edwin H.	122
Presbyterian Hospital	112
Quincey, T. S.	72
Rand-McNally Building	30
Relic House	77
Rosenthal, James	46
Rush Medical College	92
Sattley, W. N.	71
Scanlan, Kickham	48
Schiller, Statue of	10
Schiller, Theater	87
Schoeninger, Adolph, Residence	70
Schoeninger, Adolph	68
Seal Pond	17
Sherman, E. B.	45
Smith, Abner	35
Smith, Dunlap	78
Smith, Lloyd J.	55
South Water Street	20
Spalding, Dr. Homan	120
Star Accident Building	72
State Street, north from Quincy	4
Stearns, Dr. W. M.	121
Stensland, P. O.	52
Streeter Hospital, The	120
Streeter, Dr. J. W.	120
Studebaker Building, Wabash ave.	68
Studebaker Building, Michigan ave.	67
Studebaker, Peter E.	66
Studebaker Residence, South Bend	68
Studebaker Works, South Bend	67
Sudduth, Wm. X.	121
Tacoma Building	52
Taige, Wm. H.	47
Thornton, Chas. S.	49
Torrence, J. T., Residence of	74
Torrence, J. T.	74
Trainor, John C.	49
Union Park	23
Union Stock Yards	75
Unity Unitarian Church	97
Venetian Building	89
Vocke, William	49
Wacker, Charles H.	68
Wait, Horatio L.	50
Western Bank Note Co.'s Building	86
Wheeler, H. A.	58
Winston, Frederick S.	51
Wisner, Albert, Residence	86

INTRODUCTION.

THE QUEEN OF THE CONTINENT, with her throne planted on the west shore of Lake Michigan, and with a domain which extends to every part of the Western Hemisphere, which men have named "Chicago," could not have selected a more unpromising location, so far as outward appearances went, when that location was determined.

A broad swamp, threaded by sluggish bayous, rank with skunk cabbage, wild garlic, and other unsavory weeds, certainly could have given but slight grounds for predicting a future city. Moreover, it is claimed by those whose opinion is entitled to respect, that it was only through a sheer error that the city which should have grown up about the mouth of the St. Joseph or the Calumet, came to be located around here, on the western side of the lake; and that the land which the government actually bought for its fort at the mouth of the Chekagou river, was a very fair section in Indiana, and not the swamp which was inadvertently taken. In early days the ditch now known as the Chicago river reached back into the prairie within a very short distance of the Des Plaines (with which it has since been united), leaving only a short portage to be made in a journey from the far Eastern lakes to the mouth of the Mississippi. And later, when the Northwest

A BUSY CORNER — STATE AND MONROE STREETS.

took on its marvelous development, inviting the great railways of the East into harvest fields already ripe, there was no route available for them but that around Lake Michigan, and through the struggling young town just beyond the foot of the lake. But even the early residents of the place never dreamed that it would attain commercial prominence, and the time is still within memory, when the inhabitants feared the ruination of their town by canals and railways! To-day, however, it is the centre of a full third of the railway mileage of the United States, and the most rapidly prospering city on the continent.

Chicago is situated on the west shore of Lake Michigan, in latitude 41° 53' north, and longitude 87° 38' west from Greenwich. It has a frontage on the lake of about twenty miles, inclusive of the parks at either extremity of the city, affording fine dockage and harborage.

From the lake, at Water street, the Chicago river extends west about half a mile, to Canal street, where it divides into two branches, one extending in a northwesterly direction through that portion of the city, and the other southward, for about a mile and a half, to Fourteenth street, where it makes a sweep to the westward as far as Bridgeport, among the lumber yards. Here it again divides into two unimportant secondary branches (reaching one west and one south), and empties itself into the Illinois & Michigan Canal, through which it is united with the Des Plaines river.

Thus, the main stem of the Chicago river divides the eastern portion of the city into two parts, one of which is known in common parlance as the "South Side," and the other as the "North Side." These two branches, again, separate the North and South Sides from the West Side, all that portion of the city lying west of these branches being known by this title. Communication between the different portions is kept up by means of thirty-two swing bridges, and these are further supplemented by three tunnels, one at Washington street and one at Van Buren street, connecting the South with the West Side, and the third forming a similar link between the North and South Sides, at La Salle street.

Chicago is the centre of 76,865 miles of railroad leading into it from the west, and receives from the east the terminals of over 11,336 miles of through lines, exclusive of connections. Seven passenger depots accommodate the traffic of thirty companies, and receive through passengers from all points of the compass. These depots are all situated at convenient distances from the business centre. The Union Depot, used by the Pittsburgh, Fort Wayne & Chicago; Chicago, Burlington & Quincy; Chicago & Alton; Chicago, St. Louis & Pittsburgh, and the Chicago, Milwaukee & St. Paul roads,—is situated on the west side of the river, on Canal street, corner of Adams street. The Dearborn Station, which accommodates the following roads: Chicago & Eastern Illinois; Atchison, Topeka & Santa Fe; Chicago & Grand Trunk; New York, Lake Erie & Western; Louisville, New Albany & Chicago, and the Wabash roads, is on the South Side, a few squares south of the Post Office, at the intersection of Polk and Dearborn streets. The Rock Island Depot, accommodating the Lake Shore & Michigan Southern; Chicago, Rock Island & Pacific, and the New York, Chicago & St. Louis roads, is on the South Side, corner of Van Buren and Sherman streets. The Michigan Central, Illinois Central, Cleveland, Cincinnati, Chicago & St. Louis; Chicago & West Michigan, occupy the magnificent Central Depot on the lake front, at the foot of Twelfth street. The Chicago & North-Western occupies a separate depot, on the North Side, at the corner of Wells and Kinzie streets, east of the north branch of the Chicago river. The new depot of the Wisconsin Central, Baltimore & Ohio, Chicago Great Western, and Northern Pacific roads, is east of the river, at the corner of Harrison street and Fifth avenue. As before intimated, every one of these depots is within a few minutes' walk of all the important public buildings, and the business centre of the city.

Commercially, the city is well defined in its localities. Thus, the lumber, grain, and shipping interests occupy nearly the entire river frontage; the South Side, from the river to Twelfth street, is given over principally to hotels, stores, public buildings, offices, and commercial establishments; the North Side, the remaining portion of the South Side, and the West Side, west of Halsted street (about one-half mile beyond the South Branch), are given over to residences, while the manufacturing interests occupy the intervening portion of the West Side, and the outskirts of the city in all directions. A belt line railroad encircling the entire city connects all the railroads.

Intramural communication is very complete, surface or elevated railroads intersecting the city in every direction. Of elevated roads there are three—the Alley South Side Elevated, which starts from Congress street, between State street and Wabash avenue, and runs south to Jackson Park at 63d street. The Lake Street Elevated, which runs a short distance north from its terminus at Madison and Market streets, to Lake street, and thence west beyond the city limits to Oak Park; and the Metropolitan Elevated, which, starting from Jackson and Franklin streets, runs west to the city limits, a branch running north from Marshfield avenue station. This branch divides at Robey station, one division running west to Lawndale avenue station, the other north to Logan square station. There are altogether about 521 miles of street, horse, cable, electric, and ele-

INTRODUCTION.

vated railways in operation within the city limits, furnishing cheap transportation to all parts. The Chicago City Railway Company owns all the lines upon the South Side (excepting terminals of other companies), and has 162.37 miles of track, of which 34 3-4 miles are operated by cable, most of the balance being operated by electricity.

The West Chicago Street Railway Company operates the West Side horse and cable system, and owns 201 1-2 miles of track, of which 30.42 miles are operated by cable, and 122.28 miles by electricity. There are 1,901 cars, and 1,666 horses. The company has six power houses.

The North Chicago Street Railway Company operates about 107 miles of surface roads, partly by cable and partly by electricity. To this must be added 14 miles operated by the General Street Railway Company, a new rival in the field, and about 36½ miles of elevated railroads, either in operation or nearly completed. When the present system of intra-mural travel is finished, no city in the world will be better furnished than Chicago.

All of these roads have their termini within a few squares of the City Hall, and afford convenient means for reaching any part of the city. Besides these and many other minor companies, various steam roads running in different directions have local stations within short distances of each other, and run suburban trains at short intervals.

The streets are laid out at right angles, and the houses are—with the single exception of those on streets running north and south in the South Division—numbered from one regularly

THE GRANT MONUMENT, LINCOLN PARK.

upward; the east and west streets being numbered from the lake westward to the river, and, again, from the river westward; and the others from Randolph street, and, west of Ashland avenue, from Lake street, as the dividing lines, north and south. The exception noted above is, that south of Twelfth street, the streets and avenues take their initial numbers from the streets which they cross. Thus, beyond Twelfth street the numbers run from 1200 upward until Thirteenth street is reached, when they begin again with 1300, and so on. A movement is on foot to apply this simple method to the entire city; but at present a street number guide is necessary to a stranger who wishes to find his way about easily.

Chicago's rapid growth in population has be-

Pork packing is one of the principal industries, the growth of which is shown in the following table. Number of hogs packed in Chicago during the year:

    1854...................... 52,849
    1860...................... 151,339
    1871...................... 919,997
    1881......................5,752,191
    1895......................5,784,670

Beef packing has grown with like rapidity.

STATE STREET, LOOKING NORTH FROM QUINCY STREET.

come proverbial—about 20 per cent. annual increase—and her rise in wealth and importance has been phenomenal. A few figures will suffice to illustrate this development. Population:

    1830......................   70
    1840......................   4,853
    1850......................   29,963
    1860...................... 112,172
    1870...................... 298,977
    1880...................... 503,185
    1890......................1,208,669
    1894......................1,657,727

During the season of 1863-64, there were packed here 70,086 cattle, while in 1894-95, the number had risen to 1,803,466. The grain trade has increased from 6,928,459 bushels received in 1853, and 37,235,027 bushels in 1860, to 189,432,819 bushels in 1891. Shipments, which began with 78 bushels of wheat in 1838, had grown by 1870 to 54,745,903 bushels of grain of all kinds (flour included, reduced to its equivalent in grain), and in 1895 reached the sum of 171,464,137. The lumber receipts, which in 1853 aggregated 202,101,000 feet, and 93,483,000 shingles, had reached, in 1895, 1,638,130,000 feet, and 352,-

313,000 shingles. Salt receipts had increased in the same period from 81,789 to 1,994,056 barrels; coal, from 38,548 to 6,091,284 tons; hides. from 1,274,311 to 90,822,102 pounds; wool, from 1,030,600 to 51,371,694 pounds. The clearing house statement of the associated banks of Chicago for the past six years is as follows:

1887	$2,969,216,210
1888	3,163,774,462
1889	3,379,925,188
1890	4,093,145,904
1891	4,456,885,230
1895	5,614,979,203

ONE OF THE OLD-TIME GLORIES OF CHICAGO — THE GRAND PACIFIC HOTEL.

HISTORICAL SKETCH.

EARLY HISTORY.

The early history of Chicago will be a subject of increasing interest as it grows older and takes on greater commercial importance. What was it in its beginnings, what were the causes of its phenomenal growth? are questions that people will ask themselves with increasing frequency. Then the antiquarian and the archaeologist will vie in ferriting out information about its early history, its people, and their times. The Miami Confederation of Indian tribes, including the Illinois, from which the State derives its name, are generally supposed to have been the early proprietors of the site of Chicago, and the first recorded white visitor to the spot was probably the Sieur Jean Nicolet. He at least "visited the villages of the Illinois" somewhere about 1634, and among them, probably, the important settlement near the mouth of the Checagou river. Later, in 1672-74, Louis Joliet, a trusted agent of Count Frontenac—then Governor of "New France"—and Father Jacques Marquette, a devoted priest of the Society of Jesus—appear, from the French chronicles, to have visited and explored the Chicago river. Fragmentary allusions in these same records, however, tend to prove that long before this period the French trappers and fur-traders were familiar with the locality. Thus, Marquette, in 1674, falling ill on his way up the Chicago river, was visited and cared for by two trappers—one of them, fortunately for him, a surgeon—who had their cabin near by.

Nicholas Perrot, also, is said to have visited the place in 1671; and, after the death of Marquette, in 1675, Father Claude Allouez, succeeding him in the mission of the Illinois, made several trips hither.

By some, again, it is confidently asserted that La Salle preceded Joliet in his first visit; but, however the honors may stand in point of time, to Joliet certainly belongs the credit of having first given to the Chicago river a definite position in the geography of our country, and to him also pertains all the honor of first proposing the canal that now connects the waters of Lake Michigan with those of the Gulf of Mexico, a scheme which required nearly 200 years to convince engineers of its feasibility.

The stories of these early explorers and missionaries read more like romances told by some ingenious fabricator of adventures, than sober fact; and there is no page in American history more fascinating than those relating to the French explorations in the Northwest; nor are there to be found instances of greater hardihood, grander perseverance in the face of well-nigh insurmountable difficulties, or nobler self-sacrifice in the cause of duty, than the lives of these voyageurs and missionaries furnish. Often disappointed, almost constantly suffering, these brave men pressed onward to the martyrdom which they knew as a rule awaited them. Especially is this true of the Jesuit missionaries, who, for the generous purpose of saving the souls of unknown and unwilling savages, freely laid down their lives in the trackless wilderness; and, as one fell beneath the burden of his labors, or under the treachery of his flock, another eagerly and enthusiastically took his place, and followed him to a similar death.

There was nothing in the site of Chicago as these early explorers saw it, to tempt the eye or hint of future importance—a sluggish estuary creeping tortuously through marshes and sands into the desolate lake, and behind it, as far as sight could reach, nothing but sandy barrens, malarious marshes, and trackless prairies; the very name, signifying in the Miami tongue, "skunk cabbage, wild onion, or garlic," might have been repulsive enough to discourage them. But, to our advantage, visitors continued coming.

In 1678, La Salle, having secured from the French King a patent of nobility, as well as a grant of seigniory for Fort Frontenac, on Lake Ontario, undertook in earnest the exploration of the Mississippi and Illinois rivers. With him, among other followers, came three Flemish friars, two of them, Fathers Membre and Ribonrde, being the immediate successors of Fathers Marquette and Allouez in the Illinois mission. The expedition encountered many difficulties in its wanderings; but, during the period between 1678 and 1683, La Salle crossed the Chicago portage several times.

Sometime during 1685, a fort was built here by Durantaye, one of La Salle's followers, and the letters of the French Catholic missionaries of the time show that in 1699 there was a flourishing Jesuit mission at the same place.

As time passed, the locality of Chicago saw many changes of ownership, and had successive visitors. In 1773 a large tract of land, including the site of the present city, was purchased by William Murray, for five shillings, and "certain merchandise," from its red proprietors. This purchase, in turn, passed into the hands of an American company, but the government finally refused to confirm the title, and in 1795 the United States secured by treaty a tract of land six miles square, surrounding the mouth of the Chicago river, intending to establish here a military post.

1795 TO THE INCORPORATION.

An Irishman said that "the first white settler in Chicago was a black man." Writing on July 4, 1779, the then British Commander at Fort Michilimackinac mentions this "oldest inhabitant" as "Baptiste Point De Sable, a handsome negro, well educated, and settled at Eschikagou, but much in the French interest." This Point De Sable was a Santo Domingoan slave, who had probably fled from his Spanish masters to the kindlier protection of the French in Louisiana. Anyway, he became a trapper, and established his cabin at the mouth of the Chicago river, and there remained, following his calling, until 1796, when he sold out to Le Mai, a French trader, and rejoined at Peoria an old Santo Domingoan companion, in whose cabin he died. Meanwhile, during the years of De Sable's residence here, Chicago had become a somewhat familiar trading point, and Le Mai, succeeding him, added considerable impetus to its growth and importance. He made some improvements, and carried on his business until 1804. But in the meanwhile three or four neighbors had settled down beside him, and in 1803, Captain John Whistler, in command at the U. S. army post at Detroit, was ordered hither to erect a fort. It was finished in the fall of the same year, and was called Fort Dearborn, in honor of the Secretary of War, General Henry Dearborn. In 1804, John Kinzie, an Indian trader from St. Joseph, Mich., bought out Le Mai's cabin, and brought his family hither, after improving the Jean Baptiste cabin into a tolerable dwelling. His son, John H., who was but a few months old at the time of the removal, subsequently became one of the most prominent men of the city.

For about eight years things rolled along smoothly. The garrison was quiet, and the traders were prosperous, the number of the latter having been considerably increased. Then the United States became involved in trouble with Great Britain, which finally broke out into the war-flame. The Indians took the war-path long before the declaration of hostilities between the two civilized nations. On the 7th of April, 1812, they made an attack on one of the outlying houses, and killed and scalped the only male resident, then descended toward the fort, but refrained from making an attack, finding that the soldiers were ready to give them a warm reception. For some months they continued to harass and rob the outside settlers. The government finally decided to abandon the fort, as it was too remote from headquarters to be successfully maintained in a hostile country. On the 7th of August, 1812, Captain Heald, the commander, received orders to evacuate the fort, if practicable; and, in that event to distribute all the United States property among the Indians in the neighborhood. He hesitated for five days, knowing that a special order had been issued by the War Department to the effect that no fort should be surrendered "without battle having been given." He then reluctantly decided to comply, as his little force of seventy-five men was evidently unable to cope with the Indians.

On the 12th instant the Indians assembled in council, and Captain Heald informed them that he would distribute among them, on the next day, all the ammunition and provisions, as well as the other goods lodged in the United States factory, on condition that the Pottawatomies would furnish a safe escort for him and his command to Fort Wayne, where they should receive a further liberal reward. The Indians acceded to these terms; but Mr. Kinzie, who had learned by long experience the treachery of Indian character, afterward prevailed on Captain Heald to destroy all the liquor and the ammunition not needed by the troops on the journey.

The next day the blankets, calicoes and provisions were distributed as agreed upon, and in the evening the liquors were thrown into the water, with all the ammunition, except twenty-five rounds, and one box of cartridges. They also broke up all the spare muskets and gun fixtures, and threw them into the well. So much liquor was thrown into the river that the Indians drank largely of the water, saying that it was almost as good as "grog."

The next morning Captain Wells, a relative of Captain Heald, arrived from Fort Wayne

Note.—It may be well to state that Prof. A. D. Hagar, late Secretary and Librarian of the Chicago Historical Society, after extensive and thorough research and personal investigation came to the conclusion that it is not the Chicago river at all which is so often alluded to in the writings of the early explorers, but the Calumet river, at the south end of the lake. Since that time, the Great Calumet has disappeared through the artificial drainage of the marshes in which it had its springs; but, with the exception of its point of entry into Lake Michigan, the present feeder of the Illinois and Michigan Canal, from Lake Michigan via the Little Calumet, Stony Creek and the "Sag Ditch," lies over the route of the old Checagou Portage. This position Prof. Hagar so minutely fortified that it is well-nigh impossible to assail it in any way except by stating that both ancient maps and ancient writings seem to indicate a confusion of the present Chicago and Calumet rivers with one another. Prof. Hagar's paper may be found in the library of the Society, and will repay careful reading.

with fifteen friendly Miamis. In the afternoon another council was held, at which the Pottawatomies professed to be highly indignant at the destruction of the whisky and ammunition, and made numerous threats, which plainly showed their murderous intention. On the morning of the 15th of August, 1812, the troops left the fort. Mrs. Kinzie, with her family of four children, two domestics and two Indians, took a boat, intending to cross the lake to St. Joseph, but remained at the mouth of the harbor during the subsequent carnage, then returned to their home. The military party went southward, intending to march around the head of the lake. They had only proceeded about a mile and a half, when they were attacked by a party of Indians, concealed behind a sand ridge, whom they charged and dislodged from the position; but the Indians were so numerous that a party of them were able to outflank the soldiers, and take the horses and baggage. A severe fight followed, in which the number of the soldiers was reduced to twenty-eight; and during that action a young savage tomahawked the entire party of twelve children in the baggage wagon. Captain Heald then withdrew his troops, and a parley ensued, the consequence of which was that the troops surrendered on condition that their lives should be spared, and were marched back to the fort, which was plundered and burned the next day. Mr. Kinzie did duty as surgeon, extracting the bullets with his penknife.

Accounts vary somewhat as to whether the Indians kept faith in their agreement, some charging that they massacred the children and some of the women after the surrender; but the facts appear to have been as above stated. The total number of killed was fifty-two, which included twenty-six soldiers, twelve militiamen, two women and twelve children. The prisoners were ransomed some time afterward, the Kinzie family being taken across the lake to St. Joseph, and thence to Detroit, a few days after the massacre.

For four years the place was deserted by all save Indians. Even fur-traders did not care to visit the scene of so much disaster. In 1816 the fort was rebuilt, under direction of Captain Bradley, and was thereafter occupied continuously by United States troops for twenty-one years, excepting a short time in 1831. In 1837, it was abandoned, the Indians having been removed far to the westward. The fort stood, however, till 1856, when the old block house was demolished. Its position was on the south bank of the river, just east of the place where Rush street bridge was afterward built. One old building, however, remained, almost rotten with age, till the great conflagration swept it away, as the last relic of military rule. It was a small wooden structure that had formed part of the officers' quarters, and stood almost in the apex of the sharp corner formed by the meeting of Michigan avenue with River street.

But the rebuilding of the fort failed to re-establish the entente cordiale that had existed between the Indians and whites previous to the spring of 1812. Mr. Kinzie did not return till some time after the fort was reconstructed. Gurdon S. Hubbard, Esq., who was a resident of Chicago until he died a few years ago, visited the place in 1818, as agent of the American Fur Company, of which John Jacob Astor was then President. He came in a small schooner which was sent here once a year with provisions for the garrison. On his arrival he found only two families on the site of the future city outside the fort. John Kinzie lived on the north side of the river, nearly on the line of Michigan avenue; and Antoine Ouilmette, a French trader, who had married an Indian woman, resided on the same side, about two blocks further west. J. B. Beaubien arrived about the same time. In 1823 one more white resident appeared on the scene, Archibald Clybourne, who established himself about three miles from the fort, on the North Branch. In 1827 he built a slaughter-house, and entered into business as butcher for the

MAP OF THE MOUTH OF THE CHICAGO RIVER,
WITH THE PLAN OF THE PROPOSED PIERS FOR IMPROVING THE HARBOR.
BY WM. HOWARD, UNITED STATES CIVIL ENGINEER.
FEBRUARY 24, 1830.

EARLY HISTORY.

fort. He resided here continuously until the day of his death, August 23, 1872. In the same year (1827) Chicago was visited by Major Long, on a government exploring expedition, who drew a sorry picture of the place, which then contained only three families, all occupying log cabins. He said, in his subsequent report, that Chicago presented no cheering prospects, and contained but a few huts, "inhabited by a miserable race of men, scarcely equal to the Indians from whom they had descended," while their houses were "low, filthy and disgusting, displaying not the least trace of comfort." His opinion of the site as a place for business was equally poor. He spoke of it as "affording no inducements to the settler, the whole amount of trade on the lake not exceeding the cargoes of five or six schooners, even at the time when the garrison received its supplies from the Mackinac." How wonderfully the aspect of the place changed within half a century from the time of Major Long's visit, has been written with a pen of iron—the record graven so deeply that not even the great conflagration could efface it.

After the evacuation of Fort Dearborn, the land and property remained in charge of the government officials conducting the harbor improvements. However, in 1835, "Gen." John B. Beaubien had managed to buy the entire property for $94.61, and subsequently divided it up and sold lots on it; but in 1840 the Supreme Court annulled his claim, and he received back his money without interest. Meanwhile, in 1839, most of the property was resold by the government to individuals, and later the balance was granted in sections to the Illinois Central Railroad Company, the United States Marine Hospital, which stood upon Michigan avenue, and was burned in the great fire, and the balance to Gen. Beaubien. Dearborn Park was a result of the same legal dispute.

On the site of the fort itself now stands a

OTTAWA INDIAN MONUMENT, LINCOLN PARK.

large grocery store, with a memorial tablet let into its wall. It may be seen at the corner of Michigan avenue and South Water street.

FROM THE INCORPORATION TO THE GREAT FIRE.

In 1837, Chicago became a city. It was incorporated by act of the Legislature, passed March 4, which extended the limits to include an area of about ten square miles. It was bounded as follows: On the south by Twenty-second street, on the west by Wood street, on the north by North avenue, and on the east by the lake, except the fraction of section ten occupied as a military post. It included, in addition, the ground on the lake shore lying east of Clark street, extending half a mile north of North avenue, since occupied as the old city cemetery, and now a portion of Lincoln Park.

The corporation was divided into six wards, each of which was empowered to elect two aldermen.

From this period to the date of the great fire, the onward march of the city is well known. Its marvelous growth in population, wealth, internal resources and improvements, and everything that goes to make up a great and mighty municipality, are matters of history. Its wholesale trade in 1871 was about $450,000,000. Its progress astonished the world, and was scarcely credible to its own citizens.

By the first city census, taken in 1837, its population was 4,170, inclusive of 140 sailors belonging to vessels owned here; and in 1871 it had grown to 334,270, with a corporate valuation of $289,746,470. The first railroad out of the city, the Galena & Chicago Union, now a part of the Chicago & North-Western Railway, was opened in 1848, and the Illinois & Michigan Canal was also completed in 1848; but railroad connection with the East was not established until 1852, on February 20 of which year "the first through train from the East, via the Michigan Southern Railroad, entered Chicago, and was greeted with a salvo of artillery." Several successive extensions of the city limits had taken place in the interval, so that in 1871 Chicago embraced the total area of thirty-five square miles. She had a total tonnage of 95,395.95 tons; imported goods to the value of $2,042,499, and exported to the amount of $5,580,174. Then, at the very height of her good fortune and in the midst of her onward career, came the great conflagration, which in a single night effaced all signs of her prosperity, and awoke the commiseration and active sympathy of the entire civilized world.

STATUE OF SCHILLER, LINCOLN PARK.
The statue of the great poet stands among the flowers facing the Lincoln Park Conservatory. It is a reproduction of the famous work of Ernst Raus. The statue is the gift of the Schwaben Verein, and was unveiled with imposing ceremonies May 15, 1886. It cost $8,000.

THE GREAT FIRE.

The great fire, memorable in the history of

the city as the first bar to its progress, occurred on the night of October 8, 1871, and is yet fresh in the minds of our citizens, as well as in the hearts of all the people of the earth, whose charity poured in to the assistance of the sufferers.

We can not better describe its horrors than by the following abstract from "Chicago and the Great Conflagration," by Messrs. Colbert and Chamberlain:

"There had been, on the previous evening (that of Saturday, the 7th of October), an extensive conflagration, which the journals had recorded in many columns, devoting to it their most stunning headlines, their most ponderous superlatives, and their most graphic powers of description. The location of this fire was in the West Division, between Clinton street and the river, and running north from Van Buren street, where it caught, to Adams street, where, fortunately, it was checked, rather by the lack of combustible material than by any ability of the Fire Department to obtain the mastery. * * * * The damage by this fire was nearly a million dollars.

"* * * A little while after nine o'clock on Sunday evening the lamp was upset which was to kindle the funeral pyre of Chicago's pristine splendor. The little stable, with its contents of hay, was soon ablaze. By the time the alarm could be sounded at the box several blocks away, two or three other little buildings —tinder boxes—to the leeward had been ignited, and in five minutes the poor purlieu in the vicinity of De Koven and Jefferson streets was blazing like a huge bonfire. * * *

"The first vault across the river was made at midnight from Van Buren street, lighting in a building of the South Division gas works, on Adams street. This germ of the main fire was not suppressed, and from that moment the doom of the commercial quarter was sealed, though no man could have foretold that the raging element would make such complete havoc of the proudest and strongest structures in that quarter. The axis of the column, as it had progressed from the starting point in the southwestern purlieu, had varied hardly a point from due northeast. Having gained a foothold upon the South Division, its march naturally lay through two or three blocks of pine rookeries, known as 'Conley's Patch,' and so on for a considerable space through the abodes of squalor and vice. Through these it set out at doublequick, the main column being flanked by another on each side, and nearly an hour to the rear. That at the right was generated by a separate brand from the western burning; that at the left was probably created by some of the eddies which were by this time whirling through the streets toward the flame below and from it above. The rookeries were quickly disposed of. Beyond them, however, along La Salle street, was a splendid double row of 'fireproof' mercantile buildings, the superior of which did not exist in the land. * * *

"One after another they went as the column advanced; and the column was spreading fearfully—debouching to right and left, according as opportunities of conquest offered themselves. It was not long after one o'clock before the Chamber of Commerce was attacked, and fell a prey to the on-advancing force. Soon the Court House was seized upon; but it did not surrender until near three o'clock, when the great bell went down, down, and pealed a farewell dying groan as it went. The hundred and fifty prisoners in the basement story were released to save their lives. They evinced their gratitude by pillaging a jewelry store near by. * * *

"From the Court House the course of the main column seemed to tend eastward, and Hooley's Opera House, the Times building, and Crosby's fine Opera House (to have been reopened that very night) fell rapidly before it. Pursuing its way more slowly onward, the fiery invader laid waste some buildings to the northeast, and, preparatory to attacking the magnificent wholesale stores at the foot of Randolph street, and the great Union Depot adjoining, joined forces with the other branch of the main column, which had lingered to demolish the Sherman House—a grand seven-story edifice of marble—the Tremont House, and the other fine buildings lying between Randolph and Lake streets.

"The left column had, meantime, diverged to pass down LaSalle street and attack all buildings lying to the west of that noble avenue— the Oriental and Mercantile buildings, the Union Bank, the Merchants' Insurance building, where were Gen. Sheridan's headquarters, and the offices of the Western Union Telegraph, and in fact an unbroken row of the stone palaces of trade which had already made LaSalle street a monument of Chicago's business architecture, to which her citizens pointed with glowing pride, and of which admiring visitors wrote and published warm panegyrics in all quarters of the globe. The column of the left did its mission but too well, however, and by daylight scarcely a stone was left upon another in all that stately thoroughfare. But one building was left standing in this division of the city—a large brick structure, with iron shutters, known as Lind's Block. This was saved by its isolated location, being on the shore of the river, and separated by an exceptionally wide street from the seething furnace which consumed all else in its vicinity.

"The right column started from a point near the intersection of Van Buren street and the river, where some wooden buildings were ignited by brands from the West Side, in spite of the efforts of the inhabitants of that quarter to save their homes by drenching their premises with water from their hydrants; and, we need hardly add, in spite of the desultory though desperate efforts of the Fire Department. The right column had also the advantage of a large area of wooden buildings on which to ration and arm itself for its march of destruction. Thus fed and equipped, it swept down upon the remaining portion of the best-built section of the town. It gutted the Michigan Southern Depot and the Grand Pacific Hotel, and the tornado soon made them shapeless ruins. It spared not the unfinished building of the Lakeside Publishing Company, which had already put on a very sightly front, and which had scarcely anything to burn but brick and stone. It licked up the fine new buildings on Dearborn street near the Post Office.* * *

"The Post Office was seized upon and gutted like the rest, some two millions of treasure being destroyed in its vaults, which proved to have been of flimsy construction. It swept down upon the new Bigelow House, a massive and elegant hotel which had never yet been occupied, and demolished that, together with the Honore Block, a magnificent new building, with massive walls adorned with hundreds of stately colonnades of marble. It reached out to the left, and took McVicker's new theatre in its grasp for a moment, with the usual disastrous result. It assaulted the noble Tribune building, which the people had been declaring, even up to that terrible hour, would withstand all attacks, being furnished with all known safeguards against destruction by fire; but the enemy was wily as well as strong. It surrounded the fated structure, and ruined it too. It threw a red-hot brick wall upon the building's weaker side, a shower of brands upon the roof, a subterranean fire under the sidewalk and into the basement, and an atmosphere of furnace heat all around. It conquered and destroyed the Tribune building at half-past seven in the evening. It marched on and laid waste Booksellers' Row, the finest row of bookstores in the world. It fell upon Potter Palmer's store of Massachusetts marble, for which Field, Leiter & Co., dry goods importers, were paying the owner $52,000 a year rent. This splendid building, with such of its contents as had not been removed in wagons, went like all the rest. It deployed to the right, in spite of its ally, the wind, and destroyed the splendid churches and residences which adorned the lower or town end of Wabash and Michigan avenues. Among these were the First and Second Presbyterian Churches, Trinity Episcopal Church, and the palatial row of residences known as 'Terrace Row.' Finally, its course southward was stayed at Congress street by the blowing up of a building. The southern line of the fire was for the most part, however, along Harrison street, which is one square further to the south.

"This is a brief sketch of the operations of the fire in the West and South Divisions. It effected a foothold in the North Division as early as half-past three in the morning; and it is remarkable that almost the first building to be attacked on the north side of the river was the engine house of the Water-works; as if the terrible marauder had, with deadly strategy, thrown out a swifter brand than all others to cut off the only reliance of his victims, the water supply. The Water-works are nearly a mile from the point where the burning brands must have crossed the river. The denizens of the North Division were standing in their doors and gazing at the blazing splendor of the Court House dome, when they discovered, to their horror, that the fire was already raging behind them, and that the Water-works had gone. A general stampede to the sands of the lake shore, or to the prairies west of the city, was the result.

"Besides its foothold at the Water-works, from which the fire spread rapidly in every di-

THE HERALD BUILDING, 154 WASHINGTON ST.

rection, it soon made a landing in two of the elevators near the river, and organized an advance which consumed everything left by the scores of separate irruptions which the flames were constantly making in unexpected places. This was the system by which the North Division was wiped out: Blazing brands and scorching heat sent ahead to kindle many scattering fires, and the grand general conflagration following up and finishing up. Within the limits shown upon the appended map nothing was spared; not any of the elegant residences of the patricians—not even those isolated by acres of pleasure grounds; not even the 'fire-proof' Historical Hall, with its thousand precious relics; not even the stone churches of the Rev. Robert Collyer and Mr. Chamberlain, protected by a park in front; not even the cemetery to the north, whither many people removed a few of their most necessary effects, only to see them consumed before their eyes; not even Lincoln Park, whose scattering oaks were burned to dismal pollards by the all-consuming flames—nothing but one lone house, the Ogden residence, lately torn down,* as the sole survivor of the scourged district. The loss of life and the sufferings of those who managed to escape with life were most severe in this quarter of the city. They will be long remembered by all our people, the human element of the tragedy having been purposely omitted from this as far as practicable. Only at the lake and the northern limits of the city was the conflagration stayed—or rather, spent—for lack of anything to consume.

"The sensations conveyed to the spectator of this unparalleled event, either through the eye, the ear, or other senses or sympathies, can not be adequately described, and any attempt to do it but shows the poverty of language. * * *

"The total area burned over, including streets, was nearly three and a third square miles. The number of buildings destroyed was 17,450; persons rendered homeless, 98,500; persons killed, about 200. Not including depreciation of real estate or loss of business, it is estimated that the total loss occasioned by the fire was $190,000,000, of which about $44,000,000 were recovered on insurance, though one of the first results of the fire was to bankrupt many of the insurance companies all over the country. The business of the city was interrupted but a short time, however. Before winter, many of the merchants were doing business in extemporized wooden structures, and the rest in private dwellings. In a year after the fire, a large part of the burnt district had been rebuilt, and at present there is scarcely a trace of the terrible disaster, save in the improved character of the new buildings over those destroyed, and the general better appearance of the city—now architecturally the finest in the world."

THE FIRE OF JULY, 1874.

On July 14th, 1874, within three years, as if the demon of destruction were not yet satiated, still another great fire swept over the devoted city, destroying eighteen blocks, or sixty acres, in the heart of the city, and about $4,000,000 worth of property. Over 600 houses were consumed; but fortunately, by far the larger number of these were wooden shanties. Nearly all the magnificent structures of the rebuilt section escaped.

---

* Washington square, between Clark street and Dearborn avenue.

THE NEW CITY.

"It is an ill wind that blows no one good," and the fearful calamity which destroyed the great city of wood, made possible the greater city of stone and iron which has replaced it. of the old city had not ceased to smoke ere the new city began to grow, like a "Jonah's gourd," out of its ruins. The magical growth of modern Chicago has been sung far and wide, and has gained for her the title of "the Phoenix of cities"; and truly, in the solidly and compactly built city of to-day, there is little to remind one that twenty-five years ago the very streets were burned out of recognition.

If Chicago had not already received its poetical title, "The Garden City," it might be appropriately called the "City of Palaces"; for there are few modern cities which even approach it in the number and magnificence of its fine buildings, public and private. Moreover, the generous width of its avenues contributes the perspective, absent in New York and others of the older cities, which is so essential to architectural effect. The materials and designs are various, running all the way up the scale, from the iron fronts of the business portion, on the South Side, to the marble, granite, brown stone, brick, serpentine and Bedford sandstone of the finer residences and the various public buildings.

THE MONADNOCK BUILDING, JACKSON, DEARBORN, AND VAN BUREN STREETS, AND CUSTOM HOUSE PLACE.

Had Chicago not been Chicago, and had Chicago not made herself indispensable to the world, such a blow might indeed have effectually prostrated her. But, as it was, the ashes

However, the title "Garden City" is equally deserved; for there are few cities in which more

space is allotted to yards, lawns and parks. The parks being usually regarded as the principal attraction of the city, it may be well to place them first among our descriptions, following with accounts of the public buildings and institutions.

THE PARK SYSTEM.

The system of parks and boulevards which girdle the city, is an institution peculiar to Chicago. Though the prairies on the one hand, and the lake on the other, keep the air of Chicago delightfully wholesome, the dwellers in a great city require an occasional glimpse of green, and these are supplied in the "Garden City" by the most extensive and elaborate system of parks and drives in the country. The parks proper include 1,879 acres of land, and the connecting boulevards will, when finished, comprise a total length of about thirty miles. These improvements, though far advanced, can not be completed within a number of years, as they involve large and elaborate works.

There are a number of small "parks," "places" and "squares" distributed through the various sections of the city; but these, not belonging to the boulevard system, shall have separate mention.

The park system proper, including the boulevards, is under control of commissioners appointed by the State, and supported principally by direct tax upon the divisions of the city in which they are situated. Thus, Lincoln Park and the Lake Shore drive are under control of a separate commission, as are the parks situated on the West and South Sides respectively.

Lake Shore Drive.—The North Division begins with the Lake Shore drive, a boulevard leading from the Water-works, through Lincoln Park. It may be reached from the South Side by way of Rush street bridge and Pine street, though Dearborn avenue is generally preferred, on account of its handsome residences. It is a beautiful drive, running for more than two miles directly beside the lake and along the eastern border of Lincoln Park, and is continued beyond under the name of Sheridan Drive.

Lincoln Park.—This, the first finished of the Boulevard Parks, occupies a space of 250 acres, one-half mile wide by one and one-half miles long, bounded on the east by the lake, and on the west by Clark street, and extending from North avenue on the south, to Diversey avenue on the north. The southern portion of the present park was formerly occupied by the old Chicago Cemetery, but it was finally condemned for public use, and the bodies were transferred. A single reliquary grave remains as a reminder of the past. In 1869 the Legislature appointed its first Board of Commissioners, and provided for its maintenance and improvement, and since that time it has had constant care and labor, until it is the most complete of the entire system. On one side, the Lake Shore drive, continuing from the entrance, extends from Oak street to its northernmost limits, and commands, on one hand a panoramic view of the great lake, and on the other the varying scenic beauties of the park itself. Within its boundaries beautiful lawns alternate with picturesque, artificially broken grounds, flower-beds of the most elaborate patterns, intricate walks, and magnificent winding drives. Noble trees and fine shrubbery are grouped in the most effective positions, and twenty acres of beautiful lakes add the picturesqueness of water to the general effect. Still further heightening the attractiveness of the resort, there are a refreshment pavilion, a plentiful supply of boats, an interesting zoological collection, a magnificent conservatory and palm house, the museum of the Academy of Science, and, in the summer, frequent musical entertainments. There are also a striking bronze Indian group, of life size, mounted on a massive granite pedestal—presented by Mr. Martin Ryerson; and a bronze statue of Schiller, erected by the German citizens in 1886, on the anniversary of the great poet's death. It stands at the south end of the large flower beds. To these works of art have been added a Lincoln monument, by St. Gaudens, and a drinking fountain, as provided for in a munificent legacy of the late Eli Bates; the La Salle monument, presented by Lambert Tree; and the equestrian monument to General Grant, erected by the city in 1891.

Humboldt Boulevard.—There is, at present, no completed boulevard connection between Lincoln and Humboldt Parks, the best practicable route being North avenue, a well-paved drive from the southern limit of the former to the northern border of the latter park. This gap it is intended to supply in the future, by the completion of Diversey boulevard. From Lincoln Park, west to the north branch of the Chicago river, there is a break in the continuity of the boulevard plans. Eventually this gap will be filled by the utilization of Diversey avenue. At present Humboldt boulevard begins on the west side of the river, where Diversey avenue crosses it, and from there runs west a mile and a quarter to Logan Square, then south one-half mile to Palmer Place, which, extending north two blocks, opens into a third division, running south three-quarters of a mile into Humboldt Park, at North avenue. The boulevard proper is 250 feet wide, while Logan Square is 400x800 feet, and Palmer Place 400x1,750 feet; total length of the drive, about three miles. It is paved with granite, macadam, flanked with cedar blocks on either side, for a greater part of its length and is beautified by four rows of lawns and planted with trees.

Humboldt Park, the northernmost of the

system, lies four miles northwest from the City Hall, between West North avenue on the north, Augusta street on the south, North California avenue on the east, and North Kedzie avenue on the west. It may be reached from the South Side by the Milwaukee avenue and West North avenue street cars, on Randolph street. It is beautifully laid out, and contains 200 acres of land. It is one of the most attractive of all the parks, being well wooded, and provided with fine lawns, and having a large area of lake surface, admirably adapted for rowing. There is a refreshment pavilion close to the boat landing; a band stand, on which Sunday concerts are given during the summer months; and a beautiful conservatory to delight the lovers of flowers. It contains also a famous artesian well 1,155 feet in depth, which furnishes a fine grade of rich in the sulphates, chlorides and carbonates, at a temperature of 63.5° Fahrenheit.

Central Boulevard, a little over one and a half miles in length, is the connecting link between Garfield and Humboldt Parks. It leaves the latter at Augusta street, and, running south to Sacramento Square, at Indiana street, proceeds west along the latter street to Central Park avenue, where it again turns to the south, and enters Garfield Park at West Kinzie street. The Chicago, Milwaukee & St. Paul Railway tracks are bridged, just south of Grand avenue, by a handsome viaduct, which adds greatly to the picturesque variety of the drive. The average width of the boulevard is 250 feet, including the completed driveway, 38 feet wide, bordered on each side by a narrow ribbon of turf, with a bridle path accompanying it along its outer edge, and a double colonnade of handsome elms affording fine shade and enhancing its beauty.

Garfield Park, formerly known as "Cen-

A SEAL POND, LINCOLN PARK.

tral Park," had its title changed in memory of the martyred President. It is the most westerly of the parks, and lies about four miles west of the City Hall, between West Kinzie street on the north, and Colorado avenue on the south. It extends one and a half miles from north to south, and contains 185 acres of ground. Three large lakes add the beauty of water effect to the scenery. In the lakes are several pretty miniature islands, one of them holding the band stand. There are plenty of boats to be hired at very reasonable rates, and there is a roomy landing 300 feet in length. The landing reaches back to the casino, a refreshment pavilion with

minute. It has a high reputation for cases of anaemia and diseases of the stomach and kidneys, as well as for rheumatic and kindred constitutional disorders. The rapidity with which what was wild prairie a few years ago has been transformed into an exquisite health and pleasure resort is truly remarkable. The Central Driving Association occupied a portion of the southern wing as a speeding park, and the track of the Garfield Park Club adjoins it on the west. Garfield Park is reached by the North-Western Railway to Central Park Station, also by street cars on Lake and Madison streets, or by way of

Washington Boulevard.—This boulevard, a

ELK IN LINCOLN PARK.

broad verandas and breezy balconies. Through the elaborate shrubbery, woods, flower-beds, lawns and shady borders, wind three miles of walks and two miles of driveways, enmeshing the completed portion of the park; wood, stone and iron bridges, mazes and rustic seats, add variety to the scenery; and a handsome drinking fountain for horses, provided by the Illinois Humane Society from funds contributed by Mrs. Mancel Talcott, furnishes refreshment for the animals. But the centre of attraction is the 2,200 feet artesian well, supplying a valuable mineral water, at the rate of 150 gallons per

continuation of Washington street, commences at Halsted street, a little less than one mile directly west of the City Hall, whence it extends through Union Park, westward to Garfield Park, and on to 52d street. Its total length is nearly five miles, and it is a beautiful driveway, averaging about 100 feet in width, bordered on each side by a ribbon of turf, set with handsome trees, and built up for a great part of its length with magnificent residences, many of them surrounded by beautiful grounds. It is the popular drive of the West Side, being macadamized or asphalted and finely kept.

Union Park, which, until the spring of 1886, was one of the city parks, but at that time it passed into the hands of the West Side Commissioners, by whom it has been greatly improved. The boulevard runs directly through it, bordered by walks, lawns and variegated flower beds, and in full view of the lake, pavilion, ornate fountain, and picturesque hills with which its surface is broken. It is in the heart of the residence portion of the West Side, being bounded on the north by Bryan Place and Lake street, on the east by Ogden avenue, on the south by Warren avenue, and on the west by Ashland avenue. It is one and three-fourths miles west from the City Hall, and will repay a visit. It may be reached within a half-hour by electric cars on Randolph or Madison streets, or Ogden avenue.

Douglas Boulevard.—This is an L-shaped boulevard connecting Garfield and Douglas Parks, and extends from Colorado avenue south seven-eighths of a mile, then east seven-eighths of a mile to Albany avenue, where it enters Douglas Park. It is 250 feet wide, embracing in its plan a driveway (already completed) thirty-eight feet in width, bordered by strips of sward on either side, and accompanied by a bridle-path on its outer edge, the whole beautifully colonnaded with a double row of elms. It is now practically completed, and is one of the most popular of the boulevards on the West Side.

Douglas Park is a prairie park, situated at the limit of the built-up streets of the city, on the open plain, free to all breezes from any direction. It lies four miles southwest from the City Hall, between West Twelfth street on the north, Albany avenue on the west, West Nineteenth street on the south, and California avenue on the east. Though comparatively small—only 180 acres—it is a beautiful and popular park, and is especially notable as the spot selected by the Chinese of Chicago for their annual "Festival of the Kites," which is religiously observed with each returning August. Eleven acres of the park are covered by a picturesque lake, fed with the mineral water of an artesian well, gushing out in a romantic grotto. The water is medicinal, with properties similar to those of Garfield and Humboldt Parks. There is an inviting refectory, from the balconies of which a fine view is had of the park scenery, and there are a conservatory and propagating houses which furnish 60,000 plants annually for transplanting.

Douglas Park is reached by the Twelfth street cars, which run on Randolph street to Fifth avenue; by the Ogden avenue cars, which run on Madison street, and by the local trains of the Chicago, Burlington & Quincy Railway, which stop at Douglas Park Station. The depot is the Union, at Canal and Adams streets. The Chicago Passenger Railway Company's tracks have been extended to Douglas Park, via Western avenue and Twelfth street. The driving route is along Washington boulevard to Garfield Park, thence to Douglas Park by the Douglas boulevard.

Southwest Boulevard is still, for the most part, on paper, but the contemplated plan is for a boulevard on a grand scale. The proposed route is about five miles in length, reaching from Douglas Park south to Gage Park, at the terminus of Garfield boulevard. Starting from Douglas Park, at Sacramento avenue, it runs south about one-half mile to Laughton street, on which it continues eastward for a short distance, to California avenue. Proceeding southward along this avenue about three-fourths of a mile, it reaches Thirty-first street, which is utilized for about one-half mile to Western avenue, on which it completes the link with Gage Park and Douglas boulevard, crossing the Illinois & Michigan Canal just west of the Bridgeport lumber wharves. The boulevard will be 200 feet in width, with a broad central driveway, bordered by wide strips of sward, shaded by double rows of elms, and outside of these still other roads for equestrians and general travel. Though a very small portion of this boulevard has been completed, it is possible to drive on Western avenue from Nineteenth street to Gage Park, at Fifty-fifth street. The road, of course, is not very good, but it affords an opportunity to follow the boulevard route, and passes through Brighton Park and the Town of Lake; while it is possible, as well, to reach in this way the sewage pumping works at Bridgeport, the West Side Waterworks, and the Union Stock Yards. The South Parks are best reached from Douglas Park, however, by way of Eighteenth street and Michigan avenue boulevard.

Gage Park, the smallest park in the boulevard system, forms the junction of Western avenue boulevard, which enters it from the north, and Garfield boulevard, into which it opens at the east. It contains twenty acres of ground, but so far not much has been done in the way of improving it. This park was named in memory of George W. Gage, one of the first Commissioners, who died September 24, 1875. It may be reached by drive, as above described, or by the Chicago, St. Louis & Pittsburgh Railway to Forty-ninth Street Crossing, which is within a mile, or by way of Garfield boulevard from Washington Park.

Garfield Boulevard is completed on an elaborate scale, with a commodious central driveway, bordered by grass and rows of trees. Outside of these, there will be on the one side a roadway for equestrians, and on the other a highway for traffic, the whole being hedged in with colonnades of elms. This boulevard is 200 feet wide, and extends along Fifty-fifth street from Gage Park to Washington Park, a total length of about three and a half miles. The improvements are far advanced, and the entire boulevard is in excellent condition for driving.

Washington Park.—Garfield boulevard gives entrance at its eastern extremity to Washington Park, and this park, Jackson Park, and Midway Plaisance (the connection between them) are known under the collective title "South Parks." The total cost to the city of the grounds alone for these parks was $3,208,000, and the improvements have considerably more than doubled that sum. Though the work is not entirely completed, the result is most gratifying, and the South Parks are a continual source of pleasure to our citizens, and a principal point of attraction to visitors. Washington Park lies nearly six miles south and east from the City Hall, and is bounded by Fifty-first street, Kankakee avenue, Sixtieth street and Cottage Grove avenue, a space of 371 acres, somewhat over a mile west from the lake. The extent of the grounds has given an opportunity for breadth of treatment which the landscape artists have not neglected. Among the most attractive features are the "Meadow," a famous stretch of sward, covering 100 acres; the "Mere," a meandering sheet of picturesquely distributed water, thirteen acres in extent; the conservatory, a handsome building, 40x120 feet,

connected with eleven propagating houses and a cactus house, and containing an interesting collection of tropical plants; the artesian well 1,643 feet deep, which furnishes a mineral water; and the stable, built of stone, in the shape of a Greek cross, to accommodate over

A LILY POND, WASHINGTON PARK.

100 horses, the stalls being arranged circularly about a central space, into which the phaetons with their loads are driven when horses are to be changed. This stable covers a space of 325x 200 feet, measured through its greatest diameters, and shelters the 130 fine Norman blooded

horses owned by the Commission. Flowers are tastefully distributed at the most effective points throughout the park, 200,000 plants being propagated and set out annually. Boats may be hired for rowing on the Mere, and lunches may be had at the Refectory, in which also is the Superintendent's office. Afternoon concerts are usually given at frequent intervals through the summer months during the season, from about June 1 to the middle of October, or later.

Washington Park may be reached direct by taking Cottage Grove avenue cars. This line extends along the entire eastern border of the park. If driving is preferred, there are several routes to follow, either of which will furnish a good view of the residence portion of the city of the South Side. Starting from Michigan avenue and Jackson street, Michigan avenue may be followed to Thirty-fifth street, then turning to the east along the latter street to Grand boulevard, and thence to the Fifty-first street entrance of the park. Traversing the park and returning, Drexel boulevard at the eastern entrance may be taken, turning out to the right on any of the avenues leading to the starting point. In this section are the homes of many of Chicago's leading citizens, the diversified architecture of the residences along the route making the drive a pleasant and enjoyable one. Another and more direct route is along State street or Wabash avenue to Fifty-fifth street, thence along Garfield boulevard to the park. The Alley South Side Elevated Railroad is now equipped and running from Congress street to Sixty-third street, and these cars may be taken from Congress street to Washington Park. The cable-car fare is only 5 cents each way, and in

CHICAGO ATHLETIC ASSOCIATION BUILDING, 124-126 MICHIGAN AVENUE.

the warm, pleasant days of summer the ride on the open cars affords a delightful recreation to the poor, or, for that matter, to the rich. Constant improvements are being made in the park, tending to make it more beautiful every year. The race track of the Washington Park Club is said to be one of the finest in the world. And finally, the regular suburban trains on either the Lake Shore & Michigan Southern Railway or the Chicago, Rock Island & Pacific Railway (running out of the same depot, at Van Buren and Sherman streets) will land passengers on Garfield boulevard (Fifty-fifth and Clark streets) about one mile west of Washington Park.

Jackson Park, when completed, will be by far the most attractive of the entire system, as it will be also the largest, covering the 524 acres bounded by Lake Michigan, Fifty-sixth street, Stony Island avenue and Sixty-seventh street. Of its entire acreage, only 150 are at present improved, though it is intended to push the plans rapidly to completion. They include a system of sinuous interior lakes, covering 100 acres, beautified with numerous islands and bridged passages, and connected at either end with Lake Michigan. A breakwater protecting the entire frontage has been constructed, and a fine pier for excursion steamers and pleasure craft will

VIEW IN UNION PARK.

Midway Plaisance.—At the present time the two South Parks—Washington and Jackson—are connected by a beautiful drive, formerly amounting to little more than a country road. The plans of the Commissioners, however, include elaborate improvements for this connecting link. They comprise finely boulevarded, well-shaded driveways, and a handsome waterway connecting the lake systems of the two parks. It formed the Street of Nations during the progress of the great Columbian World's Fair in 1893. The Plaisance is located between Fifty-ninth and Sixtieth streets, is one and one-tenth miles in length, between the two park entrances, and contains eighty acres of ground.

be added. This beautiful pleasure ground has attained additional prominence from being chosen as the site of the great Columbian World's Fair Exposition, held in 1893.

Jackson Park may be reached from Washington Park, by the routes mentioned in that connection.

Drexel Boulevard.—Washington Park is entered from the north by two magnificent boulevards—Drexel on the east, and Grand on the west. They parallel each other at a distance of a little more than one mile apart, and are connected at a point one and three-eighths miles north of Washington Park by Oakwood boulevard, at which Drexel boulevard ends. This last named is the most exquisite of the boulevard system, and has a wide fame. It opens into Washington Park at its northeastern angle, from the east, by a wide plaza, through the centre of which extends a broad lawn, richly ornamented by the gardener's art. On either side of this lawn are the broad driveways, and at Drexel avenue stands the famous fountain presented by the Drexel Brothers, the Philadelphia bankers, in memory of their father, after whom also the boulevard was named. Here, at Drexel avenue, the boulevard turns directly north on that avenue, entering Oakwood boulevard at the junction of Thirty-ninth street and Cottage Grove avenue. The boulevard is laid out on the plan of the Avenue l'Imperatrice, in Paris, and has two broad drives, one on either side of a central space, finely swarded, and filled with various species of trees, and ornamented with flower beds, among which wind the well-gravelled promenades, with bowers and rustic seats. The entire boulevard is 200 feet wide, and is bordered by rows of well-grown elms. The tasteful villas along this boulevard are one of its principal attractions.

Oakwood Boulevard is the connecting link between the boulevard last named and Grand boulevard. It is a fine drive, 100 feet wide, and half a mile long, and enters Grand boulevard at Thirty-ninth street. "The Cottage" stands at its junction with Drexel boulevard, whence the phaetons start for the tour of the park.

Grand Boulevard, entering Washington Park at its northwestern angle, extends thence northward two miles to Thirty-fifth street, where it connects with a short boulevard on that street. It is 198 feet wide, a broad driveway bordered by strips of lawn, with double colonnades of elms, outside of which are roadways thirty-three feet wide, the one on the west for equestrians, and the other for traffic. Still outside of these are ribbons of turf with single rows of trees separating the roadways from the foot-

STATUE OF LINNE, LINCOLN PARK.

ways, which have yet another line of trees on their outer borders.

Thirty-fifth Street Boulevard, running westward on the street of that name, connects Grand and Michigan avenue boulevards. It is about one-third of a mile in length, and sixty-six feet wide.

Michigan Avenue Boulevard occupies the avenue from which it takes it name, between Garfield boulevard on the south and Jackson street on the north, a distance of three and a quarter miles. The roadway is 100 feet from curb to curb, and is bordered by strips of green, with elms, and broad stone sidewalks. It is the most fashionable drive in the city, and upon it are situated many fine residences.

The City Parks.—The oldest of Chicago's parks are the small, isolated squares of lawn and shrubbery scattered at various points through the city, but they do not belong to the system proper, being under the city government. They are, in general, very attractively laid out — some of them with lakes and fountains, most of them having fine trees—and are fairly well kept. They include, on the West Side, Jefferson Park, five and a half acres, bounded by Adams, Throop, Monroe and Loomis streets, a mile and a half west and south from the City Hall. It is charmingly arranged with a lawn, a lake, a grotto, hills, trees, etc. Vernon Park is on the north side of Polk street, between Centre avenue and Loomis street, nearly two miles southwest from the City Hall, and about half a mile south of the park last named. It covers nearly four acres, has a lake and some fine trees. On the North Side, Wicker Park fills the triangle made by Park, North Robey and Fowler streets, three miles northwest from the City Hall, and contains four acres of ground, attractively laid out. Washington Square, bounded by Clark street, Dearborn avenue, Washington Place and Lafayette Place, is

COLUMBUS MEMORIAL BUILDING, STATE AND WASHINGTON STREETS.

about one mile north from the City Hall, and contains two and a quarter acres, well filled with fine trees.

On the South Side, Lake Park, the most central of the parks, lies between the Michigan avenue boulevard and the lake, and extends from Randolph street to Lake Park Place. It is now being extended into the lake, and will be greatly beautified. Groveland and Woodlawn Parks, adjoining each other, and facing the grounds of the old Chicago University, lie between Cottage Grove avenue and the lake, beyond Thirty-third street. The two parks and the University grounds were a gift from Stephen A. Douglas, whose mausoleum and monument occupy a space of elevated ground contiguous to Woodlawn Park, and overlooking Lake Michigan. The mausoleum and shaft, 104 feet high, are of granite, and the latter is surmounted by a bronze statue of the great Senator, while four corner pedestals are occupied by figures, representing "Illinois," "History," "Justice," and "Eloquence," respectively. This magnificent memorial cost $100,000. Groveland Park is a grove of fine elms, well interlaced with vines, and threaded by picturesque walks. Ellis Park, lying between Vincennes and Cottage Grove avenues, at Thirty-seventh street, four miles south from the City Hall, contains three and three-eighths acres. Aldine Square, at Thirty-seventh street and Vincennes avenue, close to the last-named park, is a beautifully kept enclosure, surrounded by handsome resi-

SOUTH WATER STREET, LOOKING WEST FROM DEARBORN STREET

dences. Besides these, there are several other small public grounds, including Congress, Campbell, and Union Parks on the West Side. There are a great many other parks, but of less importance.

THE WATER SUPPLY.

No attempt will be made here to detail the history of the growth of the water system from the small requirements of a village population, when water was drawn through wooden pump-

crib was built two miles out, which served as an intake for two tunnels, each of seven feet in diameter, running under the bed of the lake to pumping stations on the land. Subsequently another tunnel of five feet in diameter was built to the same crib. Even this proved inadequate; and, at times, there was found to be danger from shore contamination. So, another crib was built four miles out, which was completed in 1892, with an eight-foot tunnel. In addition to these there are two, the Lake View and the Hyde Park cribs, the first with a 6 and the other with a 7-foot tunnel, each two miles out. Altogether there are fourteen miles of lake tunnels completed and in operation, and six miles of land; to which must be added eight miles of land tunnels and three of lake, in course of construction.

The water is drawn through these tunnels to pumping stations on shore, six in number, known respectively as the "Chicago Avenue," the "West Side," the "Central," the "Fourteenth street," the "Lake View" and the "Sixty-Eighth

INSURANCE EXCHANGE BUILDING, LA SALLE AND ADAMS STREETS.

logs, to that of a city of 1,750,000 inhabitants, requiring iron mains up to four feet in diameter. We can only give the present development. Broadly stated, the water supply of Chicago is taken from Lake Michigan, from two to four miles out from shore. The first

street," having a total pumping capacity of 338,000,000 gallons of water every twenty-four hours. In connection with the tunnel extensions before mentioned, two more pumping stations are projected, each of 60,000,000 gallons capacity, which, when completed, will make a total capacity of 458,000,000 gallons of water daily for the City of Chicago.

At these pumping stations the water is pumped, by means of tremendous engines, directly into the mains, by which it is distributed to all parts of the city for all purposes. The mains are the pipes which are laid under the streets, and which are tapped at desired points for private service or hydrants. Those mains are of iron; and vary in size, the smallest being four inches in diameter and the largest four feet. Some are four, six, eight, twelve, sixteen, twenty-four, thirty-six and forty-eight inches, inside diameter; and the total length of water main in the city, at the end of 1895, was 1,940 miles. The Fire Department is supplied through 16,466 hydrants.

Next to the water supply system comes those of the sewers and streets. At the close of the year 1895 there were in Chicago about 1,284¼ miles of street sewers, which had been built at a cost of $16,587,184. There were also 1,123.54 miles of street paving of different kinds; and 4,624.82 miles of sidewalks. From this, some idea can be formed of the aggregation which goes to make up the City of Chicago.

THE DRAINAGE SYSTEM.

Closely connected with the water supply and the sewage systems of the city is that of drainage. The growth of the city, so much beyond the wildest anticipations of the most sanguine, developed problems which at first were not dreamed of. The outlets of the sewers were into the lake, at the shore, and into the Chicago river, which itself emptied into the lake. No one supposed that this would ever be sufficient to contaminate the water supply taken so far out. But it was. In times of freshet, the danger became imminent; and it was made apparent that this must become more so as the city continued to grow. Much was accomplished by the establishment of pumping works at Bridgeport to lift the water from the south branch of the river into the Illinois and Michigan Canal basin, and so, to turn the current of the river backward, and carry the sewage which flowed into it from hundreds of sewer openings, into the canal instead of into the lake. But in times of freshet the volume of water poured into the river was sufficient to overcome this artificial current and send the sewage into the lake. At such times the water became unfit for use. It became evident that nothing short of an entire change in the system of drainage would be adequate, one that would permanently send the Chicago river backward through an artificial channel cut to the valley of the Desplaines and onward to the Illinois, and which would draw a sufficient volume of water from the lake itself to create a current inshore, and so render contamination impossible. After a long period of agitation, promoted mainly by Hon. Harvey B. Hurd, and a few other broad-minded and public-spirited citizens, a great sanitary district was organized, comprising most of the City of Chicago and parts of Cook County. Commissioners were elected charged with the work of cutting a great drainage canal from the south branch of the Chicago river, across the divide to the valley of the Desplaines and from there on to Joliet and the Illinois river. Taxes were levied, bonds issued, contracts let and the work begun for one of the greatest engineering works of modern times. The work is now under contract, and being prosecuted with the utmost vigor from the point of beginning at Robey street and the Chicago river to Joliet, including the controlling works which are to control the descent into the basin at Joliet. These works will consist of gates or movable dams by which the flow of water from the main channel into the tail race, which is to deliver the outflow into the Desplaines river, can be controlled.

The river below Lockport follows the trough of the valley down a steep declivity into the canal basin at Joliet. The fluctuations in Lake Michigan, by varying slope of water surface, will be felt at the controlling works, and provision must be made to meet these fluctuations covering a range of thirteen feet.

Earth was first broken September 3, 1892, since which time there has been expended up to January 1, 1896, for all purposes, $19,319,-033.87. The estimated cost of construction of the work, including right of way, is something like $28,000,000 to $30,000,000. While this vast outlay has reference solely to providing a suitable drainage system for the City of Chicago, it is intended to utilize it as a great waterway for inland navigation, between Lake Michigan and the Mississippi river by way of the Illinois. It will be large enough to float the largest vessels which can navigate the Mississippi from St. Louis to New Orleans as soon as the general government shall improve the river by the necessary locks and dams between Lockport and La Salle. The fall between these two points is one hundred and fifty feet. Sooner or later the general government must take the entire work off the hands of the State of Illinois and the City of Chicago, and assume control, making it a part of the water-ways for inland navigation of the country. Ultimately the navigation feature will become its most important feature, while yet affording a means of drainage for the City of Chicago. There is reason to believe that its commercial value will exceed that of the Panama or the Suez Canals.

But there is still another advantage which is expected to come from this work. The fall from Lockport to Joliet will give water-power of almost unlimited extent which can be made available for manufacturing purposes on the ground; and which can be used to generate electricity to be conducted to Chicago and used for power, for lighting and for all the purposes to which electricity is now applied.

TRACK ELEVATION.

There is another public improvement which is rapidly assuming large proportions. The population of the city has become so great and the railroad crossings within the city so many as to constitute a serious public danger of accidents, whereby life and limb were sacrificed daily. The number of killed and injured at these crossings has run up to thousands yearly. And, besides, the delays to travel and traffic are so great from these grade crossings as to become a public nuisance. It was found that the only way to cure, or even lessen, the evil, was to elevate the tracks. The Rock Island and the Michigan Southern have already elevated their tracks for a considerable portion of the distance within the city, and the work is being carried on to complete it. Other roads have already consented to do the same thing, and some of them have begun it. There is no doubt that, in the near future, every steam railroad in the city will have raised their tracks sufficient to do away with the danger to life and limb, and to give to traffic freedom from delay from this cause.

POLICE.

The first policeman of Chicago was O. Morrison, who was elected "Police Constable" in 1835, three years after the incorporation of the town. After the organization of the city, "Police Constables," one from each of the young city's six wards, upheld the municipal dignity until 1855, when the Police Department was created. As now organized, this department is under the control of a General Superintendent, appointed by the Mayor. The city is divided into five precincts, which are again subdivided into districts, each precinct, with one exception, containing three districts. The first precinct contains four districts. The headquarters of the department are in the City Hall; each precinct (excepting the fifth, recently created) contains a police court, in which there are daily sittings, and each district contains a station house. The total number of men in this department on January 1, 1896, was 3,255. The efficiency of the force is greatly enhanced by the now famous police telephone and signal system, with the wagon patrol belonging to it. It is purely a Chicago invention, though it has been adopted in Philadelphia and elsewhere, and was put into operation by Mr. Austin J. Doyle, former chief of the department, and since Superintendent of the Chicago Passenger Railway. It includes signal boxes at prominent street corners, containing telephones and alarm dials registering "fire," "thieves," "murder," etc., and connecting with the district station. They have each a gas lamp on top, and replace the ordinary lamp post. In response to a signal call, the patrol wagon is promptly dispatched with its proper detail to the spot. These patrol wagons, containing stretchers, manacles, lanterns, blankets, medicine chests and coils of rope, and having broad, well cushioned seats along their sides, serve equally well as ambulances or police vans, and for use at fires. Patrolmen are required to report by telephone from the signal boxes, at regular intervals during patrol service. The total value of property belonging to the department January 1, 1892, was $1,139,208. The total number of arrests made and prosecuted during the preceding year was 83,464, on the subjects of which fines to the amount of $301,555 were imposed.

FIRE DEPARTMENT.

The Chicago Fire Department owes its efficiency and thoroughness to the lessons the city has learned from terrible experience.

In 1833, three months after Chicago acquired the right to call herself a town, she enacted a fire ordinance, requiring that stove pipes be protected by sheet iron or tin, six inches from wood, where they passed "through the roof, partition or side of any building," and providing a penalty of five dollars for violation of this law. Four fire wardens were also appointed, but found no call for their services until a year after, when, in the early part of October, 1834, four buildings at Lake and La Salle streets were burnt down. The Democrat of the next week, reporting the fire, said: "A building on the corner, occupied as a dwelling, lost $300. There was in the house $220 in money; $125, being in Jackson money, was found in the ruins. The remainder, the rag currency, was destroyed." Thus it appears that, even so early as 1834, our citizens had discovered some of the advantages of "specie payment." In November of the same year a fine of five dollars was affixed as the penalty to an ordinance against carrying "firebrands" or coals of fire from one house or building to another, unless the same be carried, or conveyed in a covered earthen or fireproof vessel."

As now organized, the Fire Department is divided into sixteen battalions, each under a chief of battalion, and the entire force under charge of a fire marshal. Mr. Denis J. Swenie is present holds this office, and his record in the service dates back to its beginning, in 1858, when he was Chief Engineer. The working force consists of 1,116 men and officers, and the department owned, at the close of 1895, 84 steam fire-engines, 27 chemical engines, 4 powerful fire-tugs, 2 stand-pipe and water towers, for reaching lofty buildings; 33 hook and ladder trucks, 100 hose wagons, carts, and carriages; 470 horses, 2 life-saving guns, 12 life-saving nets,

7,000 feet of ladders, and 28 miles of hose. The fire alarm system is very thorough, and includes 2,396 automatic signal boxes, 2,375 miles of wire, and an elaborate network of overhead and under-ground telegraph lines. The South Division contains 38 steamers and 14 hook and ladder outfits; the West Division, 30 steamers and 10 hook and ladder outfits, and the North Division, 13 steamers, and 5 hook and ladder outfits. The celerity with which responses are made to alarms is astonishing, and it is well worth a visit to one of the prominent engine houses to see the crew get under way. Steamer No. 32 is located at foot of Monroe street, within convenient walking distance of all the centrally located hotels.

THE HARBOR

The Chicago river, at the time of the first occupation of the site, was entirely devoid of natural advantages for harborage, and it would have saved the city much embarrassment had the ditch never been opened to admit a sailing vessel or steamer. It would be a great blessing if this foul gutter could be converted from an open into a closed sewer, but, once made a "navigable stream," that became impossible.

In 1812 the soldiers at Fort Dearborn cut a channel through the sand bar opposite the fort, and thus made the first "improvements" looking toward its present greatness and disgrace.

In 1833, the scheme for the Illinois & Michigan Canal having been pretty generally accepted, the government opened its preliminary operations by appropriating $25,000 for rendering the mouth of the Chicago river practicable. Accordingly the two piers were begun, and carried about 500 feet out into the lake, while the spring freshets of 1833 saved the necessity of dredging away the bar.

RAND-McNALLY BUILDING, 160-174 ADAMS STREET

The work was continued intermittingly until 1870, when it was decided to extend the original plans, and include a commodious exterior harbor. These plans were again finally modified in 1878, so that the completed harbor will include a sheltered area sixteen feet in depth, covering 270 acres, with communicating slips along the lake front covering 185 acres, making a total of 455 acres; this, in addition to the river proper, with which the outer harbor communicates. There is, also, an exterior breakwater, one-third of a mile north of the end of the north pier, so situated as to protect vessels entering the mouth of the river. The length of this outer breakwater will be 5,436 feet, of which 3,136 feet have been completed. The north pier, measuring from the outer end of the Michigan street slip, is 1,600 feet long, and extends 600 feet beyond the easterly breakwater, which latter, beginning at the outer end of the south pier, extends directly south 4,060 feet, and is distant 3,300 feet from the present shore line south of Monroe street. A channel 800 feet wide intervenes between this and the north end of the southerly breakwater. This latter breakwater continues for a short distance due south, then turns at an angle of 30°, and extends in a southwesterly direction to within about 1,550 feet of the present shore line, and 500 feet from the dock line. This breakwater is 3,950 feet in length. The line of wharves and slips will be ended, and the southern end of the harbor completed, by the magnificent wharf to be built by the Illinois Central Railroad Company at Thirteenth street. It will extend to the government dock line. There is a lighthouse on the shore end, and a beacon light on the lake end of the north pier, and a beacon light on the north end of the easterly breakwater. The Life Saving Station is at the lake end of the northernmost railroad wharf, directly adjoining the south pier.

On the inner harbor, the wharfing privileges occasioned much dispute, until 1833, when they were defined, the wharves being sold or leased in perpetuity, on payment of their value, and an annual rental of one barleycorn. In 1857 there were but six miles of dock, while at the present time there are twelve miles of slips and slip-basins, and the twenty-nine miles of river front are mostly docked. It happens not infrequently that more than a thousand vessels winter in this harbor.

THE GOVERNMENT BUILDING.

This is an immense stone structure, built in the Romanesque style, with Venetian modifications, and, with its grounds, covers the square bounded by Clark, Jackson, Dearborn and Adams streets. The building proper covers a ground space of 342x210 feet, not inclusive of the elevated lawns which surround it on three sides. It is three stories high, with basement and attic. The building and site together cost the government over $6,000,000, but the work is so imperfect that it is condemned, and is being removed to make room for a new structure.

The Post Office.—The old Kinzie house appears to have served, among its multifarious and successive uses, as Chicago's first Post Office. Anyway, when, in 1831, this city was given a place among the postal towns, Jonathan N. Bailey was appointed Postmaster, and, as there is no record of any special office being secured, it is probable that the mails were distributed from the new official's residence, the old Kinzie house. At this time Niles, Mich., was the nearest distributing office, and from that place the mails came fortnightly by horseback to Chicago. But by 1833 the horseback mail service from Niles had doubled in frequency, while the office had risen to the dignity of occupying half a log cabin, 20x45 feet in extent, near the corner of Lake and South Water streets, the portion on the opposite side of the official partition being occupied as a store by Brewster, Hogan & Co., the second member of which firm—John S. C. Hogan—was then Postmaster. From this date until 1860, when the Government Building was completed, seven or more different removes were made to accommodate the growing business of the office. This first Federal building stood on the northwest corner of Dearborn and Monroe streets, and was burnt out in the fire of 1871, the mails, however, having been saved. The building was afterward repaired, and became the new Adelphi, afterward Haverly's Theatre, until 1881, when it was torn down, and replaced by the First National Bank building.

After the fire, the Post Office occupied successively, Burlington Hall, corner of Sixteenth and State streets, and the Wabash Avenue Methodist Church building, northwest corner of Wabash avenue and Harrison street, until that building was destroyed in the conflagration of 1874. After this, it was located in turn at Washington and Halsted streets (now the West Division sub-office); in the Honore building, northwest corner Dearborn and Adams streets, where it was again burnt out, the basement of the Singer building (now Marshall Field & Co.'s retail store), corner of State and Washington streets; in the Government Building, southeast corner of Clark and Adams streets, and at present in temporary quarters on Michigan avenue, between Madison and Randolph.

The development of the business done by this office has been little short of phenomenal. In 1871, forty years after its establishment with a fortnightly horseback mail, it had become the second in importance under the government. Chicago is the postal distributing centre of one-seventeenth of the inhabitants of the United States. It is the postal centre, territorially considered, of one-fifth of this country. It is the

distributing centre of nearly 5,000,000 people, and the great proportion of its business is of that character. It contributes one-fifteenth of the postal revenue of the United States. Its net profit is second to that of New York, while its percentage of profit is not equaled by any of the large cities of the country. Its total receipts are about $5,000,000 a year, showing an increase of 235 per cent. within the last ten years. It contributes to the government as much as do the cities of St. Louis, Cincinnati, San Francisco, Brooklyn, and Pittsburg together. The allowance for clerk hire at the Chicago Post Office is more than that of all the Post Offices in the States of Alabama, Arkansas, California, Colorado, Connecticut, Delaware, Florida, Georgia, Idaho, Kansas, South Carolina, Utah and Washington.

Chicago as a post office is, territorially considered, with its 187 square miles, the largest in the world. One hundred and twenty-five square miles are served by carriers, of whom there are 1,092 in number. There are now made in the city 3,500 deliveries a day, and about 1,100 collections, and the wagon collectors cover in the neighborhood of 3,800 miles a day, traveling miles enough to encircle the world once a week. The number of persons employed in the Chicago Post Office is about 2,600, and the number of persons paid by the Postmaster of Chicago is about 3,100, which includes the clerks of the railway mail service who radiate from Chicago. The amount of money handled by the money order division of the Chicago Post Office this year will be, in round figures, $30,000,000, or $100,000 a day. The money order business of Chicago is forty times as large as that of Brooklyn. The postal receipts of this office this year will be $5,000,000; the percentage of expense to receipts will be about 55 per cent. in Chicago, considering its enormous mileage (nearly 4,000 miles of which is covered by free delivery. This is a remarkable showing. Last year there were handled 700,000,000 pieces of mail matter. There are in the service 106 wagon collectors, who have 156 horses.

There are in Chicago ninety-two places where money orders can be purchased and mail matter registered, and 190 places where stamps are sold. There are handled on an average in this city 2,000,000 pieces of mail matter daily. There are collected on an average daily, 700,000 pieces of first-class mail matter, meaning letters, of which about 500,000 are for delivery outside the city, and about 200,000 for delivery within the city. In addition thereto there are letters and newspapers (local and otherwise, pieces of mail matter delivered by carriers) enough to make the grand total of 1,000,000 pieces handled by the carriers. Nearly 40,000,000 pounds of second-class mail matter were handled at the Chicago Post Office last year. This amount is enormously large, and when reduced to figures can be estimated at 160,000,000 newspapers, or 500,000 a day.

The number of third and fourth-class pieces, such as catalogues, books, and merchandise, amounted to more than 12,000,000, thus making a total of bulky matter, on the average, of more than 1,000,000 a month.

The honor of devising distribution cars and perfecting the railway mail service is usually given to Col. George B. Armstrong, Assistant Postmaster of the Chicago office in 1864. He was made the first Superintendent of that branch of the service as soon as it was organized, and died on May 5, 1871. There is a bust of him standing on the government grounds, at the corner of Clark and Adams streets.

The Custom House.—Prior to 1846, the port of Chicago was a tributary of the Detroit district, but on July 16th of that year it was made, by Act of Congress, a port of entry, and on August 10th William B. Snowhook, previously special surveyor, was appointed Collector of the Port. The Custom House was then located at 3 Clark street. In 1852 it was removed to 129 South Water street, again removed, in 1856, to 13 La Salle street, where it remained until 1866, when it was transferred to the new government building, at the corner of Dearborn and Monroe streets. After the fire, temporary quarters were occupied during seven months, in Congress Hall Hotel, at the corner of Michigan avenue and Congress street. These quarters proving inadequate a change was made to the Republic Life Insurance building, where the department remained until 1885, when a transfer was made to the now abandoned government building, and is at present temporarily at the corner of Harrison street and Pacific avenue.

The following shows the business transacted in the Inspector's Division of the Custom House during 1895: There were weighed 29,617,861 lbs. of tin-plate; 4,966,877 lbs. of soda; 3,102,959 lbs. of tobacco; 36,678,232 lbs. of miscellaneous matter, making a total of 74,365,929 lbs. There were gauged 315,046 gallons of spirits, and 6,238 packages stamped. There were 2,517,379 cigars received, and 66,747 boxes stamped. The number of vessels measured was 20, number discharged, 303; cars transferred, 469; cars discharged, 7,702; cars inspected, 2,340; consignments, 8,889. There were 929,194 packages delivered to consignee, 26,145 to appraiser, and 334,153 to warehouse.

The growth of the department is shown by the following figures:

Exports, 1836, $1,000.64; imports, $325,203.90; 1857, exports, $1,585,096; imports from Canada, $326,325; duties collected on all importations, $143,000.23; while, by 1871, the value of imports had reached $3,989,860, on which there were collected $1,985,370.10. During the same year there arrived 12,320 vessels, with 3,096,101 tonnage, and cleared 12,312 vessels, of 3,082,235 tonnage. By 1891 the value of imports had risen to $16,828,394, paying in duties $5,920,166.02. The number of vessels owned in Chicago at the close of the same year was 360, with a total tonnage of 72,600. This port registers more entries and clearances than any other in the country.

MILITARY.

Major-General Wesley Merritt, who, on the transfer of Major-General Nelson A. Miles, assumed command of the Department of the Missouri, U. S. A., has his headquarters on the fourth floor of the Pullman building, corner Michigan avenue and Adams street.

The new Post at Fort Sheridan, twenty-four and one-half miles north of the city, on the Chicago & North-Western Railway, and overlooking the lake, quarters ten companies of the regular United States army.

The First Brigade of the Illinois National Guard has its headquarters in Chicago. This Brigade comprises the First Regiment of Infantry, with a granite armory at Sixteenth street and Michigan avenue; the Second Regiment of Infantry, occupying a splendid brick armory at the corner of Washington boulevard and Curtis street; the Third Regiment of Infantry, the Fourth Regiment of Infantry, the First Regiment of Cavalry, occupying a stone armory on Michigan avenue, north of Monroe street; Battery C and Battery D, whose stone armory is at the corner of Michigan avenue and Monroe street, adjoining that of the First Cavalry. The Brigade headquarters are in the Pullman building, corner Michigan avenue and Adams street. This Brigade numbers about 2,500 men, 1,500 of whom are residents of Chicago. Beside these, there are in the city several detached military companies, all liable to State service.

CRIMINAL COURT AND COUNTY JAIL.

These departments of justice occupy three buildings, covering about two-thirds of the square bounded by Michigan street, Dearborn avenue, Illinois and Clark streets. The criminal court building has a frontage of 140 feet on Dearborn avenue, and 65 feet on Michigan street. This building is of limestone. The county court sessions begin on the first Monday of each month. The jail, on Illinois street, is of brick, and contains 198 cells, of which 136 are for male, 48 for female, and 16 for juvenile offenders. The buildings cost $375,000.

PUBLIC BUILDINGS AND INSTITUTIONS.

Trade, as well as society, has grown luxurious in its tastes during these latter days. Time was when the great financiers, at the helms of important mercantile enterprises, were contented with the meanest of quarters, on the theory that the beauty of the oyster has nothing to do with the value of the pearl. But tempora mutantur, et nos mutamus in illis (times change, and we change in them), the merchant prince now prefers to occupy a mercantile palace, and the great generals of finance want something more than shabby tents for their departmental headquarters. Therefore it is that Chicago, being the most modern of all the four great commercial centers of America, more than any of her sister cities reflects this modern idea, and has to show such a great number of handsome and imposing blocks and buildings devoted to purely commercial uses. If there is a typical American city, it is this. America's youngest daughter; and, if there be such a thing as American architecture, it is to be seen in the buildings of Chicago. Their materials are brought from every field, and their designs from every source. As the bulk of Chicago's business is done within the two square miles bounded on the east by the lake, on the south by Twelfth street, on the west by Halsted street, and on the north by the river, the blocks and buildings here described are nearly all within easy walking distance of the City Hall, or any of the hotels.

The foregoing gives a tolerably fair idea of the official organization and governmental departments of the city. Closely connected with them are the courts and those who are entrusted with the administration of the law. And, inasmuch as a city depends, not so much on its great buildings and improvements, as upon the men who maintain its activities, we hereby present the portraits and biographical sketches of some of Chicago's representative men who are intimately connected with its official and administrative functions, the lawyers.

BIOGRAPHICAL SKETCHES.

HON. ABNER SMITH.

The position of judge on the bench, when clothed with its true purity and strength, ranks first among the callings of men. Law is the voice of God and the harmony of the world; and its administration should be by conscientious men who are calm in the strength of flawless rectitude. Judge Abner Smith, who was elected to the Circuit Court bench in November, 1893, has evidenced the possession of qualities and abilities which place him in the rank of such judges. He has served with great satisfaction in the law, chancery and criminal courts, and has won the esteem and high praise of the bar, on account of his legal ability, judicial temperament and fairness. His work, say the lawyers, is performed with the utmost sincerity, never slurred over or hastened as a lawyer or judge; and into it, he puts the best of himself—his best thoughts, his acute observation, his close knowledge of law and of human nature. As a judge, his acts are strong and full of breadth, accuracy and force. Since jurisprudence is the foundation of the commonwealth, and indispensable to its growth,

HON. ABNER SMITH.

prosperity and advance, it is well that such judges represent and enforce it.

In sound judgment, in patient industry, in clear conception of the spirit and scope of jurisprudence and intuitive perception of right, Judge Smith already ranks high in the estimation of bench, bar and public.

Abner Smith was born at Orange, Franklin County, Massachusetts, August 4, 1843. His parents were Humphrey and Sophronia (Ward) Smith, who moved to Middlebury, Vermont, to educate a large family. Abner was graduated from Middlebury College, in 1866, after which he taught in Newton Academy, Shoreham, Vt. He came to Chicago in 1867 and entered the law office of J. L. Stark, a prominent lawyer; studied law, was admitted to the bar in 1868, and entered into partnership with Mr. Stark. When the latter died in 1873, he succeeded to the business of the firm. He has been in active practice since; has devoted himself to his profession; and has been rewarded by a most satisfactory success in all respects. He has won a competence, not one dollar of which was ever rusted with tears, or stained with blood. He has merited and won the esteem of his fellow-citizens because of his uprightness in business and his straightforward conduct. For several years after the dissolution of the firm of Stark & Smith, by the death of Mr. Stark, he practiced alone. In 1877, he formed a partnership with Mr. J. M. H. Burgett, under the name of Smith and Burgett, which continued until 1887. His ancestry, on the paternal and maternal side, are among the oldest and most substantial families in Massachusetts, the latter, the Ward family, known in the annals of the Revolution, before and since, in public positions of trust and honor in legislature and the judiciary. Abner Smith's legal acumen and ability were inherited and have been multiplied by his own attainments. As a lawyer he engaged in a high order of litigation and with a marked degree of success. His upcome has been gradual, permanent and sure. So far as a judge goes, he has met the expectations and sanguine prediction of his friends. In 1869 he married Ada C., daughter of Sereno Smith, of Shoreham, Vt.; and resides at No. 15 Aldine Square.

GEORGE EVERETT ADAMS.

George Everett Adams was born June 18, 1840, in Keene, New Hampshire. He is a descendant, in direct line, from the original Adams family, which settled at Cambridge, Mass., in 1628. His father, Benjamin F. Adams, came to Chicago in 1835 and made some investments; but did not remove here with his

GEORGE EVERETT ADAMS.

family until 1853. Young George received the first rudiments of his education in the common schools of his native town and afterward at Phillips Exeter Academy and Harvard College, where he graduated in the class of 1860. He also graduated from the Dane Law School in 1865. For a short time he was a member of Battery A, Illinois Artillery, in the early part of the war, since which he has devoted his energies to the practice of the law when not serving in official stations. Mr. Adams was elected to the Illinois State Senate in 1880. In 1882 he was elected to Congress and re-elected in 1884, 1886 and 1888, where he served with distinction on the committee on banking and currency, and on the committee on judiciary. He is now a member of the Board of Overseers of Harvard College, a trustee of the Newberry Library, a trustee of the Field Columbian Museum and a member of the Chicago Board of Education.

CHARLES H. ALDRICH.

Charles H. Aldrich was born August 26, 1850, in La Grange County, Indiana, and is a graduate of the University of Michigan. He began the practice of the law at Fort Wayne, Indiana, in 1876. He removed to Chicago in 1886, and soon took high rank at the

CHAS. H. ALDRICH.

bar. He is connected with much of the most important litigation pending in the State and United States courts in Chicago; and is often engaged in contest in other jurisdictions. He served as Solicitor General of the United States during the latter part of Harrison's administration and the first part of Cleveland's second administration. He was married October 13, 1875, to Miss Helen Roberts, a beautiful and accomplished woman, to whom he attributes such success as has come to him. They have three children--one son and two daughters—and reside at Evanston, Illinois.

EDGAR A. BANCROFT.

Edgar A. Bancroft, though a resident of Chicago for but little over four years, is already one of its best-known and popular lawyers. He is the general solicitor of the Chicago & Western Indiana and "The Belt Line" railroads. For three years he was the solicitor for Illinois of the A., T. & S. F. R. R. Company; and as such he had a prominent part in the contempt proceeding in the United States courts, growing out of the Chicago strike of 1894.

Mr. Bancroft graduated from Knox College in 1878, after winning first honors in the interstate oratorical contest. In 1880 he received the degree of LL. B. from the law school of Columbia College, New York. His career as a lawyer began at Galesburg, and his ad-

EDGAR A. BANCROFT.

vancement in his profession has been constant. He is a member of the Union League, the Chicago Literary, the Caxton, the Marquette and the Law Clubs.

WILLIAM H. BARNUM.

William H. Barnum was born in Onondaga County, New York, February 15, 1840. His parents removed to

WILLIAM H. BARNUM.

Belleville, St. Clair County, Illinois, when he was about two years of age. As he grew up, he attended private schools; and, at sixteen, entered the State normal school at Ypsilanti, Michigan, where he spent two and one-half years. He then began teaching at his home, at Belleville, in order to earn the money to continue his studies. He entered the sophomore class of the University of Michigan in the fall of 1858, and, although compelled to relinquish his studies there during the junior year, he has since been accorded the honorary degree of Master of Arts by that institution. On leaving college he resumed teaching at Belleville, at the same time continuing his classical, literary and historical studies under competent instructors.

In 1860 Judge Barnum began the study of the law under Hon. George Trumbull, a brother of Ex-Senator Lyman Trumbull. He was admitted to practice in 1862, and began at Chester, Randolph County, Illinois. In 1867 he removed to Chicago and formed a partnership with Lawrence J. J. Nissen; and continued in the active practice of the law under various connections until 1879, when he was elected to the bench. For six years he filled the judicial office with satisfaction to the bar and honor to himself, when he resigned and resumed the practice of his profession.

Judge Barnum, while practicing at the bar has probably figured as extensively in the celebrated cases of his time as any lawyer in Chicago, his name being prominently associated with the legal history of the country.

LEWIS H. BISBEE.

The subject of this sketch was born in Derby, Orleans County, Vermont, March 28, 1839. He was brought up on a farm; and at sixteen began an

LEWIS H. BISBEE.

academic course of study, afterward entering St. Hyacinth College, Montreal. Here he acquired among other things, a thorough knowledge of French; when he returned to Derby and began the study of the law, supporting himself in the meantime by teaching French. He was admitted to the bar in 1862, but soon enlisted for service in the war, being made captain of Company H, 9th Vermont Infantry. He resigned in 1863 by reason of ill health, and returned to the practice of the law. In 1866 he was elected state's attorney of Orleans County and re-elected in 1867, but resigned to become collector of customs at Newport. In 1869 he was elected to the House of Representatives of Vermont, and again in 1870. During the same time he served as commissioner for Vermont under the extradition treaty with Canada. Mr. Bisbee now sought a wider field for his activities and so removed to Chicago and there again began the practice of the law. In 1875 he attacked the validity of the blanket mortgage which B. F. Allen, of Des Moines, Iowa, had placed upon his real estate before the failure, and succeeded in having it set aside. Since then he has been connected with other celebrated cases. Mrs. Hetty Green, said to be the richest woman in the world, is one of his clients.

Mr. Bisbee is the author of "The Law of Produce Exchange," which is standard on the law governing stock and grain exchanges. He is a Republican and has taken a prominent part in many Republican campaigns. In 1878 he was elected to the Illinois Legislature, receiving almost the unanimous vote of his district. He took an active part in the annexation of Hyde Park to Chicago, being one of the originators of the scheme. He was married in 1864 to Miss Jane E. Hinman, of Vermont. They have two children.

LESTER L. BOND.

Lester L. Bond was born at Ravenna, Ohio, in 1829. He received his early training in the public schools and later attended school in the winter and worked in a machine shop during the summer. He began the study of law in the office of F. W. Tappan, completing it under Beirce and Jeffries. He was admitted to the bar in 1853. He removed to Chicago in 1854 and be-

LESTER L. BOND.

gan his practice, in the prosecution of which he gradually dropped common law and devoted all his energies to patent law, on which he has come to be a recognized authority—one of the most eminent in the northwest. Mr. Bond has served two terms in the Illinois Legislature and several in the Chicago City Council, where he has made a most enviable record. He is a member of many of the powerful Chicago clubs and a Mason of high degree.

JOHN S. MILLER.

John S. Miller was born at Louisville, N. Y., in 1847. He graduated at the St. Lawrence University in 1869, when he became a professor in that institution, at the same time studying law. He was admitted to the bar in 1870, and came to Chicago to practice his profession in 1874.

In 1891 Mr. Miller was appointed corporation counsel by Mayor Washburne, and during two arduous years of labor won, amongst other victories, a recognition of the city's right to compel railroads to elevate their tracks. Mr. Miller also argued and won the celebrated "Lake Front case," involving the right of the Illinois Central Railroad to occupy the Lake front.

Mr. Miller is now a member of the eminent firm of Peck, Miller & Starr, and it need scarcely be insisted upon, as amongst the leaders of the Chicago bar. Mr. Miller married in 1887, and is the father of two children, has a large circle of friends, and is a member of the Chicago, Union League University and other clubs.

CLAYTON EDWARD CRAFTS.

Mr. Clayton E. Crafts was born July 8, 1848, at Auburn, Ohio. His earlier years were spent on his father's farm and attending the common schools. In

CLAYTON E. CRAFTS.

1864 he entered Hiram College. At twenty he graduated from the Ohio State and Union Law College, at Cleveland, Ohio, and was admitted to the bar. Shortly after he entered the law office of Judge John J. Van Allen, at Watkins, New York, remaining there until 1869, when he came to Chicago and began the practice of his profession. In 1882 he was elected to the Illinois House of Representatives; and has since served continuously. He was elected speaker of the House of Representatives for two successive terms, those of 1891 and 1893. He is a recognized leader in the Democratic party; and senior member of the law firm of Crafts and Stevens, making a specialty of real estate and corporation law. Mr. Stevens is master in chancery for the Superior Court of Cook County and one of the foremost lawyers at the bar.

GEORGE W. BROWN.

George W. Brown, County Judge of Du Page County, Illinois, and one of the foremost men at the bar in the West, was born at Winfield Township, Du Page County, May 17, 1859. He received his early training in the common schools of his county, from which he passed to the high school at Wheaton, finally graduating at the Northwestern College at Naperville. From here he entered the Union College of Law of Chicago, taking the full course. In the meanwhile he read law with Hoyne, Horton and Hoyne, of Chicago, and was admitted to the bar at Wheaton in 1883. He then entered upon the practice of his profession at Wheaton, taking a lively interest in all public matters affecting the people of Northern Illinois. In the meantime his practice rapidly increased, together with his popularity among the people. In 1890 he was elected County Judge of Du Page County, and in 1894 was re-elected by an overwhelming majority, being practically the nominee of both political parties. It is needless to say that the administration of his office has met with the hearty approval of the people. That is sufficiently indicated by the unanimity of his re-election.

Judge Brown is nearly, if not quite, as much appreciated in Chicago as he is in his own county. He is often assigned to duty on the bench of this county on the trial of important cases, where he has given uniform satisfaction both to lawyers and litigants.

Judge Brown has opened an office in Chicago in connection with Mr. J. F. Snyder, who is also a resident of Wheaton, under the firm name of Brown and Snyder. The practice of the firm ranks along with the largest and most important in the city. Judge Brown was special attorney for the Northwestern and Metropolitan Elevated Railroad Companies in most of their condemnation suits while building and extending their systems. He is a safe and cautious counsellor; a clear and logical reasoner; a fluent speaker; and before a jury a powerful and effective advocate. He takes an active interest in the destinies of the Republican party, and wields a powerful influence throughout the whole of the northern part of the state.

Judge Brown is a Mason, a Knight Templar of Bethel Commandery, Elgin, Illinois; a "Shriner," of Medina Temple, Chicago; a member of the Odd Fellows, the National Union, Modern Woodmen, Knights of Pythias and other societies. He is a man of moderate means and in the prime of life. Whatever he has and whatever he is has come from his own unaided exertions; and it is fair to expect that the same qualities of diligence and steadfast uprightness that have characterized him in the past will carry him to still greater fame and fortune in the future. Men do not stop growing in the middle of their careers. Judge Brown has still the best portion of his life before him and he confidently looks forward to a long life of usefulness and honor.

GEORGE W. BROWN.

HON. LYSANDER HILL.

Lysander Hill was born in Union, Lincoln County, Maine, July 4, 1834, the son of Isaac and Eliza M. (Hall) Hill, tracing his ancestry to the earliest settlers of Massachusetts. After passing through the common schools, he studied at Warren Academy, and entered Bowdoin College in 1854 and graduated therefrom in 1858. Choosing the law as his profession, he entered the law office of A. P. Gould, at Thomaston, Maine, and was admitted to the bar in 1860. He began practicing at once in Thomaston, forming a partnership with J. P. Cilley, under the firm name of Cilley & Hill. This partnership was dissolved in 1862 when Mr. Hill entered the Union army as captain in the Twentieth Maine Infantry. In 1863, on account of physical disability, Mr. Hill received his discharge from the army.

He resumed the practice of law at Alexandria, Virginia, and Washington, D. C., under the style of Hill & Tucker.

He was Register in Bankruptcy of the Eighth Judicial District of Virginia from 1867 to 1869, when he was appointed judge of the district to fill an unexpired term.

In 1874 Judge Hill removed to Washington, D. C., and in May, 1881, removed to Chicago.

Judge Hill was married in February, 1864, to Adelaide R. Cole, of Roxbury, Massachusetts. This union has been blessed with three children.

In politics, Judge Hill is a Republican. Judge Hill takes rank as one of the ablest patent attorneys in the entire country. He is a gentleman of pleasing address and enjoys the esteem of a large circle of friends.

EDWARD S. ELLIOTT.

Edward S. Elliott, though less than thirty-five years of age, has already achieved a record that would be creditable to an older man. As a young man he educated himself, taught school and entered the University of West Virginia, from which he graduated with the highest honors; and was for two years assistant professor of ancient languages in that institution. Then, graduating from its law school, he took postgraduate law courses at the University of Virginia and at Columbia College, New York, and began law practice in New York City. Subsequently returning to West

EDWARD S. ELLIOTT.

Virginia, he took high rank in his profession. An earnest Republican in politics, he stumped the state for the Republican ticket and made a reputation as a powerful public speaker. He was appointed assistant United States District Attorney by President Harrison, which position he filled with distinguished ability for four years, when he removed to Chicago. Mr. Elliott is a member of the Chicago Bar Association and of the Union League and Hamilton Clubs.

NELSON COWLES GRIDLEY.

At the age of eighteen Mr. Gridley began the study of law in the office of Kent and Davies, of New York, in which city he was born in 1829. When twenty years of age he was appointed Deputy Clerk of the Supreme Court of the city and County of New York, and filled the position for two years. During the last year he was admitted to the bar. He began the active practice of his profession in conjunction with Cyrus Lawton, and later in partnership with J. G. Lamberson. In 1854 he went to San Francisco and practiced there until 1856, in which year he moved to Milwaukee, and finally, in 1870, came to Chicago. Since living in Chicago, Mr. Gridley has built up a large practice, making a specialty of patent law, in which department he is an authority of national

NELSON C. GRIDLEY.

reputation. Mr. Gridley's home is in Evanston, in the advancement of which place he has taken a great interest.

GEORGE W. KRETZINGER.

George W. Kretzinger has been in the successful practice of law in Chicago for more than twenty years. His knowledge of legal matters is unusually

GEORGE W. KRETZINGER.

wide, but he is especially learned in corporation law in which branch of his profession his success has been most marked. As an advocate Mr. Kretzinger is powerful and eloquent. Among other important positions,

Mr. Kretzinger has for some time been general counsel of the Louisville, New Albany & Chicago Railroad Company. Mr. Kretzinger's determination of character was early evidenced by his entering the army at the age of fifteen. He served during the entire war, and, youthful as he was, was noted for his courage and capacity. In social circles Mr. Kretzinger is much esteemed, and his manly qualities have won him many friends.

WILLIAM SIDNEY ELLIOTT, JR.

William Sidney Elliott, Jr., son of William Sidney and Caroline (Morse) Elliott, was born at Niles, Michigan, May 1, 1849, and is a lineal descendant of John Eliot, the noted Indian apostle. His early education was acquired in the public schools of Quincy, Illinois. After leaving school he entered the banking house of L. & C. H. Bull, of Quincy, where he remained for four years. Coming to Chicago in March, 1869, he obtained a position with the old State Insurance Company of Chicago, with which he remained for one year, leaving it in 1870 to enter the insurance brokerage business in which he worked up one of the best paying patronages of the great Chicago fire period. In 1879 he began the study of law in the office of Emery A. Storrs, with whom he formed a partnership after his admission to the bar in 1882, which ended in 1887, when he was appointed assistant state's attorney of Cook County under Judge Longenecker, with whom he remained five years, during which time he prosecuted and secured the conviction of many noted criminals, among them being George Painter, executed for the murder of his mistress, Alice Martin; George Hathway, the slayer of Alderman Whalen, sentenced to life imprisonment afterwards sent, on his plea of guilty, to three years in penitentiary; John Conly, sentenced by jury for life upon purely circumstantial evidence; the murderers of Officer Adam Frier—Mortel and McGrath—sentenced to Joliet for life, afterwards given a new trial and acquitted; John Dennison, murderer of John Dillon, while attempting burglary; Meckie Rauson, for shooting Lawyer Whitney; Mathles Bush, for the most brutal murder of his wife, penalty life imprisonment; Augest Helzke, who whipped his son to death with a strap, sentence life imprisonment, which was commuted from the death penalty which had been imposed by the jury; Anarchist Hronek, charged with conspiracy to assassinate Judges Gary and Grinnell with dynamite or knife, twelve years in Joliet; Edward A. Trask, who had for years defied the law by countless crimes, was sentenced to eighteen years in Joliet, where he has since died; James Driscoe, convicted of murderous assault on Edwin Walker, thirty years in penitentiary; John Redmond, the father of the abducted Annie Redmond, who, through jealousy, killed Dr. Wilder, given a life sentence in prison. Mr. Elliott has been one of the most successful of defenders. In two cases the death penalty was imposed, those of Borveile and Nic Marzen. A motion is now pending in the Supreme Court in the former for a new trial; in the Marzen case Mr. Elliott has secured a reprieve from Governor Altgeld until next January, and will, in that time, have an opportunity to present new evidence that it is hoped will clear his client of the charge. Mr. Elliott participated in the effort for a stay of execution in the case of Pendergrast, who slew Carter H. Harrison; and to his services must be partly ascribed the success of those endeavors resulting in a postponement of the execution pending a trial of the question of the insanity of Pendergrast, which excited so much comment among the legal fraternity at the time, many having contended that the time for his legal execution having passed he was dead in the eyes of the law and could not thereafter be executed, which Mr. Elliott denied, being fully sustained in his position by the execution of Prendergast after the question of sanity had been passed upon. At the conclusion of Mr. Elliott's plea to the court for a stay of execution, which was granted by Judge Chetlain, Mr. James S. Harlan, son of Justice Harlan of the Supreme Court of the United States, and whom Mr. Elliott was assisting in securing the said stay of execution, passed to Mr. Elliott a note containing the following memoranda in pencil, of the date of March 22, 1894, which

WILLIAM S. ELLIOTT, Jr.

Mr. Elliott highly cherishes: "Abe Lincoln never made a more powerful speech than the one you have just made, James S. Harlan." This speech was made about the hour of midnight, within a few hours of the moment set for the execution, and after all other sources of relief had been exhausted. The conditions were highly tragic and dramatic, and will never be forgotten by those who witnessed them.

The trial of Windrath, the murderer of Corey B. Birch, on the question of his insanity, subsequently to his having been sentenced to death by Judge Horton, has since more fully sustained the position urged at the time on behalf of Prendergast.

He has conducted the defense in thirty-five murder cases since leaving the State's Attorney's office; of them twenty-two were jury trials, the verdict in fifteen of which was not guilty.

In social life Mr. Elliott is prominent; and, besides being a member of the Masonic fraternity, affiliates with several societies and clubs. He was one of the early directors of the Apollo Musical Club, and as such contributed greatly by his enterprise and energy in establishing that organization upon the firm basis upon which it now rests. He is an active, and has been an official member of the Royal Arcanum, the Royal League, the National Union and the Ancient Order of Foresters of America, of which latter order he was elected the first supreme chief ranger for the United States. In all church and charitable work Mr. Elliott is especially interested. He is a member and attendant of the Congregational Church, and entertains liberal, yet evangelical, views on religious subjects.

Politically, Mr. Elliott is a stanch Republican, and has for several years been a power in his party. In political campaigns his well known eloquence has brought his services into requisition, and his voice has been frequently heard on the platform in every ward, village and hamlet in Cook County, as well as in the general campaign field.

On October 14, 1871, Mr. Elliott was married to Miss Alinda Caroline Harris, of Janesville, Wisconsin. They have six children: Lorenzo Bull, Daniel Morse, Charles Sumner, Emery Storrs, Jessie Florence and Birdie Leon.

In personal appearance Mr. Elliott is a man of more than average size, being fully six feet tall and weighing about 200 pounds. He is well proportioned and of a winning, yet commanding, presence. One of his leading characteristics in his business affairs is his habit of giving careful attention to details. On his social side, he is exceptionally genial, always companionable and deservedly popular with his friends, who have never had occasion to complain of his fidelity however trying the ordeal.

JEREMIAH LEAMING.

Jeremiah Leaming was born at Cape May, New Jersey, January 20, 1831, the son of Jeremiah and Abigail (Falkenburg) Leaming. A representative of the Leaming family landed in New England in 1650 and settled in Connecticut. In 1690 Mr. Aaron Leaming settled in Cape May County, New Jersey; and it was from here that the subject of our sketch comes. His early education was obtained at private schools. At fourteen years of age he was sent to a boarding school at West Chester, Pennsylvania; then he attended school at Mount Hollay and Bordentown, New Jersey, and finally entered Princeton College, from which he graduated in 1853. He then studied law at Bordentown, and was admitted to the bar in 1856. The same year he married Miss Harriet Scovel, the daughter of Rev. Alden Scovel, of Bordentown, and removed to Bloomington, Illinois, where he entered upon the practice of the law. Here he formed the personal acquaintance of Mr. Lincoln and practiced in the court of Judge David Davis. At the breaking out of the war, Mr. Leaming was offered the command of a regiment, but circumstances were such as to preclude his accepting.

In January, 1867, Mr. Leaming removed to Chicago and entered upon a new field of legal practice. For

JEREMIAH LEAMING.

several years he has been Master in Chancery of the Circuit Court of Cook County, and enjoys to a very great degree the confidence of both bench and bar.

CLARENCE A. KNIGHT.

Clarence A. Knight was born in McHenry County, Illinois, October 28, 1853. At an early age he was

CLARENCE A. KNIGHT.

deprived, by death, of the guiding hand of a father, who was killed in battle in the Union army during the White River expedition. Young Clarence fitted himself, at the Englewood Normal School, to teach; and, in that way, maintained himself while taking his

BIOGRAPHICAL SKETCHES.

law course. He studied for two years with Spafford, McDaid and Wilson, and was admitted to the bar by the Supreme Court at Ottawa in September, 1874. He then formed a partnership with Mr. McDaid, one of his old instructors, under the name of McDaid & Knight. He was appointed, in 1879, Assistant City Attorney under Julius S. Grinnell, whom he succeeded as City Attorney in 1884; and in 1888 he was appointed Assistant Corporation Counsel by Mayor Roche. This position he held until 1889, when he resigned to engage in private practice. During his ten years' connection with the city law department, Mr. Knight, more than any one else, shaped the course of legislation relative to the city of Chicago. To him is credited the acts under which the various annexations have been made to the city, and also the shaping of most of the important franchises which were granted during his time.

Upon his retirement from public life he formed a partnership with Mr. Paul Brown, under the firm name of Knight & Brown. The practice of the firm runs largely to corporation, municipal and insurance law. It represents the interests of many of the great corporations of the city.

Mr. Knight is a Mason, a Knight Templar of Chevalier Bayard Commandery; a member of the Royal League, Independent Order of Forresters, the Iroquois and the Athletic Clubs.

FRANK ORREN LOWDEN.

Frank O. Lowden was born at Sunrise City, Minn., January 26, 1861. He is of Scotch lineage which runs back to a time prior to the British war of 1812. His parents removed to Iowa in 1868, where young Frank worked on his father's farm in the summer and attended the public schools in the winter. At fifteen he began teaching in Hardin County, thus

FRANK O. LOWDEN.

earning the money to defray the expense of his schooling. He entered college at the Iowa State University in September, 1881, taking the classical course. He graduated in June, 1885, being valedictorian of his class. He then resumed teaching at the Burlington, Iowa, High School, studying law during leisure hours.

In 1886 he entered the law office of Dexter, Herrick & Allen of Chicago, at the head of which stood the Hon. Wirt Dexter. He also took a course at the Union College of Law, from which he graduated in 1887, as valedictorian of his class. He received first prize for his oration and first prize for scholarship. He was admitted to the bar the same year after examination before the Appellate Court, standing at the head of his class. In 1890 he became a partner of Mr. E. S. Walker, which continued for two years. Mr. Lowden is now in practice by himself.

Mr. Lowden is a Republican in politics, and a liberal in religion, having been a close friend of the late Prof. David Swing. He is a member and director of the Calumet Club; member of two college fraternities; member of the Union League; Chicago, Washington Park, Sunset and the Law Clubs and of the Chicago Bar Association.

JAMES R. MANN.

James R. Mann was born near Bloomington, Illinois, October 20, 1856, from whence his father moved to Iroquois County in 1867. He was graduated at the University of Illinois in 1876, at the head of his class.

JAMES R. MANN.

In 1879 he entered the Union College of Law in Chicago; won all the prizes for scholarships in both junior and senior years; the Horton prize of $100 for best written thesis, besides being the valedictorian of his class. He was admitted to the bar in 1881, since which he has been in the active practice in Chicago. Mr. Mann has served on the School Board of Hyde Park, and attorney for the village prior to its annexation to Chicago. Subsequently he was elected in 1892 Alderman from the Thirty-second Ward to the Chicago City Council, and re-elected in 1894. He was a leading member of the City Council; and, for three years, was Chairman of the Judiciary Committee. To his efforts are due the drainage of the swampy district south of Jackson Park by a low level sewer system and pumping works; the creation of the Bureau for Street and Alley Cleaning; regulations for the inspection of milk; requiring corporations to make deposits of money to secure the proper replacement of streets torn up by them; the extension of the water pipe system by special assessment; the use of vitrified brick for street pavement, and many others of equal importance. In the Council, Mr. Mann has been the leader of the honest minority as against the boodle gang, and was a hard and resourceful fighter.

In 1894 he was temporary chairman of the Republican Convention, and made an opening speech which placed him in the front rank of political speakers. The Chicago Tribune editorially demanded that the State Central Committee should compel Mr. Mann to stump the State, which he did in the 1894 campaign, in a manner which added to his fame. In 1895, he led a revolt against the party leadership assumed by Mayor Swift in Chicago and was sustained by his party in the most hotly contested primary campaign ever known; and as a result he was elected Chairman of the Cook County Republican Convention. In the spring of 1896 Mr. Mann was nominated as candidate for Congress from the First District of Illinois, one of the strongest Republican districts in the country. He is noted as a keen thinker, forceful speaker and graceful writer, commanding attention in the court room or on the stump.

Mr. Mann was for several years a Master in Chancery of the Superior Court of Cook County, but resigned on account of his increased law practice. He is attorney of the South Park Commissioners, in Chicago; and is the head of the firm of Mann, Hayes & Miller, real estate and chancery lawyers.

He was married in 1882 to Emma Columbia, of Champaign, and has one son. He is a member of the Chicago Bar Association, Chicago Law and Art Institutes, the Union League, Hamilton, Oakland, Lakota, Hyde Park, 12:45, Unity and a number of other clubs.

HON. HARVEY B. HURD.

Harvey B. Hurd was born February 14, 1828, at Huntington, Fairfield County, Connecticut. He lived and worked on his father's farm until he was fourteen years of age, when he entered the office of the Bridgeport Standard, to learn to be a printer. Two years later, in 1844, he went to New York and worked for a time with Gould & Banks, law publishers.

HARVEY B. HURD.

While here he "set up" Daniel Webster's brief in the famous Girard case. In the fall of 1844 he returned to Bridgeport, and from there set out with ten other young men to attend Jubilee College, at Peoria, Ill. From there he removed to Chicago, in 1846. His first regular employment was on the Evening Journal, and afterward on the Prairie Farmer. He began the study of the law with Calvin De Wolf, and was admitted to the bar in 1848. While his profession has been the law and his thought has been in that direction, fortunate investments in real estate have given him an easy competence. He was an anti-slavery agitator, a member of the Buffalo Convention of 1856, and of the committee that formed the plan of organization there adopted, which resulted in making Kansas a free State. In 1869 Mr. Hurd served as one of the commissioners to revise the statutes of the State, and before it was finished the whole work devolved upon him, which he finished in April, 1874. He was then appointed to edit the edition of 1884. In 1862 he was elected to the chair of the Union College of Law, as professor of pleadings, practice and common and statutory law, which he still holds. Since that time he has taken great interest in all public matters. To him is credited the origin of the movement for the establishment of the sanitary district of Chicago and in the adoption of the Torrens system of land titles. Mr. Hurd was married in May, 1853, to Cornelia A. Hilliard, daughter of James H. Hilliard, of Middletown, Connecticut. In November, 1860, he was married again, to Sarah G., the widow of George Collins, of Chicago. Mr. and Mrs. Hurd have two living children: Eda I., the wife of George S. Lord, and Nellie, the wife of John Comstock.

WILLIAM EARNEST MASON.

William E. Mason is one of Chicago's most esteemed and foremost lawyers and politicians. He is a stalwart Republican, but has friends among all parties and classes. He was born in Franklinville, New York, July 7, 1850. The family removed to Bentonsport, Iowa, in 1865, since which time William has been practically thrown upon his own resources. By alternating periods of teaching with study he was enabled to make his way through school and support himself until he was admitted to the bar in 1871. Since that time he has been an active factor in politics as well as at the bar. He has served one term in the Lower House and one in the Upper House of the State Legislature of Illinois, and two terms as a member of Congress. In 1894 he entered the canvass for the United States Senate and made a tour of most of the counties of the State, giving his entire time to the Republican State committee, much of the time speaking in two counties a day. Out of nearly 300 Republican papers in the State there is not one which has not commended the splendid work done by Mr. Mason, even where they were opposed to his candidacy. He attacked no other candidate nor antagonized any other interest, but kept steadily to his own work. While he did not win the last time, he is still in the field, and he will be a good one who snatches the prize from him in 1897.

HENRY STANTON MONROE.

Henry Stanton Monroe, a prominent member of the Chicago bar, was born at Baltimore, Md., February 9, 1829. He graduated at Geneva College, New York, in 1850, valedictorian of his class. He then began the study of the law, and was admitted to the bar in 1853, beginning practice in Chicago in 1855. Mr. Monroe's practice has been general and extended. He has conducted some of the most celebrated cases that have ever come before the Illinois courts. Among them have been the Tilden and Myers case vs. the Chicago and Alton Railroad Company, and the Sturgess case vs. the Farwells and Taylor. He has handled many other celebrated cases in other States, notably, the Dixon Township case, tried in New Hampshire; the

HENRY S. MONROE.

Emma Mine case, tried in Utah; and the Michael Reese case, tried in California.

Mr. Monroe has always been a great lover of literature. At the great Chicago fire he lost one of the finest private libraries in the city, over 4,000 volumes of which were on law. He is an enthusiastic sportsman, especially with rod and gun. He was married in 1856 to Miss Mattie Mitchell of Akron, Ohio. They have one son and three daughters. His daughters especially have made good records in literary circles and his son ranks high in his profession.

ELIJAH B. SHERMAN, LL. D.

Elijah B. Sherman was born at Fairfield, Vermont, June 18, 1832. His first twenty-one years were spent on the farm, during which time he acquired a fair common school education which enabled him to begin teaching at nineteen. At twenty-one he went to Brandon and took a position as clerk in a drug store to earn the money which would enable him to enter college. He entered Middlebury College in 1856 and sustained himself by teaching. He graduated in 1860, and in 1861 became principal of the Brandon Seminary. In 1862 he enlisted in Company C, 9th Vermont Infantry, and was elected second lieutenant. His regiment was made prisoners at Harper's Ferry, where it was paroled and sent to Camp Douglas, Chicago. There he resigned and entered the Law Department of the University of Chicago, from which he graduated in 1864. He was elected to the State Legislature in 1876, serving as chairman of the committee in Judicial Department, and was re-elected in 1878. Mr. Sherman has filled many important official positions, having been master in chancery of the Circuit Court

ELIJAH B. SHERMAN.

of the United States since 1879. He was also Chief Supervisor of Elections for the Northern District of Illinois from 1884 to 1892. He is an Odd Fellow, a Mason, a member of the Grand Army, of the Veteran Club and of the Loyal Legion. He was one of the founders of the Illinois Bar Association, and its president in 1882-83; has been president of the Illinois Association of the Sons of Vermont, and is a member of many prominent clubs and societies. He received the degree of LL. D. from his alma mater in 1884. Mr. Sherman is a Republican in politics and has been identified with the history of the party since its organization.

ROSENTHAL, KURZ & HIRSCHL.

This is one of the foremost law firms in Chicago. It is composed of Mr. James Rosenthal, Adolph Kurz and Andrew J. Hirschl.

James Rosenthal is a native of Chicago. He was educated in the Chicago public schools, Chicago High School and Lake Forest, and graduated at Yale College Law School in 1880. He was admitted to the bar in July, 1880, and, for a time, practiced in his father's firm, Rosenthal & Pence, where he gained a large experience in probate and real estate law. The present firm was organized July, 1894. Mr. Rosenthal has always taken an active interest in educational matters, and in 1891 was appointed a member of the Board of Education for Chicago, serving for three years. He has proved himself one of the most useful members as chairman of the judiciary committee and as chairman of the committee on buildings and grounds. He was one of the organizers of the Young Men's Hebrew Charity Association and its first secretary. He is a staunch Republican and active in the councils of his party, and is a member of the Hamilton and Woodlawn Park Clubs, Chicago Bar Association, Illinois State Bar Association, and Commercial Law League of America.

Adolph Kurz, the second member of the firm of

Rosenthal, Kurz & Hirschl, was born in Germany, January 11, 1868. He removed, with his widowed mother, to this country in 1882 and settled in Chicago. His first care was to acquire a thorough education,

JAMES ROSENTHAL.

and in 1889 he graduated from the Chicago College of Law and entered upon the practice of his profession. Until then he had supported himself, while prosecuting his studies, as manager of the city collecting department of a large commercial law firm, to which he rose step by step from errand boy. Acquiring a love for

ADOLPH KURZ.

his work, he determined to make commercial law his specialty. He numbers among his clients such houses as Hibbard, Spencer, Bartlett & Co., Cribben, Sexton & Co., and other firms of like standing. He is a recognized expert in commercial law. He is a member of the Standard Club, the Chicago Bar Association and Chicago Law Institute.

Andrew J. Hirschl, member of Rosenthal, Kurz & Hirschl, was born April 30, 1853, at Davenport, Iowa. Mr. Hirschl was educated at Griswold College, Davenport, and at Amherst, Mass. He then took a course in the law department of the Iowa State University, at Iowa City. He began practice at Davenport, but, in July, 1891, removed to Chicago, mainly to be near the University of Chicago, where he desired his children to be educated.

Mr. Hirschl has had a wide experience in theoretical law, as well as a large scope of practice in the trial of cases. He was for a time a lecturer on the Law of Torts at the State University law department, Iowa City, in 1888, and declined a permanent appointment, finding it interfered too much with his practice.

Mr. Hirschl has been identified with a number of important cases in the Appellate and Supreme Courts. Among the more important Supreme Court cases are the Kean assignment case, reversing the settled practice of the Circuit and Appellate Courts; the Wrixon case, establishing the liability of street car companies for not having fenders on wheels; the Great Western

ANDREW. J. HIRSCHL.

Telegraph Company vs. Lowenthal, relating to liability of stockholders; People ex rel. Ahrens vs. English, establishing the right of women to vote at school elections (except for county or state superintendent); People vs. McConnell, mandamus establishing the duty of judge to hear and determine a motion for new trial left undecided by a deceased judge.

Mr. Hirschl is a Mason; member of the A. O. U. W.; of the "Turn-Verin" since 1857; is now a member of the Chicago Bar Association, Chicago Law Institute, Medico-Legal Club, Hamilton Club, Woodlawn Park Club, Delta Kappa Epsilon Fraternity, and always a Republican.

He was married September 27, 1876, to Charlotte Schreiner, a native of Prussia.

WILLIAM H. TATGE.

William H. Tatge was born at Crete, Illinois, November 9, 1860, of German parentage. His family came to this country in the fall of 1848. Early in life he imbibed a love for the law through working in his father's office while he was Clerk of the Circuit Court of Will County, at Joliet. He received a thorough training in the parochial schools of the Lutheran Church, and graduated at Concordia College, at Fort Wayne, Indiana. To gratify his parents he entered the Lutheran Theological Seminary at St. Louis, but his taste for the law led to its abandonment one year later, when he began to study with Hill & Dibell (now Judge Dibell) of Joliet. After a course of preliminary reading he entered Union College of Law, at Chicago, from which he graduated in June, 1883, having previously been admitted to the bar, after examination, by the Appellate Court, in March, 1883.

Having imbibed a love for politics along with that of the law, he has always taken an active part, so that, it is not surprising that he was admitted to the counsels of the Lutheran Church when its interests were attacked by the compulsory school law of 1890. Mr. Tatge was engaged to defend all the cases brought against parents in the State for sending their children to the parochial schools. In this he was eminently successful.

After Mr. Swift was elected as Mayor of Chicago he appointed Mr. Tatge as City Prosecuting Attorney, which office he has filled with credit to himself and satisfaction to his superiors. Mr. Tatge's practice is a general one. By hard work and conscientious effort he has become a successful practitioner.

WILLIAM H. TATGE.

Mr. Tatge was married May 6, 1885, to Miss Nellie Mallen, and resides with his wife and four boys in Englewood.

LORIN CONE COLLINS, JR.

Lorin Cone Collins, Jr., was born at Windsor, Connecticut, August 1, 1848. As a boy he attended the common schools of St. Paul, Minnesota, to which city his parents had removed in 1853. When nineteen years of age he went to Delaware, Ohio, and passed through a two years' course of training for college. He entered the Northwestern University, at Evanston, in 1868, graduating in 1872. On leaving college he entered the law office of Clarkson and Van Schaak, in Chicago, and began the study of law. Admitted to the bar in 1874, he engaged in the practice of his profession until 1878, when he was elected to the Legislature. He was twice re-elected and in his last term became Speaker of the House. During his service he was identified with many popular measures.

In 1884 Mr. Collins was appointed Judge of the Circuit Court of Cook County by Governor Hamilton to fill the vacancy caused by the resignation of Judge Barnum. In the following June he was elected for the term of six years. In 1891 he was again elect-

LORIN C. COLLINS, JR.

ed, and served until October, 1893, when he resigned and again entered on the practice of law.

JOHN R. PARKER.

John R. Parker has been actively engaged in Chicago legal affairs since his admission to the bar by the Supreme Court at Mount Vernon in 1875. He has won a great reputation and acquired a large practice by his ability and straightforwardness. Mr. Parker is a man of broad sympathies. He is actively interested in politics and always takes a prominent part in all campaigns as a Republican. He is one of the

JOHN R. PARKER.

most effective speakers that the State Republican campaign committee has at its disposal. He is a resident and large property owner in the Twelfth ward, and is deeply interested in its material and political welfare. He is ever a foremost worker for any movement tending toward the city's improvement. Mr. Parker is interested in literary and educational matters and is a graduate of Hillsdale College.

KICKHAM SCANLAN.

Kickham Scanlan has already acquired a fame in his profession far beyond his years. While only thirty-one years of age, he has been engaged in more of the celebrated criminal law cases in Chicago and the West than almost any other lawyer of twice his years. He was born in Chicago, October 23, 1864. His father, Michael Scanlan, of Washington, D. C., is well known as a writer and composer of music. During Kickham's childhood he accompanied his parents to Washington, where he attended the public and high schools of the Capital City. He afterward entered the University of Notre Dame, at South Bend, Indiana, where he took a three-year course, which he followed with a special course under a private tutor. Returning to Chicago he entered the office of Colonel W. P. Rend, the well-known coal dealer and operator, where he served for four years, during which time he acquired habits of business and a knowledge of affairs which has been of the greatest service in his subsequent career. His tastes, talents and inclination, however, were all toward the law as his profession in life. In 1886 he entered the law office of Luther Laflin Mills and George C. Ingham, at the same time taking a course at the Chicago College of Law, graduating in its first class. Following close in the footsteps of his eminent preceptor, Mr. Mills, Mr. Scanlan soon became famous in the handling of criminal cases. He remained with the firm of Mills & Ingham for seven years, during which he assisted in the trial of all of the important cases with which it was connected, including the McGarigle case, the first trial of the Cronin case, the Ohio tally-sheet fraud case in Columbus, Ohio, in 1888, where he was associated with Mr. Mills and Allen G. Thurman for the prosecution, the Millington poisoning case at Denver in 1891, and many others. His careful, painstaking industry and conspicuous ability soon made his services sought for; and he has, for years, been repeatedly called upon to assist the State's Attorney of Cook County in the prosecution of difficult criminal cases. In argument he is logical and eloquent, and his words always carry weight with judge and jury, seldom failing to result in victory. Mr. Scanlan was special counsel for the State in the Graham-Hank bribery case in Chicago, which prosecution resulted in the first conviction for jury bribery in the West. His connection with the two Cronin cases is well known throughout the country. His keen logic, his brilliant eloquence, and withal his masterly argument, carried conviction and made him widely known. In the second trial he made the opening speech for the prosecution, which extended over three days. His analysis and presentation of the case was acknowledged by all who heard it as one of the most masterly and convincing in the history of the Chicago bar. That the prosecution won its case is the general verdict of the public, but influences were at work below the surface which gave the verdict of the jury to the other side.

KICKHAM SCANLAN.

In 1893 Mr. Scanlan opened an office in the Ashland block, where he has met with almost uninterrupted success. One of the most peculiar cases in the history of Chicago jurisprudence was that of Edwin Kohn, who confessed to taking a decoy letter from the mail. Mr. Scanlan defended. He raised the point that the decoy letter was not such an one as was contemplated by the United States statutes under which Kohn was indicted. Judge Groscup sustained the point and discharged the prisoner.

Mr. Scanlan was married in 1890 to Miss Sadie Conway, daughter of Michael W. Conway, Fire Inspector of Chicago. She is a woman of rare attainments and has proved a helpmeet indeed. Two daughters have been born to them. Their home is pleasantly located at No. 85 Ewing Place, where literature, music and art add their charms to the other attractions, and give evidence of the refined and cultured home.

Mr. Scanlan is an active Republican, and exerts a powerful influence in the destinies of his party.

WILLIAM VOCKE.

An example of the self-made American citizen, and an exemplification of what an ambitious foreigner can do in this country is shown in the case of William Vocke.

Mr. Vocke came here from the historic Minden, in Westphalia, when seventeen years of age. This was in 1856. His father was a government secretary in the Prussian service, and after his death the son, believing that the United States offered him a future not to be found in his own country, emigrated hither. He stopped in New York for a short time, and then came to Chicago. He was for a time employed by the "Staats Zeitung," in the meantime studying law.

In 1860, he entered the employ of Ogden, Fleetwood & Co., a real estate firm of Chicago. On the day that the war broke out he enlisted. His company was soon merged into the Twenty-fourth Illinois Volunteer Infantry. After the expiration of his term of service he was mustered out as captain of Company D, of the Twenty-fourth Illinois.

WILLIAM VOCKE.

When Captain Vocke returned to Chicago, he again entered the service of the "Staats Zeitung;" this time as its city editor. For nearly a year he held this responsible chair. From April, 1865, to November, 1869, he was the clerk of the police court of this city. He resumed the study of the law in the meantime, and was admitted to the bar in 1867.

He was elected a member of the Illinois Legislature in 1870. Captain Vocke was also a member of the Chicago Board of Education from 1877 to 1880. For nearly twenty years past he has been attorney for the Imperial German Consulate at this point.

In 1867 he was joined in matrimony to Elise Wahl, a charming woman, and they have a family of six children—four daughters and two sons.

JOHN CHAUNCEY TRAINOR.

John Chauncey Trainor was born at Watertown, N. Y., in 1858, where he received his early education. He began the study of law in his native town in the law office of Hannibal Smith. His professional studies were interrupted by two terms of school teaching, after which he resumed them with E. B. Wynn, general counsel for the Rome, Watertown & Odgensburg Railroad Company. Mr. Trainor was admitted to the bar at the general term of the Supreme Court held at Syracuse, N. Y., January 6th, 1882, at the age of twenty-four, and a year later came to Chicago to practice his profession. He first opened an office at Kensington, and after establishing a permanent practice removed to the La Fayette Building, 70 La Salle Street.

Mr. Trainor is regarded as one of the prominent and successful lawyers of Chicago, having attained

JOHN C. TRAINOR.

that position by honesty and hard work. In politics he is a Republican, always active, unselfish and loyal to his friends.

CHARLES S. THORNTON.

Among the leaders of the bar of Chicago is Charles S. Thornton. He was born in Boston, Massachusetts,

CHARLES S. THORNTON.

in 1851, obtained his education in that city and at Harvard College. In 1873 he was admitted to practice in Illinois upon examination before the Supreme Court of that State, and has since been admitted to practice in the District, Circuit and Supreme Courts of the United States. He has been counsel in many leading cases in the practice of his profession, and has met with extraordinary success.

In addition to his law practice he has at times devoted some of his attention to public affairs. For three years he was a member of the Cook County Board of Education, was afterward elected a member of the City Board of Education, where he served for three years also, and in 1895 was appointed a member of the State Board of Education of Illinois, a position which he now holds. Some of the measures advocated by him will be of lasting benefit to the public school system. He is the author of the Pension Bill for teachers, the system of Truant Schools, and the Six Years' College Preparatory Court now in operation in the schools of Chicago.

HORATIO LOOMIS WAIT.

Hon. Horatio L. Wait was born in New York City, August 8, 1836. He comes from old colonial and revolutionary stock, his ancestors settling in Massachusetts early in the seventeenth century. His parents were Joseph and Harriet Helleman (Whitney) Wait, natives of Vermont, but who met with a considerable succcess in business in New York.

Young Horatio attended the Trinity School in New York, and, at fourteen, entered Columbia College grammar school, where he prepared for college. In 1856 he came to Chicago and entered the employ of J. Young Scammon. At the breaking out of the rebellion he forsook his lawbooks and joined Captain Bradley's company D, Sixteenth Illinois Infantry. But before that was ready for the field Mr. Wait was offered a position as assistant paymaster in the navy, which he accepted. He was commissioned by President Lincoln and ordered to report to Rear Admiral Paulding, at New York. Here he was assigned to duty on board the U. S. steamer "Pembina," with the rank of master, in the squadron under command of Admiral Dupont.

For a time the "Pembina" was on blockade duty off Savannah, where it frequently exchanged shots with the rebels constructing batteries to protect that stronghold, but was later sent on a cruise to the West Indies in pursuit of the "Alabama." In the winter of 1862 it reported to Admiral Farragut off Pensacola and Mobile. Here the "Pembina" engaged in several spirited engagements with the Confederate batteries, captured two blockade runners and aided in the capture of others. When the "Pembina" was laid up for repairs Mr. Wait was transferred to the "Mary Sanford," transporting ammunition to Charleston for the monitor fleet. A few months later he was ordered to report to Admiral Dahlgren for duty on the flagship "Philadelphia," where he participated in the naval events in conjunction with General Gilmore's attack upon and capture of Fort Sumter. He assisted in the ceremonies following the surrender, a part of which consisted in hoisting the same flag over the fort by Major Anderson that he had been compelled to lower in 1861. After the conclusion of peace Mr. Wait was transferred to the U. S. ship "Ino," and with the European squadron visited all the ports of note from Great Britain to Italy. The "Ino" was the first U. S. naval vessel to enter many of these ports after the war. While off Lisbon Mr. Wait was promoted to full paymaster, with the rank of lieutenant commander. He returned to the United States in 1867, and was ordered to the ship "New Hampshire," commanded by Rear Admiral Rowan, at the Norfolk navy yard, and in 1868 was transferred to the Pensacola navy yard as inspector.

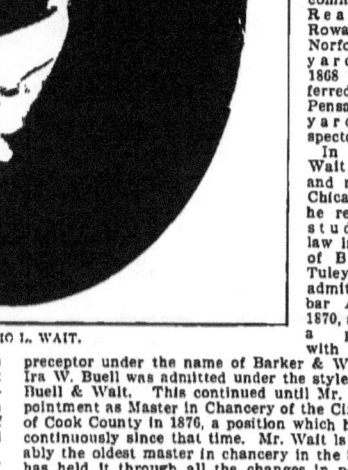

HORATIO L. WAIT.

In 1869 Mr. Wait resigned and returned to Chicago, where he resumed the study of the law in the office of Barker & Tuley. He was admitted to the bar August 22, 1870, and formed a partnership with his senior preceptor under the name of Barker & Wait. Later Ira W. Buell was admitted under the style of Barker, Buell & Wait. This continued until Mr. Wait's appointment as Master in Chancery of the Circuit Court of Cook County in 1876, a position which he has held continuously since that time. Mr. Wait is now probably the oldest master in chancery in the State. He has held it through all the changes in politics and administration, which, of itself, speaks volumes for the wisdom and integrity which he brings to the discharge of his duties. His polished demeanor, scholarly attainments and his intimate knowledge of the law are the very qualities which have made his success in every station in life which he has been called to fill. While Mr. Walt is a Republican, he is not a partisan. He has always taken an active part in social movements, being one of the organizers of the Hyde Park Lyceum, which maintained a public library until Hyde Park was annexed to the city. He is a member and has served as president of the Chicago Literary Club. In church matters, also, he has taken an active part, being a member of the Protestant Episcopal Church and formerly superintendent of the Tyng Mission Sunday School. Since then he has been active in the work of St. Paul's Episcopal Church. He helped to organize the Charity Organization Society, and helped in its work until it was merged into the Relief and Aid Society.

Mr. Walt is a member of the Illinois State and the Chicago Bar Associations, the Kenwood and the Church Clubs. He is also identified with the Loyal Legion, the Farragut Naval Association, and other naval organizations.

Mr. Walt was married May 7, 1860, to Miss Clara Conant Long, daughter of James Long, a prominent citizen and manufacturer of Chicago. They have two sons, James Joseph and Henry Heilman Walt.

FREDERICK S. WINSTON.

Frederick S. Winston was born in Kentucky, October 27, 1856. Almost the whole life of the young man has been spent in the Garden city. He was educated at Yale College, which he entered at sixteen, but left at the beginning of the senior year. He was, however, awarded his degree by the faculty upon the record of a three years' course. He then entered the Columbia College Law School at New York, and in 1878 was admitted to the bar after examination by the Supreme Court of Illinois. He at once formed a law partnership with his father under the name of F. H. & F. S. Winston at Chicago.

FREDERICK S. WINSTON.

In 1881 Mr. Winston was appointed corporation counsel for the city of Chicago, a position which he held for five years, during which time he successfully conducted a large amount of litigation for the city, saving it thousands of dollars. At the end of this time he resigned to devote himself to private practice.

Since 1886, Mr. Winston has been counsel for the Michigan Central Railroad Company. He is also counsel for a large number of the most important corporations which center in Chicago. In fact, his business has come to be exclusively corporation law. In 1886 he formed a partnership with Mr. James F. Meagher, under the style of Winston & Meagher.

BUSINESS INTERESTS.

Old Chamber of Commerce Building.—This structure, at the time of its completion, was, with a single exception, the most pretentious in the city. It was built of cut Athens marble, and occupied the space represented by a frontage of 93 feet on Washington street, and facades of 180 feet on La Salle street and Calhoun place. It was surmounted by a mansard roof, the total height of the edifice above the ground floor being 99 feet. This building perished in the fire of October 9th, 1871. The present Chamber of Commerce building was completed in 1891. It is on the corner of La Salle and Washington streets, and is thirteen stories high. It cost upwards of $1,000,000. The building is noted for its great interior court, reaching from the main floor to the skylight. Nine passenger and freight elevators are kept constantly in use. This building and the City Hall and County Court House form an imposing architectural sight.

The Board of Trade Building.—The final abiding place of the Board of Trade is one of the few structures in the United States, to which the adjective "palatial" may, without exaggeration, be applied. It is a solid-looking granite pile, occupying half the square bounded by Jackson, Sherman and Van Buren streets, and Pacific avenue, its tower and entrance portal standing exactly in front of La Salle street, which ends at Jackson street. The view down this treet closed by the Board of Trade reminds one very forcibly of Wall street, New York, looking toward Old Trinity Church.

The building is in two sections, the front one, facing Jackson street, being used for trading, etc., and the rear one devoted to offices. The total ground occupied is 175 feet frontages, by 265 feet depth. Each facade is finely finished, with handsome entrances and relieving projections. Over the main entrance are two emblematic feminine figures, representing respectively "Manufacture" and "Agriculture."

The interior is very handsome, especially the main trading hall, 175x155 feet and 80 feet high, with its glass ceiling, 70x80 feet, and its elaborate finish. In this hall there are two capacious galleries, one on the north and one on the south side. To the latter visitors are admitted at all times, while the other is reserved for members and their friends, though even an entire stranger accompanied by ladies, should find no difficulty in gaining admission. The cost of the building was about $1,700,000.

The present membership of the Board is 2,000, each member paying an annual assessment of $65. The admission fee is $10,000, though this high rate is chiefly limitary in its effects, as memberships are transferable, and command only from $2,500 to $5,000. The Board Clearing House statement for 1895 shows clearings of $78,133,437, but there are no means of guessing at the vast short-time speculative transactions that occur under its roof. Trading is permitted in not less than 1,000 bushels of grain, or 250 barrels of pork.

The Union Stock Yards.—Meat packing is the oldest of Chicago's industries. In the fall of 1832 G. W. Dole slaughtered the first lot of cattle ever packed in the county. They numbered 200 head, and cost $2.75 per cwt. About 350 hogs, costing $3 per cwt., were slaughtered and packed at the same time. Forty-eight years later, the city received within twelve months no fewer than 7,059,355 live hogs, 1,382,477 cattle, and 335,810 sheep; since which time, the proportion of the hog products of the country handled by Chicago has kept on increasing, while a great increase has also taken place in its receipts of cattle and sheep. In 1895 the figures were 7,885,283 hogs,

2,588,558 cattle, 113,193 horses, and 3,406,739 sheep, the total value being estimated at $290,584,380. The shipments for the same period were 2,100,613 live hogs, 5,784,670 dressed hogs, 785,092 cattle, 53,136 sheep, 910,339,175 lbs. of dressed beef, 74,646 barrels of pork, 387,437,699 lbs. of lard, 174,807,919 lbs. of hides, and 63,441,320 lbs. of wool.

The Union Stock Yards at Halsted street, in the former Town of Lake, in which this enormous business centres, cover no less than 400 acres of ground. In 3,300 pens, 1,800 covered and 1,500 open, provision is made for handling at one time 25,000 head of cattle, 14,000 sheep, and 150,000 hogs. The yards contain twenty miles of streets, twenty miles of water troughs, fifty miles of feeding troughs, and seventy-five miles of water and drainage pipes. Five artesian wells, having an average depth of 1,230 feet, afford an abundant supply of water. There are also eighty-seven miles of railroad tracks, all the great roads having access to this vast market. Its entire cost was $4,000,000.

The meat-packing industry is carried on in immediate proximity to the Stock Yards. The extent of this enterprise may be imagined from the fact that a single business, that controlled by Messrs. Armour & Co., occupies seventy acres of flooring, and employs 3,500 men. The Stock Yards and packing houses (admission to the former free, the latter usually shown to visitors upon application) can be reached by rail from Van Buren street depot (trains infrequent), by State street cable-line or South Halsted street horse-cars.

The Board of Trade.—The history of this institution is an epitome of the commercial growth of Chicago. The preliminary meeting of business men, having in view the organizing of a Board of Trade, was held on March 13, 1848, and the first annual meeting of the resultant Board took place in April of the following year. The first quarters occupied by it were a room over a flour store on South Water street, engaged at a rental of $110 per annum. There were eighty-two members.

On the 13th of April, 1850, the institution was formally organized under an act of legislature authorizing it, and the membership fee was fixed at $5, while

TACOMA BUILDING, LA SALLE AND MADISON STREETS.

the annual dues were raised from $2 to $3. By 1851, the membership had dropped to thirty-eight, with a deficit reported by the Treasurer.

Years passed on, with many changes of location, but little progress. Interest—during several periods fostered by the seductive allurements of free lunches,

BIOGRAPHICAL SKETCHES.

comprising cheese, crackers and ale—waxed and anon waned. The free lunches filled the board-rooms, but not the corporation coffers; in fact, we read that in 1855, "the refreshment business" being revived, "a doorkeeper was appointed to keep out the loungers who were attracted by the free lunches."

This certainly is a comical beginning, viewed in the light of the present day; but, when we remember that in those times Chicago had no communication save by lake, canal and wagon road, with the outside world, and that grain passing through the warehouses was measured by the half-bushel, an old-fashioned free lunch no longer seems anomalous.

After 1856, however, prophetic signs of the future began to show within the institution; membership increased rapidly, its voice began to be heard and its influence to be felt in every important question of trade or finance affecting the interest of Chicago.

By 1866 the membership had risen to 1,462, and on August 13th of the same year the completed Chamber of Commerce building was occupied.

The Board of Trade and the Union Stock Yards are so intimately connected that it is impossible to consider them or the men who are connected with them separately; because the transactions at the stock yards

THE BOARD OF TRADE BUILDING.

form so large a proportion of the business of the Board of Trade. For this reason it is proper that we here present to our readers sketches of a few of the business houses and men who are among the guiding spirits of both. As in the case of the lawyers, we have not taken the richest, but those who are fairly representative of the conservative, yet aggressive Chicago business man.

SCHWARTZ, DUPEE & CO.

This is one of the foremost commission houses operating on the Board of Trade. While the firm, in its present form, cannot be said to be one of the oldest, it is one of the most substantial. It was formed about 1882, by Gustavus A. Schwartz, for many years connected with H. Botsford & Co., and John Dupee, Jr., for a long time in the commission business for himself. In 1886, John W. Conley, for several years with John W. Rumsey & Co., and Mr. I. J. Bloom were admitted to partnership. The concern occupies spacious offices on the ground floor of the Board of Trade Building; and does a general commission business in stocks, grain and provisions. It also has an office at No. 7 New Street, New York. It owns and leases an extensive system of private wires connecting with New York and other important points which give facilities for business second to none in its line.

THE FIRST NATIONAL BANK.

The First National Bank is the oldest of the national banks in Chicago. It has the largest capital, resources, deposits and earnings. It was organized in May, 1863, with a capital of $100,000. This has been increased until now it has a capital of $3,000,000, with a surplus of a like amount. It occupies a building of its own on the northwest corner of Dearborn and Monroe streets, which has always been a model of convenience and beauty. The bank occupies the whole of the main floor, while the five upper floors are taken up with offices. In the basement are the safety deposit vaults. The present officers of the bank are Mr. Lyman J. Gage, president; James B. Forgan, vice president; Richard J. Street, cashier; Holmes Hoge, assistant cashier, and Frank E. Brown, second assistant cashier. The list of directors includes Samuel M. Nickerson, F. D. Gray, R. C. Nickerson, E. F. Lawrence, Norman B. Ream, L. J. Gage, S. W. Allerton, Nelson Morris, Eugene S. Pike, A. A. Carpenter and James B. Forgan.

LYMAN J. GAGE.

Lyman J. Gage, president of the First National Bank of Chicago, was born June 28, 1836, at De Ruyter, Madison County, New York; and was educated at Rome Academy. Mr. Gage was first president of the Board of Directors of the World's Columbian Exposition, and also was formerly president of the American Bankers' Association. Mr. Gage is now a member of the Commercial Club, the Chicago Club,

LYMAN J. GAGE.

the Union Club, the Bankers' Club, and the Chicago Literary Club. He has long taken an active interest in philosophical and sociological questions; is remarkably broad and liberal in his views, contact with the commercial world having added strength and depth without narrowing a character capable of the deepest development.

EDWARD F. LAWRENCE.

Edward F. Lawrence was born at Groton, Mass., October 29, 1835. He received his early education in the public schools of Belvidere, Ill., where his parents removed to in 1837. He finished his education at the Lawrence Academy, at his place of birth, in 1847. He returned, and in 1849 was placed in a country store to learn commercial business. From here he went to Boston, and was apprenticed to Whitney & Fenno, a leading dry goods and jobbing house, where

EDWARD F. LAWRENCE.

he remained for six years, a part of the time in the office and a part as a traveling salesman. In his trips he frequently came to Chicago, and in 1858 he settled here permanently. He has been, since 1859, a member of the Board of Trade. He was one of the directors of the World's Columbian Exposition; and, for more than twenty years, has been one of the directors of the First National Bank.

In politics Mr. Lawrence is a Democrat, although not a partisan. He was married May 23, 1861, to Miss Mary Ballentine, of Waukegan. They have one son, Dwight, who thus early gives promise of a life of great usefulness.

EDWARD LESTER BREWSTER.

Mr. Edward L. Brewster was born June 22, 1842, at Brockport, New York, a direct descendant of the

EDWARD L. BREWSTER.

Pilgrim Fathers. He was given a good education at the Brockport Collegiate Institute, after which he spent two years at Buffalo, as clerk in a commercial house, in the study of practical business details and in a commercial college. In 1860 he came to Chicago and entered the banking house of Edward I. Tinkham & Co. Since that time Mr. Brewster has been closely identified with the banking interests of the city. In January, 1868, he established the wholesale grocery house of Farrington & Brewster; but in 1872 he withdrew to form the banking firm of Wrenn & Brewster. A magnificent business was started which weathered the storm of 1873; and continued until 1876, when Mr. Brewster retired and created the firm of Edward L. Brewster & Co. For twenty years this has been one of the foremost financial institutions of the city. Mr. Brewster has been a member of the Board of Trade since 1873, and of the New York Stock Exchange since 1881. He is a member, and has been president of the Chicago Stock Exchange. He is a member of many of the social clubs. Among them are, the Chicago, the Calumet, the Union, and the Washington Park, of Chicago, and the Metropolitan and Union League clubs of New York.

LAMSON BROS. & CO.

The firm of Lamson Bros. & Co., composed of S. W. Lamson, L. J. Lamson and S. S. Date is one of the few firms on the Board that has retained its name, without change, for more than twenty years. Be-

THE FIRST NATIONAL BANK BUILDING.

ginning in a small way, they have by industrious labor and a strict adherence to legitimate business principles placed themselves in the front rank of the well established, conservative and responsible Commission Houses.

This firm has probably the largest private leased wire system in America, reaching eastward from Chicago to New York, down along the Atlantic and Gulf States, along the Mississippi River to New Orleans, through Texas and the central states—in fact they reach almost every business center of importance.

Having an ample force of the best brokers on 'Change, and responsible New York and New Orleans connections, they are in a position to give close attention to all grain, provision, stock and cotton business entrusted to their care.

CHARLES COUNSELMAN.

Charles Counselman, one of the foremost operators on the Board of Trade, was born in December, 1848, at Baltimore, Md. He was given a thorough education with a view to his entering upon the practice of the law. But a too close application to study impaired his health so that he was compelled to give up his chosen profession and seek a more active field of labor.

CHARLES COUNSELMAN.

He came to Chicago in 1869. For a year he occupied a subordinate position and then began business for himself as a grain and provision commission man on the Board of Trade. He met with an abundant success from the first; and to-day he is the owner of the Terminal Grain Elevators of the Rock Island system. Those elevators have a capacity of 7,000,000 bushels. In 1888 the firm of Counselman & Day was formed for the handling of stocks and bonds. Mr. Counselman has always avoided politics, never having sought or held public office.

LLOYD JAMES SMITH.

Lloyd James Smith, although a native of Indiana, has spent nearly his whole life in Chicago, his parents moving to Chicago when he was a child. He was born at Wheeler, Porter county, Ind., Sept., 10, 1863, and has lived in Chicago since 1865.

His first business venture was clerking for the Northwestern National Bank in 1880. He remained two years and then moved west and spent two years in Idaho and Oregon when he returned to Chicago and

LLOYD J. SMITH.

began as broker for the Central Elevator Co. and for Munger, Wheeler & Co. In 1889 he was made manager of the Santa Fe Elevator and Dock Co., and is now the secretary and treasurer of this company. In 1891 he was made general manager also; and still holds that position.

Mr. Smith has been a director of the Board of Trade for the past five years; and has the distinction of being the youngest man ever elected as a director of the Board of Trade. He has served on all important committees of the Directory; and has always represented the elevator interests in their controversies. He has been chairman of the Republican County Central Committee; two years as its vice-president. For five years he has been first vice-president of the Marquette Club; and is a member of the Chicago Athletic Club. Mr. Smith is a Republican and takes a great interest in politics and public affairs.

Mr. Smith was united in marriage in 1890 to Miss Sadie Hall. They have one child, a daughter, about four and a half years old. They live in Evanston Avenue, at Lake View.

SIDNEY ALBERT KENT.

One of the most conspicuous and thoroughly representative men of Chicago is Mr. Sidney A. Kent. For more than forty years he has occupied a prominent position in the business world, won for himself by his perseverance, his sterling integrity and his good judgment. He was born at Suffield, Connecticut, July 16, 1834, the son of Albert and Lucinda (Gillette) Kent. His ancestors, on his father's side, came from England about 1630, and formed one of the oldest of the New England colonial families. His mother's family was only a little less renowned in the early history of New England.

Young Sidney was trained up on the farm until he was nineteen, securing the best English education which could be afforded in the common schools and at the Suffield Academy. He then started out to make his fortune, coming direct to Illinois. He first located in Kane county, where, for a time he taught school while awaiting an opportunity to engage in mercantile business. Early in 1854 he obtained a clerkship in the wholesale dry-goods house of Savage, Case & Co., of Chicago. The city then had a population of only about fifty thousand; but it had become plain that it was destined to take the lead as a commercial center. Two years later Mr. Kent went into business for himself as a general commission merchant. He pushed his business with so much vigor and intelligence that he soon acquired a recognized position among the prominent commission houses of the city, from which he branched out into other and wider fields. He engaged extensively in the fur trade, making trips into the western country and buying in large quantities for the New York market. In this he was associated with his elder brother, Mr. A. E. Kent. In 1859, in company with his brother he engaged in the beef and pork packing business under the style of A. E. Kent & Co. This proved to be a profitable venture; and after thirteen years of successful business the company was reorganized as a stock company, as the Chicago Packing and Provision Company, of which Mr. Sidney A. Kent was made president. This too has grown until it is to-day one of the largest in the packing business in Chicago, enjoying an extensive foreign as well as domestic trade. Mr. Kent remained its president until 1888, when, owing to his many other interests and duties he resigned and accepted the position of vice-president.

Closely connected with the Chicago Packing and Provision Company were the Merchant's and Trader's Packing and Provision Company, of Nebraska City, Neb., and the East St. Louis Packing and Provision Company, in both of which Mr. Kent was largely interested. During his more than forty years in Chicago business he has been a member of the Board of Trade; and he has taken a leading part in many of the great operations in the grain market which have been a marked feature of Chicago's business, especially during the last twenty years. Much

of the time he has been a director of the Board of Trade. In 1869, along with Mr. B. P. Hutchinson and others, he organized the Corn Exchange National Bank, becoming its first president, which position he held for several years. He was also, for many years, a director in the American Loan, Trust and Savings Bank; and the Kirby Carpenter Company, which has large interests in land, lumber and mills on the Menomonee river in Michigan. Upon the organization of the Chicago Gas Trust, in 1887, Mr. Kent was made president. In 1891, he assisted in the organization of the Natural Gas Company, of Chicago, with a capital of $2,500,000. With almost unbounded resources at his command, he has a genius for great undertakings which are invariably successful. They are comprehensive in their scope, planned with sagacity and carried out with vigor and deliberate judgment. His associates have always recognized his preeminent abilities by deferring to his judgment.

Nor has Mr. Kent confined himself merely to money getting. He has always been a munificent patron of the Chicago University. The Kent Chemical Laboratory, one of the most complete in this country in all its appointments, was built from a liberal donation of $250,000, made for that purpose by Mr. Kent. He has also made several other considerable donations to the same institution.

Mr. Kent was married Sept. 25, 1864, to Miss Stella A. Lincoln, of Newark, New Jersey. They have two charming daughters as the result of this union.

SIDNEY A. KENT.

WILLIAM H. HARPER.

William H. Harper was born May 4, 1845, in Tippecanoe County, Indiana, the fifth of a family of eight children. In 1851, the family removed to Iroquois County, Illinois, and two years later to El Paso, Woodford County. Its experience was that of all pioneers, one calculated to develop hardy qualities and self-reliant characters. Young William, along with his brothers, worked on the farm in the summer and attended school at the log school house in the winter. In 1864, when nineteen years of age, he enlisted in

Company B, 145th Illinois Infantry, and served until the end of the war.

On his return from the war he entered Eastman's Business College, of Chicago, from which he graduated in 1865. He then began the live stock and grain shipping business at El Paso, where he remained three years and then removed to Chicago in 1868. Here he engaged in the grain commission business on the Board of Trade. In 1873, he was appointed chief Grain Inspector at Chicago. In 1876, he organized the Chicago and Pacific Elevator Company, of which he was made treasurer and manager; which position he still holds. The company now owns elevators A and B.

In 1890, Mr. Harper assisted in the organization of the Globe National Bank, of which he was made a director. He was elected to the lower house of the Illinois Legislature in 1882. He was the author of the high license bill which remains the law of the

WILLIAM H. HARPER.

state. Many other popular measures were championed by him, among them being the law by which fines were to be paid over to the treasuries of certain societies, such as the Humane society and the Society for the Prevention of Cruelty to Children.

In 1895, he took part in the formation of the Chicago Southern States Association, to conduct an excursion to Atlanta, Ga., to attend the Cotton States Exposition, and acted as director of the excursion.

Mr. Harper is a prominent member of the Board of Trade, the Union League, Calumet, Washington Park and Hamilton clubs. He is a mason, a K. T. and member of Oriental Consistory, and a member of Plymouth Congregational Church. He was married July, 1867, to Miss Mary J. Perry, of Metamora, Woodford County, Illinois. She died September 30, 1884, leaving three children, one of whom, Roy. B., is a member of the class of '97 in the United States Military Academy, West Point, New York.

JOHN CUDAHY.

John Cudahy was born at Callan, County Kilkenny, Ireland, November, 1843. His parents removed to America in 1849, soon afterward settling at Milwaukee, Wisconsin. Here young John obtained what education the schools ever gave him. At fourteen, he entered the packing house of Ed. Roddis, where he remained until he was nineteen. He now entered the employ of John Plankinton, afterward Plankinton & Armour. At twenty-one he learned the nursery business, with Thomas Gynne, of Milwaukee, dealing in fruit and ornamental trees. Here he spent three seasons winning golden opinions from his employer, who was satisfied to sell to him the entire plant with

JOHN CUDAHY.

only a small payment down. Three years later he had paid the debt and saved a comfortable sum over. He then sold out and accepted employment under Layton & Co., packers, from which he was appointed three years later, as provision inspector for Milwaukee. In 1875 he bought an interest in the packing house of John Plankinton, but soon removed to Chicago, and, with E. D. Chapin, carried on business under the name of E. D. Chapin & Co., packers, for two years, after which the firm became Chapin & Cudahy for about five years longer, when Mr. Chapin withdrew and left Mr. Cudahy to form a new firm with his brother under the style of Cudahy Bros., packers. The firm now owns the largest packing house in Milwaukee; an extensive establishment at Louisville, Ky., and at Nashville, Tenn. Mr. Cudahy has always been noted for his strict business integrity and probity. He is married and has reared an interesting family.

HARRIS ANSEL WHEELER.

Harris A. Wheeler was born at Orrington, Maine, July 30, 1850. He was educated in the public schools until he was seventeen years of age, when he struck out for himself. He took a position as bookkeeper in a wholesale dry-goods store. In 1869 he went to Detroit, but returned to Maine in 1871. He was appointed Second Lieutenant in the regular army March 4, 1872, resigning his commission in 1874, re-entering mercantile life. In 1878 he was appointed financial manager of the Michigan Military Academy, at Orchard Lake. In 1880 he came to Chicago and became private secretary to N. K. Fairbank, a position he still holds; but his main interests are in manufacturing. He is at the head of several important enterprises.

Mr. Wheeler was appointed upon the military staff

GEN. H. A. WHEELER.

of Governor Cullom in July, 1881, and reappointed by his successor, Governor Hamilton, and also Governor Fifer; was Colonel of the Second Infantry from July, 1884, to February, 1890; and is now Brigadier General commanding the First Brigade, I. N. G., his commission dating from June 24, 1893.

CHICAGO TELEPHONE CO.

There is no city in America which makes as great use of the telephone as Chicago. The telephone exchange, operated by the Chicago Telephone Company, was established in 1880, and since has grown steadily, until now more than 400,000 people daily talk over its lines. This tremendous amount of traffic is nearly double that of any other exchange in the country, and shows the utility of the telephone in the rapid business method and great distances to be covered in Chicago. The exchange business is carried on in nine different offices located in different parts of the city. The main office, in which nearly one-half the lines are concentrated, is in the Telephone Building at the corner of Franklin and Washington streets, and upwards of 5,000 lines are there operated.

Telephones for the use of subscribers are furnished in all modern and well-known forms, the long distance office equipment, the long distance desk telephone, the party line residence telephone, or the private branch exchange used by railroads, manufacturers and others. The telephone which is furnished to the subscriber forms the smallest part of what is necessary to make up the telephone service given by the company. This is shown by the great mileage of trunk lines made necessary by the traffic from one exchange to another and the amount of apparatus and force of operators needed to handle this trunk line business.

The main part of the plant of the Chicago company is contained in underground cables, in permanently placed subways and located underneath the principal highways and streets. Constant additions are being made to it, and the character of the service of the company is maintained at the highest standard.

Upwards of 13,000 telephones are now operated by the company within the city, while in the neighboring exchanges operated by the company at Evanston, Elgin, Waukegan, Aurora, Joliet and other important points within a radius of fifty miles, about 3,000 additional telephones are installed.

The long distance telephone lines of the American Telephone & Telegraph Company were extended to Chicago from New York in 1892, and are now operated in direct connection with the Chicago telephone exchange. The merchant in Chicago, therefore, from his own office, can converse, not only with the telephone subscribers in Chicago and vicinity, but with more than 50,000 other telephone subscribers in exchanges reached by long distance lines.

HERBERT E. BUCKLIN.

Herbert E. Bucklin, founder of the house of H. E. Bucklin & Co., was born at West Winfield, Herkimer County, New York, July 19, 1848. He was educated mainly in the common schools at his boyhood home and at the New York State Academy, which he entered in 1866. The following year he took a thorough course at Bryant and Stratton's Commercial College in Chicago. From here he entered his father's drug store at Elkhart, Indiana, as a clerk. Here he made a special study of drugs, and, in 1869, began the manufacture of patent medicines, in connection with the drug business. In 1876 he sold his interests in Elkhart, and, two years later established himself in Chicago. There are few who remember Chicago of

H. E. BUCKLIN'S BUILDING.

that day who will not recall the sensation produced when a brave spirit had the hardihood to rush into the maelstrom of financial panic and business disorder to set up a new business. He did just this— He founded a business which has grown to vast proportions; he conquered all the obstacles which lay in his way; his genius is stamped upon the city, and his name has become a household word in the homes of two continents and whose goods may be found in almost all of their drug stores.

Mr. Bucklin is the proprietor of four valuable patent medicines, which have brought him fame and fortune. One is Dr. King's New Discovery for Consumption, Coughs and Colds; Bucklin's Arnica Salve, Electric Bitters and Dr. King's New Life Pills. He also publishes the Druggist, devoted to health, business and science, and to advertise his medicines. He expends a hundred thousand dollars annually among the leading newspapers throughout the United States and territories to advertise the merits of these medicines. He has been compelled to make constant enlargements and additions to his already magnificent business building. In it he has gathered a most valuable library of rare and expensive works.

In 1877 Mr. Bucklin's marriage with Miss Bertha E., daughter of Hon. George Redfield, of Cass County, Mich., was celebrated. Three children have been born to them: Harley R., in 1879; Charlotte, in 1883, and Herbert E., in 1887. Although Mr. Bucklin is a strict business man, he never forgets to be courteous and considerate to all who are brought in contact with him. He never dreams that the fact that he has, by his own genius, established an industry here; and led it to a high and honorable place in the affairs of the city, furnishes an excuse for winning him away from the manners and methods which have given him his great success, as has been the case with so many others. On the contrary, he has broadened in the spirit of social and commercial life; opened to his view the duties which are required of the successful, and made a man young in years old in real usefulness.

H. E. BUCKLIN.

bounded by Randolph, Van Buren, Franklin and State streets. This plant was originally provided with capacity of 800 horse power, which was thought sufficient for the demands at that time. Provision was made, however, for increase; and new machinery was installed at short intervals until, in 1894, the capacity was upwards of 5,000 horse power. Previous to this those in charge, in view of the increasing demands for electric light and power, and to be ready for the load, which indications showed might be expected, had planned a much larger plant. A site was selected on the river bank, near Harrison street, and in 1892 the work of construction was begun.

The plan carried out, and which proved wise, was, to conduct electricity from this point by a heavy line through a private tunnel beneath the river, and thence to the Adams Street Station, from which it could be distributed over the existing system of feeders and mains. Allowance was made for the utmost increase in output which might be hoped for in a long time. Improved machinery of every kind was obtained and attention given to every detail, so that this handsome plant, as completed, stands a monument to engineering and architectural skill. It is one of the finest electric light and power stations in the world. Its present capacity is sufficient to develop near 1,000 horse power, and machinery for as much more can be installed in the same building. In the meantime work was in progress in other directions. A smaller district had been planned and a station for supplying light to the south side residence section had been built on Wabash Avenue, south of Twenty-sixth Street, feeding an underground system which covered the portion of the city between Twelfth Street, Lake Michigan, Thirty-fifth Street and Wabash Avenue.

THE CHICAGO EDISON COMPANY.

The Chicago Edison Company was organized and received its franchise from the City of Chicago in the spring of 1887.

The first plant was located at No. 139 Adams Street, and an underground system of feeders running from this station was laid in the streets of the district

This plant, which, while small in Chicago, in an ordinary city would be considered large, was carrying a heavy load; but a project was on foot which was to increase the range of the company. An arrangement was made by which a plant, located at the river and Washington Street, formerly operated by the Chicago Arc Light and Power Company, came under the control of the company, and the customers supplied by it became customers of the Chicago Edison Co. This meant great additions to its already broad field, both in volume of business, in systems of distribution and in styles of machinery used; for up to this time only Edison apparatus of the kind known as low tension had been used. By this move systems of high tension arc lighting, alternating incandescent lighting and 500 volt power were acquired.

This gave the company many customers on the west side, where it had hitherto made no advances, to say nothing of portions of the north side near the river, and some territory on the diagonal streets running to the northwest.

The greater portion of the north side still remained

The attention of the company has been directed to the extension of its underground systems, strengthening of its feeder capacity and the gradual interweaving of the lines of conductors between the districts originally separated, so that a few years will see one complete interlocked system extending from Thirty-ninth street on the south, to Lincoln Park on the north, and from the lake far into the residence district of the west side.

The Chicago Edison Company not only supplies current for light in its two branches of arc and incandescent, but for power of all kinds, heating devices and experimental purposes. It has already obtained and is gradually extending a foothold in the demands of the Chicago people which can never be displaced.

DYNAMO ROOM, HARRISON STREET STATION.

uncovered, but in 1893 a north side plant was determined upon. The Newberry Library, which would surely become a very large consumer of electric light, offered a rare opportunity for obtaining a nucleus around which a good business could be built up. By an arrangement with the trustees ground was secured and a compact station built, adjoining the library on the north so closely that few realized that it was not a portion of the building. From this station the territory from the river to Lincoln Park, and from Wells street to the lake is supplied, and many of the residences in this section of the city are illuminated with incandescent light.

This plant is a model of its kind, being provided with machinery, equally modern with that at the Harrison street station. It is the youngest and most pampered child of the great corporation. Since its erection there has been no necessity for further plants.

THE AMERICAN BISCUIT CO.

The American Biscuit & Manufacturing Co. has twenty-eight plants in operation in various western cities, three of which are located in Chicago. The Chicago bakeries are as follows:

Bremner Bakery, 76 O'Brien street.
Dake Bakery, Adams and Clinton streets.
Aldrich Bakery, Green and Randolph streets.

It is the largest manufacturer of fine biscuits, crackers, cakes, and candies in the world. Its older branches have fed three generations of consumers, and its different brands are recognized as standards of purity and excellence. Thrifty housewives are substituting the "A. B. C." cakes for "home cooking," thereby saving time, money, and worry.

THE WESTERN BANK NOTE AND ENGRAVING CO.

This company has had a history for more than thirty years. It is said to be the only regular and fully equipped bank note company west of New York, and the only one outside of that city whose work is accepted for listing on the New York Stock Exchange. In addition to the steel plate work turned out, the company has a large lithographic plant for the execution of all kinds of bank and commercial work. Among the many handsome specimens shown are bonds and stock certificates of railway companies, bank notes of the Bank of Hamilton, Ontario, diplomas for the Board of Lady Managers of the Columbian Exposition, honorary certificates for the Field Columbian Museum, and a magnificent collection of bankers' steel plate drafts. The work turned out embraces every variety of bonds, stock certificates, currency for foreign countries, bankers' drafts, portraits, and all the various commercial forms, which are executed in the finest manner from steel engraved plates. The officers of the company are: C. C. Cheney, president; C. A. Chapman, vice president and treasurer, and Charles Heineman, secretary. The building which is the home of the company is herewith shown.

PHILIP HENRICI, RESTAURATEUR.

Philip Henrici is one of the characters of Chicago. No person has seen Chicago unless he has visited Henrici's. For more than twenty-six years he has been catering to the tastes of those who know a good thing when they see it. For twenty years he occupied the old stand at 175 and 177 Madison street, until it became one of the landmarks of the city. About two years ago he removed to his present location, 108 and 110 Randolph street, which was fitted up expressly for him, under his own supervision. This is, without exception, all things considered, the finest restaurant in Chicago. Not that others are not more costly and expensive, but in tasteful arrangement and artistic decoration it easily leads anything else in the city. The location is an ideal one. All the cable cars from the North Side pass the doors. It is within one square of the City Hall and County Court House, and directly opposite the Schiller Theater. The restaurant proper is 40x165 feet, and has a seating capacity for 500 persons. Nearly 2,000 persons are served there, on the average, daily. A new feature, the smoking-room, has lately been added for the benefit of those who enjoy a good smoke during or after their meals. Make a note of "Henrici's, 108 and 110 Randolph street," and be sure to see it when you come to the city. It is strictly a temperance house. No intoxicants are served.

CHARLES HENRY BUNKER.

Charles Henry Bunker was born at East Troy, Walworth County, Wisconsin, September 22, 1850. His grandfather, Gorham Bunker, was one of the early pioneers of that State, and Charles Henry's

WESTERN BANK NOTE COMPANY'S BUILDING, CORNER MADISON STREET AND MICHIGAN AVENUE.

father, George Bunker, was born in the Badger State. The subject of our sketch was born on a farm, where his childhood was spent until he was about six years old. About that time his father moved to Whitewater, Wisconsin, and engaged in the lumber business; but in 1862 located at Madison, the State capital, where for twenty-five years he continued in the same business, during which he acquired a comfortable competency. In that beautiful "City of the Lakes" young Bunker took a high school course and then entered the Wisconsin State University. During his junior year he left the University, however, to engage in the lumber business, and later was one of the firm of Bunker & Shepherd, who conducted a general merchandise store at Oregon, Wisconsin.

In 1874 Mr. Bunker assisted in building a railroad from Ottawa to Burlington, Kansas. He conducted the enterprise successfully, opening up coal mines and completing the road. In 1877 he returned to Chicago and formed a partnership with Mr. A. A. Abbott in the business of handling farm machinery, wagons and carriages at wholesale. Later the firm became the well-known Abbott Buggy Co., of Chicago, of which Mr. Bunker was secretary and treasurer for about a dozen years. After building one of the largest carriage factories in the world, which employed between five and six hundred men, and after having manufactured over 100,000 wheeled vehicles for service in all parts of the world, the business was sold to a syndicate, whereupon Mr. Bunker retired

CHAS. H. BUNKER.

from its active management and became the secretary and manager of the Metropolitan Accident Association of Chicago, which position he has since held, and in the management of which his usual success has attended him.

Mr. Bunker was married in 1873 at Oregon, Wisconsin, to Miss Helen Abbott. They have three promising children: A daughter, Genevieve, born in Wisconsin, two sons, the eldest, Gerald, born in Kansas, and the youngest, Arthur Stuart, born in Illinois.

Mr. Bunker is widely known among business men. He is universally regarded as a man of sterling integrity and of the highest character. He has been an active factor in the business life of Chicago, and is known for that ability and tenacity of purpose which so potentially contributes to success; especially in the Middle and Western States his business connections have made him favorably known in almost every town and city, his enterprises being material benefit to them. Physically Mr. Bunker is a man of fine physique, standing six feet and two inches in height, and weighs two hundred pounds.

He is socially one of the most genial and companionable of men, and the circle of his friends is large and ever increasing. In politics he is an Independent, with Democratic leanings, and in religion a man of liberal humanitarian views, taking a broad and charitable view of life, and is a practical helper of his fellowmen, noted for his kindness of heart and unostentatious benevolence.

A. BOOTH PACKING CO.

Mr. Alfred Booth, of Chicago, was born in Glastonbury, England. He came to America forty-seven years ago when at the age of twenty-three. In the winter of 1850, he started buying the lake fish from the fishermen here and shipping them throughout the smaller towns in Illinois. From this small beginning has grown the enormous business of the A. Booth Packing Company, a corporation having a paid-up capital of one million dollars and a surplus of as much more.

The company has branch houses in all the principal cities of the country, where its canned goods are known and sold in almost every civilized country on the face of the earth. The company owns extensive fisheries on the lakes, oyster beds on the eastern coasts, salmon canneries on the Columbia River, fruit canneries in California, also fruit, vegetable and oyster packing houses in Baltimore and elsewhere; its own boats and steamers on the Atlantic and Pacific oceans, the chain of Great Lakes, Gulf of Mexico, and up on Lake Winnipeg, also refrigerating cars and other important adjuncts to the proper and successful working of a business involving immense detail.

Few names are more deservedly well known throughout the United States than Mr. Booth's. His enterprise in making the succulent oyster available everywhere that railways reach has made his name familiar as a household word.

When the first trans-continental railway was completed, Mr. Booth dispatched, by the first train, several cars laden with oysters through to California and the West; and, in like manner, he has always

A. BOOTH PACKING CO.'S BUILDING.

been in the van of enterprise and progress. Wherever business is to be done, even prospectively, in the numerous rapidly increasing centers of population, there the firm is ready to establish a depot to supply the local demand, these ventures, as a rule, proving profitable to themselves as well as highly beneficial to the inhabitants.

THE CHICAGO VARNISH COMPANY.

This company was established in 1865; and, as will be seen, has been an active factor in the business of the city for more than thirty years. In 1889 it built the most complete varnish works in this country, the plant covering four acres of ground, with offices in New York, Boston and Philadelphia, as well as in Chicago. While the business of the concern is purely the manufacture and sale of its staples, those staples are so intimately connected with the decorative arts that it is quite natural to find it promoting art in some practical manner; but the way it has chosen to do that is certainly unique. When it came to erect an office building in Chicago, for its own use, it selected a style of architecture as quaint, and withal as pleasing as it is rare. It is said to be the only business block in this country of the pure, classic Dutch type. It is a building which would be singled out for its beauty anywhere, even among structures costing ten times as much. It is so refreshing to look upon; such a startling departure from the hackneyed and commonplace so prevalent in all our great cities, that we herewith give an illustration of it. It is 45x90 feet, built of dark red brick trimmed with Bedford sandstone, with a red tile roof. A clock in the two corners over the main entrance considerably heightens the effect and sets off the general design.

CHICAGO VARNISH COMPANY'S BUILDING, CORNER DEARBORN AVENUE AND KINZIE STREET.

GEORGE SCHNEIDER.

George Schneider was born in Pirmaseus, Rhenish Bavaria, December 13, 1823. He received his early education in the schools of his native place. At twenty-one, Mr. Schneider engaged in journalism, and became an active revolutionist against Bavarian rule. At twenty-five, in the revolution of 1848, he was a Commissioner of the Provincial Republican Government of the Palatinate, and was under the death penalty pronounced at that time, which the Bavarian Legislature removed in 1866. Mr. Schneider came to America in 1849, and published a German daily at St. Louis, entitled "Die Neue Zeit." In 1851 he removed to Chicago, and established the Illinois "Staats Zeitung." He was one of the organizers of the Republican party. He was a member of the National Republican convention of 1856, which nominated Fremont for president, and of the convention of 1860, at Chicago, which nominated Abraham Lincoln. He was an elector at large from Illinois at the election of James A. Garfield. In 1876 he was appointed minister to Switzerland by President Hayes. At the outbreak of the war, Mr. Schneider was appointed consul to Denmark. In the fall of 1864, in fulfillment of his mission, he went to Hamburg, Bremen and Copenhagen, and assisted in changing public sentiment in favor of the Union. Mr. Schneider was an active member of the "Union Defense Committee," of 1861, in whose charge the city subscription fund for the equipment of volunteers, and the support of their families, was placed. After his return from Denmark he was appointed collector of internal revenue, by President Lincoln, the first in Illinois. When his term expired he was elected president of the State Savings Institution, and retained his interest therein until 1871, when he organized and was made president of the National Bank of Illinois. He has for several years been the president of the Bankers' Club of Chicago. Mr. Schneider was a director of the local board of the World's Columbian Exposition, and a member of the committee on ways and means and the committee on press and printing, both being important committees.

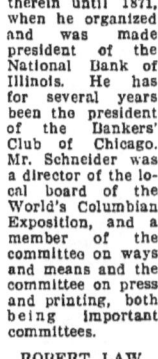

ROBERT LAW.

Mr. Robert Law was born in Yorkshire, England, February 15, 1822. He remained at home on the farm until he was twenty-one; but he started for America the day he attained to his majority. He bought a farm in Cecil County, Maryland, where he lived for five years. He was then obliged to return to England to dispose of property which came to him by the death of his father. On his return the following year he came west and located in St. Louis, engaging in steam boating between that city and Cincinnati. After two years he sold out and engaged in the business of railroad construction, from St. Louis on the Merrimack. He then took a contract on the Illinois Central, from Freeport to Dubuque, 70 miles, and was also interested in 44 miles on the same road from Ramsey's Creek to Centralia. When he had finished these contracts, he, with others, sunk a coal shaft at La Salle and formed the Illinois Coal and Iron Company. After operating this successfully for five years, he again sold out, in order to devote himself to the sale of anthracite coal, which he had already begun. It was from his mines at La Salle that the first fuel coal was sent to Chicago in quantities. And, moreover, it was when the anthracite coal business of Chicago was in its infancy that Mr. Law went into it. The annual consumption of Chicago and the west only amounted to 15,000 tons. This was in 1856. Since that time the business has grown to enormous proportions. Mr. Law has been closely identified with it during all the time since—for forty years. During all that time he has been an important factor in the growth and business prosperity of the city.

MARTIN B. MADDEN.

The universally accepted test of merit is the success that crowns the effort of the individual; and measured by this standard the highest distinction should be conferred upon Martin B. Madden, alderman from the Fourth Ward. He is Chairman of the Finance Committee of the City Council, acknowledged leader of his party in the latter body and in Cook County, and president of the Western Stone Company, the largest corporation of its kind in America.

The extraordinary career of Mr. Madden is one of those remarkable instances sometimes heard of in romance, but rarely met with in real life. He was born of poor and humble parents, John and Eliza Madden, in Darlington, England, March 20, 1855, and was brought by them to America in 1859. The family settled in Chicago, and from his sixth to his tenth year Mr. Madden attended school, never missing a single day. He then began work in the stone quarries at Lemont, Ill., of which he is now the distinguished head, and continued in the employ of the owner, Mr. Edwin Walker, for eleven years, rising from water carrier to general manager and chief draughtsman.

Severing his connection at this time with Mr. Walker, he became superintendent of the Enterprise Stone Company, and when, eight years later, this organization consolidated with several other companies as the Chicago Building Stone Co., he accepted the position of financial manager of the corporation. In 1886 the Joliet and Crescent companies combined under the name of the Joliet Stone Company, with Mr. Madden as vice president and general manager. Six years later this company consolidated with the Western Stone Company, and Mr. Madden was made its vice president, and January 16, 1895, at the annual meeting of the stockholders he was elected president.

In addition to his stone interests Mr. Madden is treasurer of the Cable Building & Loan Association, a stockholder and director in the Garden City Banking & Trust Company, stockholder in the Commercial Loan & Trust Company, and is associated with numerous other well known and successful enterprises. He is a member of the Sheridan, Concordia and Twelve Forty-five clubs, the Ancient Order of United Workmen, the Royal Arcanum, the Independent Order of Foresters, the National Union, and to other social orders; and in all of them he is popular and influential.

May 16, 1878, Mr. Madden was married to Miss Josephine Smart, of Downer's Grove, Ill., and one child, Mabel Bell, ten years old, has been born of this marriage.

Mr. Madden is a man distinctly of the people and with them. He has in no sense been lifted up of his success, but is as approachable and sympathetic as in the olden days when he labored in the quarries. Closely in touch with the people he understands their needs and has the intelligence to devise that which will best meet their wants. His management of the extensive affairs of the city as Chairman of the Finance Committee, has been characterized by the same economic measures he has evinced in the direction of the business of his company and of his own private affairs. He is honest, straightforward, active, energetic, a tireless worker and a true friend, quick in conception and in action, possessed of exceptional organizing tact and executive force. Having the advantage of youth, with great experience and sound judgment, he is a leader who directs to greater results, and his future is one of infinite promise. Yet a young man, scarcely forty, honored and trusted by all who know him, he may properly expect his fellow-citizens to call him to much higher stations than any he has filled here-

M. B. MADDEN.

tofore. Whatever his future, the record he has already made confirms the confidence of his friends that he will worthily discharge any trust, however great, that may be given into his keeping.

ADOLPH KARPEN.

We herewith present a portrait of one of the representative business men of Chicago. Mr. Adolph Karpen, born in Germany in 1860, came to this country when only twelve years of age; and, in 1880, united with his two brothers, Oscar and Soloman, to form the firm of S. Karpen & Bros., in the manufacture of upholstered goods. The firm now employs from 400 to 450 people and turns out more upholstered goods than any similar concern in America. It re-

ADOLPH KARPEN.

ceived the highest awards at the World's Fair and universal praise from the trade for the excellency of its product.

Mr. Karpen is a member of the Chicago Athletic Association; president of the Chicago Furniture Manufacturers' Association; belongs to the Masonic fraternity and is respected by all who are brought in contact with him. He has a large and growing circle of enthusiastic friends.

JACOB FORSYTH.

Jacob Forsyth came to Chicago from Ireland in 1857, to engage in the railroad business, having been born in that country in 1821. With unbounded faith in the future of Chicago, Mr. Forsyth, in 1866, purchased 10,000 acres of land in Lake County, Indiana, many miles south of the city. In 1881 he sold 8,000 acres of this tract to the East Chicago Improvement Company, the land at that time having become extremely valuable. The present Canal & Improvement Company came into possession in 1887. In 1881, Mr. Forsyth bought another large tract near his former purchase. The immense refining works of the Standard Oil Company, at Whiting, stand on a portion of this land. Mr. Forsyth's sound judgment in

real estate matters has practically vindicated itself in an extremely profitable manner. Mr. Forsyth married Miss Caroline M. Clarke, of Fayette County, Pennsylvania, a sister of General H. F. Clarke, of the United States Army, and is the happy father of nine children, five of whom are boys and four girls.

DANIEL B. ROBINSON.

Daniel B. Robinson was born at St. Albans, Vermont, in 1847, and entered the railway service at eleven years of age, rising through almost every grade from a freight clerk on the Central Vermont Railroad up to president of the St. Louis & San Francisco Railroad Company, a position which he now holds. Here is a typical instance where steady application and faithful service has brought a steady and permanent promotion just in proportion to the length of service. The railroads of the country are always on the lookout for those who, by faithful and efficient service, make themselves worthy of promotion; and such need not to lack for employment.

FRANK T. FOWLER.

Mr. Frank T. Fowler, although one of Chicago's young men, has attained a reputation and fame which many an older one may well envy. He was born at Beverly, Ohio, in 1866. He early displayed a

FRANK T. FOWLER.

love of mechanics and an aptitude for invention. He came to Chicago at twenty years of age and accepted the first situation that offered, although it paid only $4.50 per week. He afterward obtained a situation with The Crane Elevator Company, where he remained for three years, eventually abandoning it to engage in the manufacture of bicycles. Here his natural genius for invention was turned to good account. His truss frame has become famous throughout the world. The Fowler wheel is a marvel of strength and beauty. Its success has been second to none in the market. The sextuplet wheel, built by the Fowler Manufacturing Company, is a complete demonstration of the superiority of the Fowler truss frame over all others.

CHAS. KAESTNER & CO.

This is one of the oldest and most responsible machinery houses in the city. The firm was established in 1863; has grown with the growth of the city, and ships its product to all parts of the world. It manufactures machinery for breweries, malt houses, distilleries, starch works, glucose works, sugar refineries

CHAS. KAESTNER & CO.'S BUILDING.

and other manufacturing interests. We present herewith an illustration of its magnificent building, built with special reference to the needs of the firm. It is situated on Jefferson street, south of Van Buren and runs through to Law avenue, covering an area of 45,000 square feet. It is equipped throughout with electric power and light and is, beyond question, one of the most complete plants in the country. Messrs. Kaestner & Co. make a specialty of complete plants, including buildings guaranteeing capacities and costs. Parties requiring the services of experts in their line will do well to correspond with them.

GEORGE M. HARVEY.

George M. Harvey, of the firm of George M. Harvey & Co., was born at Niagara-on-the-Lake, Canada, of English and Scotch parents; and was educated at Phillip's Academy. He entered the insurance office of Rounds & Hall, Buffalo, at fourteen. He came to Chicago in 1870 and engaged with S. M. Moore & Co., founding his present firm about 1882. It represents the following companies: Mutual Fire Insurance Company of New York, Globe Fire Insurance Company of New York, L. & L. & G. Insurance Company of England, Palatine Insurance Company of Manchester, England, Mercantile Fire and Marine Insurance Company of Massachusetts. Mr. Harvey is manager for the Western Department of the Mutual Fire Insurance Company of New York.

PETER E. STUDEBAKER.

Peter E. Studebaker, second vice president, treasurer and general manager of the great Studebaker Bros. Manufacturing Company, was born in Ashland County, Ohio, from whence his parents removed, in his infancy, to South Bend, Indiana. Peter's early advantages were limited. While his brothers were attending school or learning a trade, Peter was his mother's errand boy. Then he set out from home to make his own way. He spent a year as clerk in a small store

PETER E. STUDEBAKER.

for $25, and in the time managed to save a dollar. From this he started out as a peddler. While his father and brothers were laying the foundation of the great manufacturing enterprise at South Bend, Peter was developing other qualities which were to prove just as important. He was learning practical business, which became an element of vast power in the final success of the South Bend institution. It was finally through the executive ability manifested by Peter that the Studebaker works became world famous.

Peter E. Studebaker is now a recognized leader among the large body of American manufacturers. Since he has been a resident of Chicago he has taken a great interest in local charities. He has been the staunch friend of the Waif's Mission and has contributed to many other eleemosynary institutions; so that he has come to be known as one of the largest hearted and most generous men of Chicago, one whose heart is always open to the cry of the needy.

THE STUDEBAKER BUILDING,

MICHIGAN AVENUE

It stands upon an area of 107x171 feet. The first two stories (the building being eight stories high) is of Syenite granite, from the quarries in Missouri. From the third story up it is composed of Bedford stone, and is in modern architecture as fine a facade as can well be designed. The structure presents a massive appearance. There are two polished columns

THE STUDEBAKER BUILDING, MICHIGAN AVENUE BETWEEN VAN BUREN AND CONGRESS STREETS.

at the large entrance resting on pedestals measuring each nearly four feet in diameter, and twenty-two feet high. The ground floor has, so to speak, a glass front. The interior, so far as pertains to finish and decoration, is in excellent harmony with the building; there

keepers, telephone chamber and private consultation rooms, the shipping and entry clerks' offices, the main part of this floor being employed as the repository of their several styles of carriages, coaches, victorias, landaus, carts and vehicles.

SOUTH BEND, IND.

The firm of Studebaker Bros.' Manufacturing Co. began business in a small shop in 1852. A few tools and $68 in cash constituted its capital. During the first year the output amounted to two wagons. The annual product now is about fifty thousand vehicles. The growth was at first slow. Twelve years found them making a few wagons, but struggling for recognition abroad. In 1857, a contract for wagons for the use of the United States troops in Utah gave them their first strong impetus. The company was incorporated in 1868; and the force of workmen increased year by year, by natural accretions, until those employed at home and at the various branches reached a total of 1,860 men.

While the construction of vehicles by the Studebakers was at first confined to wagons, they very early engaged also in carriage making, especially of the medium and high grades. The works are employed in the production of all the leading kinds of vehicles, embracing every variety in common use, for pleasure or road driving, from the state landau of a president, down. In wagons, every variety in demand, for the farm, the mountain, the mine, the plain, and for business use in cities, are here turned out. A very important branch is also the manufacture of street sprinklers, for which the Studebaker Company has become known the country over.

THE NEW STUDEBAKER BUILDING.

WABASH AVENUE, CHICAGO.

The building fronts 120 feet on Wabash avenue, and has a depth to the alley of 170 feet, and is ten stories and basement in height. To properly support a struc-

THE STUDEBAKER WORKS, SOUTH BEND.

is nothing cheap about it; the walls and ceilings are all hand plastered and ornamented in latest designs. The floors are all of hard wood, polished and finished in the best manner. On the north side of the building is an arch passageway, which allows a side entrance to the office and first floor. On this floor are also the offices of the company, the cashier, book-

ture of its weight, great care was bestowed upon its foundation. Heavy piles 45 feet long were driven down to hard-pan to a depth of 61 feet below the street level, and cut off 16 feet below grade and capped with timber grillage below city datum and lowest sewer point. Upon the grillage the heavy stone foundation wall and piers were started.

The front is a very graceful and ornamental design, in French Gothic, and built entirely of white terra cotta and plate glass. The important consideration of light has been the governing influence in the design.
The structure is of steel beams and steel Z bar col-

THE NEW STUDEBAKER BUILDING, WABASH AVE., CHICAGO.

umns, all embedded in brick, concrete and fireproof tile. The floor systems are of advanced type, heavy steel wires are strung from end to end of building on the suspension-bridge principle, and Portland cement concrete is laid between the steel beams, thoroughly encasing them, and supported by the steel wires.

RESIDENCE OF MR. CLEM STUDEBAKER AT SOUTH BEND.

This house, in its proportions and appointments, probably surpasses anything in Indiana. The material is native cobble stone, irregular in form and varied in color. It stands upon a natural elevation, surrounded by smoothly shaved lawns, which slope to the north and east, and are broken here and there by beds of brilliant flowers. There are several fine old oaks to the south and east. With its massive walls, its turrets, and the irregular roof, it looks like some feudal castle which has been set down in the midst of a busy nineteenth century town; and yet it produces no effect of incongruity.

CHARLES H. WACKER.

Charles H. Wacker was born in Chicago in 1856. He received his education in the public and high schools of this city, attending the Lake Forest Academy, and, for several terms, a business college. He studied music at the conservatory at Stuttgart; and attended lectures at the University of Geneva, in

CHAS. H. WACKER.

Switzerland. He began business life as an office boy with Moeller & Co., of Chicago, in the grain commission business. In 1880, he was taken into partnership by his father in the malting business, under the style of F. Wacker & Son. In 1882, the Wacker & Birk Brewing and Malting Company was organized, of which Charles H. Wacker became secretary and treasurer. In 1884, he was elected president and treasurer, which he has held ever since.

He was nominated in 1888 on the Democratic ticket for State treasurer. He has been tendered many positions of trust and honor, but has always declined to enter politics, on account of the pressure of private business.

He is a director in the Corn Exchange Bank, the Chicago Title and Trust Company, the Western Stone Company, Germania Safe Deposit Company, and president of the Chicago Heights Land Association. He is a member of the Athletic Association, the Art Institute, the Turn Gemeinde, and several German singing societies, besides being a member of the Iroquois, Waubansee, Union League, Germania, Union, Bankers', Fellowship, and German Press Clubs.

Mr. Wacker married Miss Otillie M. Glade, on May 10, 1887, and has two sons—Frederick G. and Charles H. He is a gentleman of deserved popularity with all classes and a prominent figure in the best development of his native city.

ADOLPH SCHOENINGER.

Adolph Schoeninger, President of the Home Rattan Company and formerly President of the Western Wheel Works, may be taken as a fair type of the self-made man of Chicago. He was born at Wiel, one of the old free cities of Schwaben, on January 20, 1833. He received a liberal education in his native country, passing through the high schools, from whence he entered a large dry-goods house conducted by his uncle, David Gall, of Rastadt, Baden. Here he was entered as an apprentice, but proving his worth by his work, he rapidly rose to the position of head salesman. Here he was enabled to obtain an insight into business correspondence, bookkeeping, and other branches of mercantile life. Of all this he availed himself eagerly; and when, after seven years of service, he resigned his position, he considered himself thoroughly proficient in all branches of mercantile affairs.

During Mr. Schoeninger's residence in Baden, Brentano was named Dictator, and our young merchant witnessed the court-martial and execution by the Prussians, after they had taken possession, of a number of men innocent of any crime save their failure to free their people of the oppressors. This produced such an impression upon his mind that he determined to emigrate to America. In 1854, in company with a younger brother, Mr. Schoeninger set out. He came to Philadelphia, where he found employment in various business houses until 1857, when he started in business for himself. In this he was prosperous, which gave him entré into many of the German societies of both social and benevolent character, where he soon became prominent. At the breaking out of the late Civil War, he was offered command of a company in the Seventy-fifth Regiment of Pennsylvania Volunteers, which he accepted. Here he rendered gallant service until 1864, when he returned to Philadelphia, only to find himself penniless.

He now decided to locate in the West, and came to Chicago, and obtained employment with Albert Pick, in the chinaware business, where he remained for one year. He then started a small furniture factory on Desplaines street; but this was destroyed by fire a year later. In the fall of 1866, Mr. Schoeninger took charge, on his own account, of a factory previously run by Vergho, Ruhling & Co., for the manufacture of toys, baby carriages, etc. Under his management it steadily increased until the great fire of 1871, which laid everything in ashes, including a new factory which had just been completed. As his insurance had all been placed in home companies, he lost all, because the magnitude of the fire was enough to destroy them all. Mr. Schoeninger again faced disaster, as he had so often done before, with an undaunted courage. He had made for himself a reputation for honesty and integrity which was now of value. A banking firm in Europe, knowing his reputation, offered him financial assistance, with which he rebuilt his factories and had his engines running again January 1, 1872, in less than three months. The following February he made his first shipment. Since then his success has been phenomenal. Within three years he had repaid his creditors from before the fire, and within ten years he had repaid every dollar borrowed for the rebuilding of his works. He had also made extensive enlargements, which have gone on since, until the Western Wheel Works has come to be the largest wheel manufactory in the United States. It employs 1,500 men, mostly in the manufacture of bicycles, of which it turns out 350 per day. It recently made one shipment of one solid trainload of fifteen cars, loaded solely with bicycles, from the Western Wheel Works to its general store in New York, the shipment representing over $100,000 in value.

Mr. Schoeninger has now transferred his interests in the Western Wheel Works to his sons-in-law, and has retired from this part of the business which he has built up.

In 1893, Mr. Schoeninger established the Home Rattan Co., for the manufacture of baby carriages, chairs, toy furniture, and other reed and rattan goods. This has also met with the usual success that has attended Mr. Schoeninger's other ventures. He has since added the manufacture of juvenile bicycles, which now makes such a demand

ADOLPH SCHOENINGER.

upon the company's resources that it is found almost impossible to meet that demand. In all his great work, he is assisted by his nephew, Louis, and Henry Richmann and the superintendent of the factory, Mr. Henry Henneberg, an old-time associate in business with Mr. Schoeninger.

Mr. Schoeninger was married August 20, 1857, to Miss Augusta Richmann, of Philadelphia. They had three children—one son and two daughters. One married daughter and the son died. In the loss of his son Mr. Schoeninger suffered the greatest disappointment of his life. He had hoped that he would succeed him in his business and perpetuate his name. His loss has rendered him well-nigh inconsolable. He has now transferred his hopes and affections to his little grandson, Adolph Schoeninger, the child of his son. The remaining daughter, the wife of Richard Boericke, of the Western Wheel Works, also has a son, who shares, in a large measure, the affections of his grandfather.

B. F. JACOBS.

Mr. B. F. Jacobs for many years has been one of the foremost real-estate men of the city. His firm is agent for the new Atwood Building, and is a large dealer in and subdivider of Chicago property.

Mr. Jacobs came to Chicago in 1854, and immediately identified himself most actively with the business interests of the city, as well as various lines of benevolent and patriotic work. His abilities have not only given him a goodly measure of business success, but have made him an honored leader in movements of world-wide interest and importance.

ISAAC N. CAMP.

Isaac N. Camp was born in Elmore, Lamoille County, Vermont, December 19, 1831. He is the son of Abel and Charlotte (Taplin) Camp, both of whom were natives of the Green Mountain State. He prepared for college at Bakersfield Academy, Vermont, paying for his board by teaching music. At the age of twenty he entered the University of Vermont, and earned in his spare time the money required to meet his current expenses. After four years he graduated with the class of 1856. He was then offered and accepted a position as assistant principal in the Barre Academy. Here he remained, teaching mathematics and music, until 1860, when he became principal of the high school at Burlington, Vermont, a position which he filled until his removal to Chicago, in 1868, forming a partnership with Mr. H. L. Story, under the style of Story & Camp. This partnership continued until the spring of 1884, when the Estey Organ Company purchased Mr. Story's interest in the business, and the firm became Estey & Camp, under which style it continued until it was incorporated. The business was commenced with a small capital, but by energy, perseverance, and enterprise the firm became one of the most substantial and reputable in the city of Chicago; and, at the time of Mr. Story's withdrawal, its capital exceeded half a million dollars, he receiving as his portion two hundred and fifty thousand dollars. The capital of the firm to-day amounts to something over one million dollars.

Mr. Camp was always prominently connected with public enterprises, long being a director in the Chicago Theological Seminary, and of the Chicago Guarantee Life Association, and also of the Royal Safety Deposit Company. In April, 1891, he was elected a director of the World's Columbian Exposition, and was a member of its Committee on Agri-

RESIDENCE OF ADOLPH SCHOENINGER, 1839 MELROSE STREET.

culture and Liberal Arts, ably assisting its work.

Mr. Camp has traveled extensively with his family, both in Europe and the United States. In personal appearance he was of medium height, with fair complexion and of robust physique. He had a pleasing presence and address, and was social and genial in manner. He was a man of generous impulses, and contributed generously to church, charitable and benevolent enterprises. The architect of his own fortunes, he built up a large and solid business; and, as a citizen of Chicago, he was always deservedly popular and highly esteemed.

Mr. Camp died at Lake Geneva, Wisconsin, his summer home, on Sunday morning, July 12, 1896. His death was so sudden and unexpected that it produced a severe shock to his family and a wide circle of loving friends. He had been boat riding on the lake on Saturday morning, when he was attacked with severe pains in the stomach. These continued all day. At 11 P. M. he retired, hoping that sleep would restore him. At 3 A. M., on Sunday, anxious friends thought to see how he was resting, and found him cold in death.

Mr. Camp was a member of Union Park Congrega-

I. N. CAMP.

tional Church and president of its board of trustees. He was also a member of many social clubs and benevolent organizations. He was married January 1, 1862, to Miss Flora M. Carpenter, daughter of Hon. Carlos Carpenter, of Barre, Vermont. Three of the four children born of the union are still living: Mrs. M. A. Farr, a daughter; the oldest son, Edward N., and the youngest, William Carpenter Camp.

WINFIELD NEWELL SATTLEY.

Winfield N. Sattley, the general Western manager of the Manhattan Life Insurance Company, whose portrait is herewith shown, is recognized among insurance men as a man of conspicuous ability, so marked as to make him a leader in his business. He is eminently a self-made man. Whatever he has achieved has been by his own native energy and indomitable perseverance. He started a poor boy, with no fortune but his own sterling qualities. He has won his way in spite of every difficulty. He was born in Vermont; obtained only a meagre schooling and began the study of the law. In order to earn the money to prosecute his studies he took a position with the Vermont Life Insurance Company; but young Sattley applied himself so diligently and acquitted himself so well that, instead of his position being temporary, it became, in a measure, permanent. In 1881 he was sent to Chicago by the company as general agent for Illinois. Here he attracted the attention of other companies on the lookout for men of talent, and he was appointed general agent of the Massachusetts Mutual in 1884, a position which he held for three years. He was then offered and accepted a position as superintendent of agencies of the New York Life Company

for Illinois. This he again resigned in 1889 to accept the general management of the western business of the Manhattan Life Insurance Company. By the same

W. N. SATTLEY.

zeal and energy which he has always displayed in other cases, he has been enabled to largely increase the business of the company, notwithstanding all the unfavorable conditions of general business.

J. M. W. JONES.

Mr. J. M. W. Jones, the master spirit in the J. M. W. Jones Stationery and Printing Company, was born in Hoosack, Rensselaer County, New York, January

22, 1821. He has been a resident of Chicago since 1857, and during the whole period since has been identified with the printing and stationery business.

THOMAS STEWART QUINCEY.

Thomas Stewart Quincey is a good type of the active, pushing, self-made man. He was born in Belville, Ont., May 28, 1852. From his earliest boyhood he has been compelled to look out for himself. Whatever of schooling he obtained was before he was twelve years of age and in his native town. He was completely thrown on his own resources. He obtained a situation as commercial traveler; and in that capacity, came to Chicago. Since 1875 he has made this his home. He was active in the organization of the Northwestern Commercial Traveler's Life and Accident Insurance Company, and was elected its manager. It came to absorb his entire time. He has now become secretary and manager of the Star Accident Company of Chicago, whose handsome new building herewith shown, is a conspicuous ornament to Dearborn street, and the city of Chicago.

Mr. Quincey is a member of the Oakland and Review clubs, and first lieutenant of Cavalry Troop A,

THE STAR ACCIDENT COMPANY'S BUILDING,
356 DEARBORN STREET.

Illinois National Squadron. He was in command of the Chicago Hussars, stationed at the stock yards during the Pullman strike. He is married and resides at 472 Forty-second street.

JOSEPH THATCHER TORRENCE.

General Joseph T. Torrence was born in Mercer County, Pa., March 15, 1843. He was employed for three years in a blast furnace at Sharpsburg, Md., owned by Mr. John P. Agnew. From here he went to Briar Hill, Ohio, where he worked again in a furnace until he learned the blacksmith's trade, becoming assistant foreman before he was seventeen years old. It was here he obtained a practical knowledge of mechanics. At the breaking out of the war he enlisted in Company A, One Hundred and Fifth Ohio Infantry. He was wounded at Perryville four times and was granted an honorable discharge from the army, with a life pension. He returned to Ohio just before the famous raid of General Morgan into the state. Although suffering from his wounds, he promptly took command of a volunteer force and assisted in the pursuit and capture of the rebel.

During the next five years Mr. Torrence was employed by Reis, Brown & Berger, at New Castle, Pa., first in charge of their furnaces and later managing the sales of their entire product.

In 1869, Mr. Torrence removed to Chicago, where he took charge of the furnaces of the Chicago Iron Works; and a year later, became connected with the Joliet Iron and Steel Company; built furnaces at Depere, Wis., and Menominee, Mich., and acted as consulting engineer for the Green Bay & Bangor Furnace Company, at Chicago. He was also made colonel of the Second Regiment of the Illinois Guards, and was promoted to brigadier general of the First Brigade. Since 1881, General Torrence has been instrumental in the promotion of several great enterprises, such as

the organization of the Joseph H. Brown Iron and Steel Company, on the Calumet River; the South Chicago and Western Indiana Railroad; the Chicago and Calumet Terminal Railway Company; the Calumet Canal and Improvement Company; the Standard Steel and Iron Company, and the Chicago Elevated Terminal Railway Company.

General Torrence is a Republican in politics; takes a lively interest in all public questions, and is a born leader of men. He is generous to a fault, his hand always being open to help the deserving. He was married September 11, 1872, to Miss Elizabeth Nor-

GEN. JOSEPH T. TORRENCE.

ton, daughter of Jesse O. Norton, of Chicago. One daughter blessed the union. Mrs. Torrence died October 12, 1891, the result of an accident while taking a drive with her daughter. She was mourned by a wide circle of devoted friends.

WILLIAM HOUSER GRAY.

William Houser Gray was born at Piqua, Ohio, September 23, 1847. He graduated from the Piqua High School and entered the Denison University, where he remained for three years. His father, being engaged in building, William assisted him for a time after completing his education, until an opening presented itself on the Lake Erie and Western Railroad as civil engineer. When the company failed, William went into the lumber business at Piqua until 1871. He then became interested in life insurance, in which he developed rare abilities. In 1877 he organized the Knights Templar and Masonic Aid Association of Cincinnati, which, under his management, became the leading company of its class in the United States. In 1883 he withdrew from the company and came to Chicago; and, in the spring of 1884 organized the Knights Templars and Masonic Life Indemnity Company of Chicago, of which he became a director and general manager. Its history has been one of conspicuous success from the start. It now stands as guarantee for upwards of twenty-six millions of dollars of insurance.

Mr. Gray has also large interests in other directions.

He took an active part in developing the natural gas fields of Indiana; is a large holder of lands in Indiana and also in Texas and Illinois and Arkansas. He originated the scheme of the removal of the old Libby prison of Richmond, Va., to Chicago. He is a mem-

WILLIAM H. GRAY.

ber of the Union League and Marquette clubs; of St. Bernard Commandery and of other Masonic bodies.

In religion Mr. Gray is a Baptist and in politics a Republican. He was married February 17, 1881, to Miss Orpha E. Buckingham. They have three children, Ina, Willie and Ralph B. Gray.

ANDREW DUNNING.

Among the conspicuous real estate men in Chicago, Mr. Andrew Dunning occupies a high place. He is essentially a self-made man. He served his country in the War of the Rebellion, being mustered out as a first lieutenant at the close of the war. Since then he has devoted his energies to floriculture and real estate, in both of which he has made a great success. Large tracts of fertile lands throughout the state have been placed in his hands for sale. It will pay investors to call on him.

WILLIAM W. KIMBALL.

William W. Kimball, founder of the piano and organ making industries of Chicago, was born in Oxford County, Maine, in 1828. The name Kimball is eminent as giving title to the pioneer firm in the wholesale music trade of the Northwest; and to-day it is generally conceded that the establishment of the W. W. Kimball Company is the largest and most complete of its kind in the world. This company was the first to manufacture and job organs in Chicago, and the growth of the business has always kept pace with the rapid increase of the city at large. The floorage space utilized by the firm covers over eleven acres, a fact which speaks stronger than words as to the vast business transacted. In 1857 Mr. Kimball began business in Chicago as a dealer in pianos and organs and seven years later established the wholesale trade. Within forty-eight hours after the subsidence of the great fire Mr. Kimball had converted his private residence

BIOGRAPHICAL SKETCHES.

into a musical warehouse, with the billiard room for an office and the 'barn' for a shipping department.

W. W. KIMBALL.

What could be more typical of the energy of a Chicago business man?

JAMES F. KEENEY.

James F. Keeney was born at Crawfordsville, Ind., September 15, 1840. His parents moved to Des Moines, Iowa, in 1850, where he prepared himself for

JAMES F. KEENEY.

college. He entered the University of Rochester, N. Y., in 1862, from which he graduated in 1866. He studied law two years and then removed to Chicago in 1868, and began the real estate business.

His first venture was the purchase of 210 acres at Ravenswood. South Evanston was next founded. He built a depot, a fine business block and upwards of fifty large houses, which placed it in the front rank of Chicago's suburbs.

Mr. Keeney was an active promoter of the present park system. He bought, in 1871, in Trego County, Kan., five townships on the Union Pacific Railroad, which he colonized with Chicago and Eastern people. In the center of this tract he built the city of Wa Keeney, the county seat of Trego County, and secured for it the U. S. land office, which added much to its importance.

Mr. Keeney was elected to the Kansas Legislature in 1878 and 1879, and became a leader in the House. He was a useful member of the ways and means committee. He was also made a member of the State Board of Agriculture. He was elected president of the State Fair in 1880, held in Lawrence, Kansas, and delivered the inaugural address at the opening of the fair. He returned to Chicago in 1881, and again entered the real estate business. Since then he founded Hermosa, and, in connection with others, Chicago Heights and Columbia Heights, where are located many factories, and where he still is engaged in building up this manufacturing town.

HAYMARKET SQUARE.

Herewith we give an illustration of one of the old landmarks of the city, as it appears to-day. In the early days it was the place where farmers, from the surrounding country, brought in their hay for sale to those who wished to buy. At that time the Haymarket Square was situated on the very outskirts of the city. The hay was brought, piled loosely on wagons, which here stood packed in long rows, awaiting customers. In time other farm products were brought to the same market, until now, business is so changed that little hay is ever seen awaiting purchasers here. But the entire square is given up to teams loaded with garden truck brought here for sale. Hours before daylight the arrivals begin, until, at the commencement of business a double row of farm wagons, piled high with all kinds of produce, extends, on each side of the square, from Desplaines street to Halsted. As fast as they find buyers they drop out until, by noon, there are few to be found where a few hours before there were crowds.

A double line of street cars runs through the middle of the square; but there still remains room enough on each side of it for the double row of teams standing end to end.

It was near this famous Haymarket that the tragedy of 1886 occurred, known as the Haymarket riot, where the bomb was thrown that killed and wounded nearly a whole platoon of police which attempted to disperse a meeting of workingmen. The statue near the front and right of the picture is the one erected in memory of the police that were slain by the bursting of that bomb. It stands near the west line of Desplaines street and at the entrance of the square.

So that this Haymarket square is an historic spot. Some of the most eventful occurrences have taken place in its vicinity; and it has seen all the great changes which have come to the business and social life of the great city. It is full of quaint, startling and even happy memories. It is here that the great city and the country meet day by day in the everlasting clash of separate interests, to higgle the market over greens and garden sass. It is in places like this that the student of human nature will find an inexhaustible fund of amusement and instruction in the hundreds of eager huxters who throng the walks and gather around the loaded wagons. Here is where human nature manifests itself without the restraints which surround society in its more formal aspects. Here humanity stands unveiled.

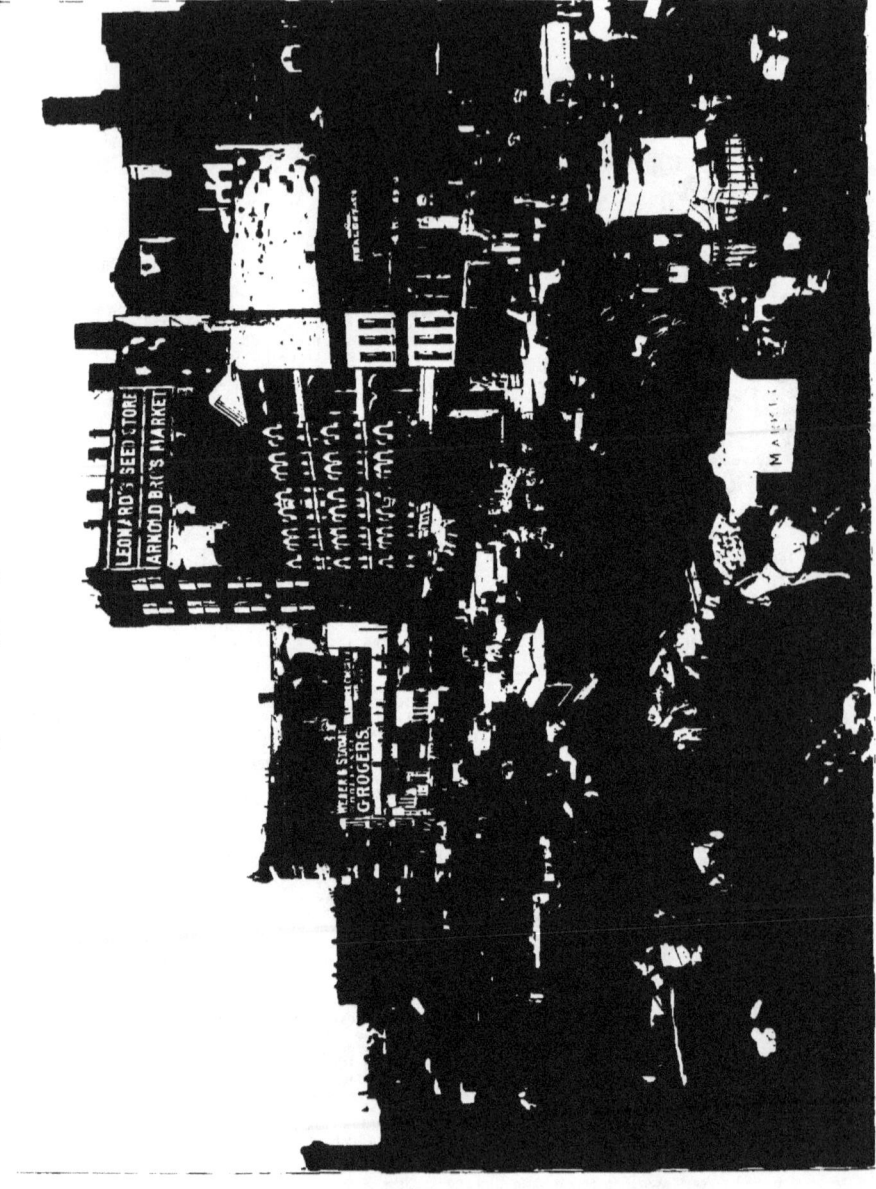

MILWAUKEE AVENUE.

Running northwest from the heart of the city, far away into the suburbs, is one of the most unique business thoroughfares in Chicago. It has a life and character all its own. It runs through a great section of the city thickly settled by foreigners, mostly Germans, Irish and Scandinavians, with a considerable sprinkling of other nationalities. These are uniformly honest, industrious and frugal people, far beyond the average. They are among the last to abandon old habits and methods and still cling tenaciously to their little stores and shops, which line this thoroughfare to the very outskirts of the city. They have been able to withstand the changes in business methods which have destroyed the small stores along other business streets, which were settled by Americans. One of the most striking and peculiar sights to be seen in the city is the flood of humanity which pours northwestward along Milwaukee avenue about six o'clock every evening after the close of business. The walks are crowded on both sides and often great numbers take to the roadway on foot. So great is the throng that it is often impossible for pedestrians to make any headway at all in the opposite direction. One can only take refuge in some open doorway or branch off to other streets, or else wait until the throng passes. This will not be until near seven o'clock. The throng is mostly made up of people too poor to pay fare upon the street cars.

ALBERT L. COE.

A. L. Coe was born in Talmage, Ohio. His early life was spent in Ashtabula County, on the Western Reserve. He removed to Chicago in July, 1853, engaging in the coal business, until the breaking out of the war. He entered the service with the Fifty-first Illinois Volunteers, in September, 1861, and continued in the service for more than four years. The firm of

ALBERT L. COE.

Mead & Coe, of which Mr. Coe is a member, was organized immediately after the war, and has continued until this time without change, doing business in the management of estates for non-residents; also in placing capital in loans and investments, which have proved successful. Careful management has added to the success of that business. Mr. Coe has been identified with several enterprises of public interest. He was one of the early members of the Union League Club. He has taken part in the Citizens' League, the Young Men's Christian Association, of which he has long been a trustee, and other organizations. He was also one of the promoters of the great Auditorium building enterprise. He has always been actuated by a desire to promote the public good, rather than private gain. Warm hearted, courteous, and generous in his intercourse with others, he is an honor to his calling, and to the city of Chicago. He has a commanding presence, and distinguished appearance, which make him a conspicuous figure in any gathering, or on the street.

THE RELIC HOUSE.

This is a place of popular resort located near the Center street entrance to Lincoln Park. It is literally built of relics of the great fire of 1871; and all around the entrances and grounds are arranged some of the

THE RELIC HOUSE.

most remarkable specimens, which will well repay the study of the curious. Every visitor to Lincoln Park should make it a point to visit the Relic House while in the city.

GRACELAND CEMETERY.

One of the most beautiful of the objects of interest around Chicago is Graceland Cemetery. It ranks on a par with Greenwood Cemetery in Brooklyn, Forest Hill of Boston, and Spring Grove of Cincinnati. For the last fifteen years the new system of cemetery adornment has been practiced, which discourages the setting up of unsightly headstones and gaudy monuments, and which cultivates the most pleasing park effects so as to produce upon the visitor a sensation of rest and peace. The utmost care is taken in the selection and planting of every tree and shrub in order to preserve the most natural effects, strengthen the picturesque and maintain a general harmony. No pruning is permitted, only the removal of dead limbs. Great elms have been so transplanted as to give dignity and grace, so that the cemetery becomes an ideal park. Near the chapel stands one of these great elms, 2½ feet in diameter and 60 feet in height. This was planted in 1889. It was then thought to be the largest tree that was ever transplanted, but a still larger one has since been planted at Graceland.

The most has been made of all irregularities of surface, the treatment being such that a slight elevation becomes, in effect, a hill—much after the Japanese method of making a landscape of great diversity of level, and variety of scope within the space of a few

SCENE IN GRACELAND CEMETERY.

feet, by judicious arrangement of surface, placing of buildings and planting. In addition to all the other ornamentation a beautiful artificial lake has been excavated, with the foliage on its banks coming down to the waters' edge, and with its outlines so broken and irregular that from no point can the visitor see it entire. On the whole, this beautiful spot must be seen to be appreciated; and it will repay the visitor to Chicago to make a trip to Graceland Cemetery.

DUNLAP SMITH.

Mr. Dunlap Smith has had a wide range of experiences during his short but eventful life. He was born in Chicago, July 14, 1863. He began his education in the public schools of the city and continued it in the schools of Belgium. He was in Paris and Brussels during the Franco-Prussian war and the Paris Commune. Later he returned to this country and graduated from Harvard University in 1884. Since 1886 he has been engaged in the real estate business in Chicago, and has become connected with many of the great interests which center in this city. He has been a director in the Chicago Elevator Company, the Iowa Central Railway Company, The Barnum and Richardson Manufacturing Company, The Wilmington Coal Company, and president of the Real Estate Board of Chicago. He is also a member of the valuation committee of the same board. He was one of the men selected by Mayor Swift for the tax commission appointed by him. Notwithstanding his present attainments, he has yet the best years of his life before him.

DUNLAP SMITH.

He is one of the youngest among those who have attained distinction.

J. GRAFTON PARKER.

J. Grafton Parker came to Chicago in the spring of 1861. He was, for many years, engaged in business

J. GRAFTON PARKER.

in Boston, being a partner in the firm of H. Jacobs & Son, wholesale provision dealers.

His connection with this firm brought him to Chicago so frequently, that he almost claimed residence here, although he did not move his family here until the fall of 1879. He then became associated with his brother, A. A. Parker, in the well-known firm of Holden & Co., remaining with him until the spring of 1888, when he entered the real estate business, associating with him his son, J. Grafton Parker, Jr., under the firm name of J. Grafton Parker & Co. Mr. Parker's genial manner, honesty and prompt business methods have won for him an enviable position with his associates in business. He has negotiated some of the largest real estate transactions in the city. Mr. Parker was born in Chelmsford, Mass., February 29, 1836. His father, Mr. Artemus Parker, and mother, Lorinda Healy, were well-known in New England for their sterling integrity and Christian bearing.

SENECA D. KIMBARK.

Mr. Seneca D. Kimbark is the pioneer of the iron and steel trade in Chicago, he having been actively engaged in that business for over forty-three years. He was born at Venice, Cayuga County, N. Y., March 4, 1832. He obtained such an education as other country boys of a persevering nature achieved. He began in the district schools and afterward attended the Genesee and Canandaigua academies, earning the money, in the meanwhile to pay his expenses. When he was eight years old his parents removed to Livingston County, and four years later he was set to work on the farm. Here he remained when not teaching in the winter, or attending school, until he was twenty-one. In 1852 Mr. Kimbark removed to Chicago, where he engaged in the iron business, becoming the junior member of the firm of E. G. Hall & Co. In 1860, the firm name was changed to Hall, Kimbark & Co.; and in 1873 to Kimbark Bros. & Co. In 1876 Mr. Kimbark became sole proprietor. The great fire of 1871 had inflicted a heavy loss upon the business; but through tact, courage and perseverance he pulled through and soon recovered the ground lost. He built up in his time one of the greatest iron, steel and heavy hardware trades in this country; also established an extensive carriage woodwork factory in Michigan, to manufacture a large line of the goods he already sold in his trade. In 1891 this was removed to Elkhart, Ind., where conditions were more favorable. This is now one of the largest of its kind in America. Mr. Kimbark has always been an enthusiastic iron man. The iron business has always been his special care. Although not a politician, he takes great interest in all questions of municipal reform. He has always refused to go into partisan politics or run for office, although he has been, from early manhood, a consistent Republican. He was one of the commissioners who located the South Park system; and, during the war, took an active part in raising troops and sending them to the front. The Kimbark Guards organized by his brother, George M., and named for him, received his aid. He was identified with the Union League Club from the time of its organization. He was one of the original members of the Chicago Club; a charter member of the Washington Park Club, and a member of the Calumet Club.

S. D. KIMBARK.

Mr. Kimbark was married September 25, 1856, to Miss Elizabeth Pruyne, daughter of Peter Pruyne, at one time state senator of Illinois, and a friend and colleague of Stephen A. Douglas. Mrs. Kimbark was born the day the first mayor of Chicago was installed. Four children have been born of this union, two daughters and two sons. The oldest son, Charles A. Kimbark, is now the financial manager of his father's business and a young man of great promise. The other, Walter, is equal in promise to his brother. He is at the head of the carriage goods department of the business, and is a skillful manager.

JOHN DUNN.

Mr. John Dunn is an English gentleman who became known to the people of Chicago through his connection with the consular service of Great Britain and by his official position with the Illinois Central Railroad Company. He has many warm friends wherever he is known. He was born in Devonshire, England, April 24, 1840, and came to America in 1869.

He resided in New York until 1873, when he moved to Chicago to enter the service of the Illinois Central Railroad as private secretary to the president. In January, 1883, he was promoted to the post of assist-

JOHN DUNN.

ant to the president and continues to hold that office at the present time, besides being assistant secretary of the company, a position he has filled since November, 1880. Mr. Dunn was British vice consul for a period of seven years, from 1878 to 1884. Since his retirement from that office he has given his whole attention to the affairs of the railway corporation by which he is employed. By profession Mr. Dunn is an attorney-at-law, having been admitted to the Illinois bar in 1875, but of late years he has not actively practiced that profession. Mr. Dunn stands high with the railroad company, and has the unbounded confidence of the president and directors.

JOHN FREDERICK EBERHART.

John Frederick Eberhart was born January 21, 1829, in Mercer County, Pa. His early life was taken up by attendance at school, work on the farm and in teaching, by which he supported himself while carrying on his studies. In this way he developed mental and physical strength, for both of which he was widely noted. He graduated at Alleghany College July 2nd, 1853. On September 1, 1853, he became principal of the Albright Seminary, at Berlin, Pa., the first educational institution founded by the Evangelical Association. Here the tax upon his energies was so great that, after two years, he was forced by failing health to resign.

Mr. Eberhart came west in the spring of 1855 and located at Dixon, Ill. There he edited for a time the Dixon "Transcript," and delivered courses of scientific lectures before institutions of learning; then spent a year in traveling for some New York publishing houses and finally settled down in Chicago to the publication of the "Northwestern Home and School Journal." For about fifteen years Mr. Eberhart was then engaged in educational work, in the editorial chair,

the lecture field and as superintendent of the schools of Cook County, Ill. It was mainly by his efforts that the public schools throughout Cook County were organized and developed into a practical system, and a normal school for the training of teachers was established. He was also an early advocate and promoter of teachers' institutes, which have exercised a powerful influence in developing improved methods of teaching.

In 1860 Mr. Eberhart turned his attention, to a considerable extent, to real estate. In this he has been reasonably successful. He has acquired a competence, and spends it in ways which he believes will bring the most good to humanity.

In politics Mr. Eberhart is a Republican, but is not a partisan and has never sought political preferment. In religion he is a Methodist, but with broad humani-

JOHN F. EBERHART.

tarian sympathies. He is a prominent member of the People's Church, whose pastor, Rev. H. W. Thomas, was his pupil and h is been his life-long friend. He was married in 1864 to Miss Matilda C. Miller, a lady of refinement and who has proved a worthy helpmeet in all his work. Four children have graced their union.

PAUL O. STENSLAND.

Paul O. Stensland was born in Sandied, near Stavanger, Norway, May 9, 1847, the youngest in a family of nine children. He was reared on a farm in his native land and obtained such schooling as he could in the district.

At the age of eighteen he left home for travel in Hindostan and farther India. He became interested in the cotton and wool industries as a buyer of staples, traveling extensively in the prosecution of his business, from Cape Camorin to the Himalayas, and from the Indus to the Bramapootra. After five years he returned to Norway, on a visit to his parents, whom he found in failing health. Both of them died within three months after his return. Soon after he set out for America, arriving in Chicago in the spring of 1871. Here he engaged in the dry goods business, which absorbed his energies for fourteen

years; but in 1885 he left it for insurance and real estate. Since then he organized the Milwaukee Avenue State Bank, of which he became president.

Mr. Stensland was a member of the Chicago Board of Education for nine years, serving on several important committees. He also served on a select committee of citizens to revise the charter of the city

PAUL O. STENSLAND.

and was a director of the World's Columbian Exposition.

Politically Mr. Stensland is a Democrat and in religion a Lutheran. He is also a member of the Iroquois Club and several Scandinavian organizations. He was married in August, 1871, to Karen Querk, of Sonhordland, Norway. They have two children.

DEPOTS.

Chicago is abundantly supplied with depot facilities. While all the older depots which were built, like the Union, at Canal street, and the Rock Island, on Van Buren street, are crowded to their utmost capacity, those built in later years, like the Grand Central and Illinois Central, are capable of affording facilities for many years to come, whatever the growth of the city or increase of roads. The following is a brief summary:

There are six railroad depots in Chicago, all but one of which are union depots—that is, they furnish terminal facilities for a large number of railroads which use them in common. The Northwestern alone, at the north approach to the Wells street bridge, accommodates the Chicago & Northwestern Railroad system. Then comes the Union Depot, on Canal street, extending from Madison to Adams streets, where the Chicago, Milwaukee & St. Paul, the Chicago, Burlington & Quincy, the Chicago & Alton, and the Pennsylvania Railroads terminate. At Harrison street and Fifth avenue is the Wisconsin Central, that accommodates several others—the Baltimore & Ohio, the Chicago & Great Western Railroad, and the Northern Pacific. The Chicago, Rock Island & Pacific is located on Van Buren street, between Sherman and Pacific avenue, which also receives the Lake Shore & Michigan Southern. The Polk street depot, at Polk and Dearborn, gives facilities to the Atchison, Topeka & Santa Fe, the Chicago & Eastern Illinois, the Wabash, the New York, Lake Erie & Western Railroad, the Chicago & Western Indiana, the Grand Trunk, and Louisville, New Albany & Chicago Railroads. And the new Illinois Central depot, at Twelfth street and Michigan avenue, one of the finest in the country, accommodates the Michigan Central and other roads. All these depots are within a few minutes' ride from the central or business part of the city, where the great hotels are all located.

HOTELS.

Chicago is noted, the world over, for the great number, the size, and the excellence of its hotels. It is impossible to give a minute description of all or even any number of them, as it would take a volume for that alone. The most that can be done is to mention, in a general way, a few of the most conspicuous and those which serve as a type of the others.

The Auditorium, with its Annex, stands easily at the head of the list, both in size and appointments. It is one of the largest in the world. It occupies that part of the Auditorium Theater building not given up to office purposes or to the uses of the theater. It rises to eleven stories in height, and has more than 1,000 rooms given up to the use of guests. The American dining-room is on the top story and commands a fine view of Lake Michigan. The European restaurant is on the ground floor, and is the largest and handsomest in the city. The hotel is run on both the American and European plans, so that guests can take their choice. The Auditorium is one of the points of interest that every visitor to Chicago wants to visit.

The Wellington is the place where the men of great wealth put up when they come to Chicago, if they happen to be of a retiring disposition. Here they can be sure of the best that the country affords without undue ostentation. It caters strictly to the ultrafashionable element, and to that it offers the most perfect of home-life comforts.

The Richelieu is another of the swell hotels. It, however, caters more to the showy and ostentatious patrons. Then comes the Palmer House, the home of the politicians; the Great Northern, and others of that class.

Then come the great middle-class hotels, of which there are hundreds, that cater to the commercial traveling public and that furnish good home-like accommodations at a very reasonable price. Of this class the Clifton, at the corner of Monroe and Wabash avenue, and McCoy's, at the corner of Clark and Van Buren streets, are good representatives. And below these there is almost an infinite variety, both in number and grade, which offer accommodation to every class and condition of people, down to the West Madison street lodging-houses, where bunks can be had for a dime.

PLACES OF AMUSEMENT.

Closely related to the hotels are the theaters. And there is a perfectly parallel gradation in the quality and prices of these with the hotels. They range from the Auditorium, the Columbia, McVicker's, the Opera House, the Schiller, and the Great Northern, down through all shades of gradation to the concert hall in a beer garden. Then, in addition to the theaters, are the race tracks, the ball grounds, the Ferris Wheel, and, in summer, the picnic grounds. They all vie with one another to offer attractions that will prove drawing cards and help to win nickels and dimes from the pockets of pleasure seekers. The roof garden is another form of amusement which is gaining in popularity. At the top of the Masonic Temple a place has been fitted up where music, dramatic entertainments,

etc., are given, far above the noise and tumult of the street. Another at the top of the new Great Northern has also been recently completed. It is 205 feet above the sidewalk, the only open-air roof garden in Chicago.

The Auditorium.—As before stated, the Auditorium, for dimensions and magnificence of appointments, easily takes first place. It ranks along with the greatest theaters in the world—the Paris Opera House and La Scala, at Milan. It was begun in 1887, and the construction was carried forward so vigorously that the great audience room was opened to the public on December 9, 1889. The entrance to the theater is from the Congress street side, near Wabash avenue. The ticket offices are located on either side of the grand vestibule that leads to the lobby. The house will seat upwards of four thousand people. There are forty boxes, elaborately furnished and hung with plush curtains. Fifty-five hundred incandescent electric lamps light the house and stage. The organ is said to be the largest and finest in the world. It contains 7,193 pipes. The stage, from foot-lights to wall, is 69 deep by 98 feet wide in the clear. It is sufficient for the grandest scenic displays that are ever necessary in a theatrical production.

The Auditorium is the home of the Orchestral Association, supporting the Chicago Orchestra, conducted by Mr. Theodore Thomas, which was incorporated in 1891. It is one of the two permanent orchestras in America. At the very beginning its financial basis was firmly established, when about fifty of Chicago's wealthiest and most public-spirited men created its "guaranty fund," thereby obligating themselves for any deficits which might remain at the end of each season. The orchestra is composed of about eighty-five members, and for twenty-two weeks of each year since its establishment two concerts per week have been given at the Auditorium—a Friday matinee and a Saturday evening concert. The best solo talent available has appeared from time to time at these concerts. The season sale for 1896-7 is already larger than ever before. A special chorus has been made an adjunct to the orchestra this season. This is under the direction of Mr. Arthur Mees. Besides its forty-four Chicago programmes, the orchestra will also visit many of the leading cities, such as Ann Arbor, Toledo, Cleveland, Milwaukee, and other places of prominence.

The purpose of the Chicago Orchestra is to furnish good music for the West, and the stability which the

THE MASONIC TEMPLE, STATE AND RANDOLPH STREETS.
Home Office of Knights Templars and Masons Life Indemnity Co.

THEATERS.

names of its guarantors has given it has led these surrounding cities to avail themselves of the opportunity furnished them.

Next to the Auditorium and its various attractions comes McVicker's Theater, with a seating capacity of about 2,000. It is one of the oldest theaters in the city. It was the fifth, in order of time, built in Chicago. It was destroyed in the great fire of 1871, but rebuilt larger and finer, so that it was again opened to the public on August 15, 1872, having been rebuilt at a cost of $200,000. Important improvements and additions have been made since, which keep it in the front rank of Chicago play houses. It is one of the most favorably located of any in the city, being convenient to street cars from all parts of Chicago, and to all the great down-town hotels.

The Columbia is situated just one square south of McVicker's, on Monroe street. It is the legitimate successor of the New Adelphi, which, for a time after the fire, occupied the present site of the First National Bank, in the old Postoffice building, the ruins of which were rebuilt after the great fire and were occupied by J. H. Haverly as a play house. When the ground lease expired, the Adelphi was demolished and the Columbia was built on its present site by Mr. Haverly, who managed it until February, 1885, when it passed into the hands of the Columbia Theater Company. In 1890, Messrs. Hayman & Davis took charge, and still control the property. It enjoys a wide and deserved popularity, not only for the completeness of its appointments, but for the uniform excellence of its attractions.

fied by the public verdict. It has come to be known as "the Parlor Home of Comedy," and justly so, for "Hooley's" is known among theater-goers and the theatrical profession as one of the most popular and successful play houses, not only in Chicago, but in the United States. The late Mr. R. M. Hooley began his

MARSHALL FIELD'S BUILDING, WABASH AVE. AND WASHINGTON ST.

Hooley's Theater. — The Chicago Tribune says: "Hooley's has become to Chicago like Daly's and the Lyceum of New York rolled into one—more than that, like six of the best Eastern comedy theaters in their combined essence." But this is no more than is justified career in Chicago in 1870, at Hooley's Opera House, situated where the Grand Opera House now stands. After the fire of 1871, Mr. Hooley made a trade of that ground for the Randolph street site and built Hooley's Theater, which was opened on October 17, 1872. It is

RESIDENCE OF MR. ALBERT WISNER, 4825 DREXEL BOULEVARD.

the home of the great dramatic stock companies of New York and London. Among its permanent attractions are Ada Rehan and Mr. Augustin Daly's company, the New York Lyceum Theater Company, the New York Empire Theater Company, Mr. and Mrs. Kendal, Mr. E. S. Willard, Mr. John Hare, Miss Olga Nethersole, Mr. John Drew, Mr. Nat C. Goodwin, Mr. E. H. Sothern, and the leading comedy attractions of Messrs. Daniel and Charles Frohman. Also the latest successes in comedy and the drama of New York and London.

Mr. Harry J. Powers is the manager and Mr. Francis J. Wolf the treasurer. The theater has been frequently remodeled, and is perfectly adapted to all the requirements of the modern stage and the comfort of the public.

The Chicago Opera House comes next in order of size. It is located on the corner of Clark and Washington streets, and has a seating capacity of about 2,300 persons. Its stage construction is remarkably perfect. Every device which modern theaters have found desirable is included. No expense has been spared in making the stage one of the finest in the West. Nothing is lacking which would add to the scenic effect or increase the comfort and convenience of the players. The interior decoration is strikingly original and appropriate, although chaste and refined. It is now running as a continuous show, without doubt the best of its class in Chicago.

The Grand Opera House is another of the old play houses of the city. It has been frequently remodeled to bring it up to modern requirements. In this way it has kept up with the march of improvements. It is located on Clark street, between Washington and Randolph streets.

The Schiller Theater is situated on Randolph Street, between Clark and Dearborn, and is one of the finest and most popular of Chicago places of amusement. It has recently passed into the hands of Mr. Robert Blei, who, in a short time, has established a reputation of giving the best vaudeville entertainment furnished in the country. The prices range from 20 cents to $1, and all seats are reserved. One beauty about the Schiller auditorium is that there are no posts or columns in any part of the house to interfere with the view of the stage. The seating capacity is about twelve hundred, and there are six boxes. The chairs are large and comfortable, with plenty of space between each row. Improved ventilating systems, including a perfect heating system for winter and refrigerating system for summer, together with suction fans in the roof that secure a continuous supply of fresh air, which renders it pleasant at any season of the year. The Schiller forms one of a circuit of vaudeville houses which extend from New York to San Francisco, and secures the first option on all the new attractions which come from Europe.

The Great Northern Theater, just completed, while

SCHILLER THEATER, RANDOLPH STREET, BETWEEN CLARK AND DEARBORN STREETS.

making no pretensions to being a great theater, is one of the finest in the city. Completeness in all its details, beauty and elegance in all its adornments, and the convenience and safety of its patrons have been the points aimed at. All the stage fittings and fixtures are of fire-proof materials, and everything from pit to gallery is fire-proof, even to floors and ceilings. It has a seating capacity of about 1,500. It contains sixteen boxes; and the chairs are exactly alike throughout the entire house. The ventilation is so arranged that fresh air is taken from the roof and forced downward throughout the whole house, there being three independent systems, one for the stage and one each for the auditorium and the gallery.

In addition to these there are numerous theaters of first-rate importance in each of the three sections of the city, which depend upon local patronage for their support, like the Standard and Haymarket on the West side. These are followed by a multitude of smaller places of every kind and quality to be found in every conceivable place where people congregate, so that there is no difficulty in satisfying the most varied tastes of resident or visitor in the matter of amusements.

A GREAT EDUCATIONAL CENTER.

Chicago has become one of the greatest centers of learning in America. In this respect, it has kept pace with its development in other and more material things. Early in its history, certain sections of land were set aside as an endowment of its common school system. Several of those sections are located in the heart of the business portion of the city; and although much of this land has heretofore been sold, there still remains enough to constitute a magnificent endowment. The rents which are received form an important part of the fund for the support of the schools. And, on top of that, the Legislature has been liberal in making provision for the raising of sufficient means, by taxation, to sustain the finest system of common schools in America. The schools are under the control of a Board of Education, consisting of twenty members, who are appointed by the Mayor and confirmed by the Common Council. The direct administration of the affairs of the schools is entrusted to one superintendent of schools, one superintendent of high schools, ten assistant superintendents, six supervisors and an extensive corps of lesser officials and employes. Four thousand three hundred and twenty-six teachers are regularly employed, and the total expenditures of the school board for the fiscal year ending June 1, 1895, was $6,334,328.10. There were, according to official reports of the same date, 281 school buildings in the city, valued at $7,273,490.

In addition to the common schools, there are fourteen high schools, where pupils are carried through the grades preparatory to entering college.

The curriculum of the public schools, embracing both the common and high schools, covers a very wide range. There are kindergarten, evening, primary, grammar, manual training, normal, college preparatory and physical culture classes, that would seem to cover the whole possible scope of an English education. In addition to English, German, Latin, music and drawing are taught as voluntary branches.

THE HIGHER INSTITUTIONS.

Beyond and above the regular public school system comes the various universities, with their colleges of law, medicine, arts, theology, science and literature, furnishing facilities for the most general and special training of every variety conceivable. The oldest of these is the Northwestern University, having its seat at Evanston, twelve miles north of Chicago, although in its strictest sense it is a Chicago institution. The Northwestern University has a liberal endowment, which has been contributed by friends of the institution from time to time since its starting. It is under the dominant influence of the Methodist denomination. Its funds are carefully invested, mainly in remunerative property in Chicago and Evanston. It is presided over by Henry Wade Rodgers, LL. D., who was called to his present position from the deanship of the Law School of the Michigan University, at Ann Arbor. The university was organized under a special charter from the Legislature of Illinois, dated January 28, 1851, but it was not opened until November, 1855.

The College of Liberal Arts, together with the university campus, is situated at Evanston on a beautiful tract of wooded upland on the shore of Lake Michigan. By the provisions of the charter, no intoxicants can be sold within a radius of four miles from its campus. The college offers four courses of study, each requiring four years for their completion, the classical, the philosophical, the scientific, and the course in modern literature. Each of these courses are open alike to persons of either sex, the instruction being the same in both cases; and the same honors are bestowed for efficiency. Post-graduate work is done in all the departments of the university, leading to the degree of Ph. D.

The Woman's College, the Academy and the Theological School, are also located at Evanston.

The Medical School is located in Chicago, on Dearborn Street, between Twenty-four and Twenty-fifth streets. It was formerly known as the Chicago Medical College, under which name it has a history of nearly fifty years of successful work behind it. This school was the first in this country: 1, to enforce a standard of preliminary education; 2, to adopt longer annual courses of instruction; 3, to grade the curriculum of studies.

Its laboratory building contains laboratories of physiology, histology, anatomy, pathology, bacteriology, chemistry, pharmacology and pharmacognosy of the most modern form and with best equipments.

Davis Hall is a very perfect out-patient infirmary, where twenty-five thousand patients are treated annually. Forty clinics are conducted weekly at Mercy and St. Luke's Hospitals and Davis Hall.

Instruction is given by lectures, recitations, conferences, laboratory and clinic methods. Numerous elective courses are offered to students who desire them, either that they may obtain "honors" or special knowledge. These courses are chiefly laboratory or combined laboratory and clinic.

The faculty consists of thirty-seven professors and forty-three instructors and demonstrators.

The Law School of the University is located in the Masonic Temple, occupying one-half the seventh floor of that building, and was formerly known as the Union College of Law. The faculty includes some of the most prominent jurists in the West. No pains are spared to retain the most eminent specialists in every branch of legal practice; and many of those who have achieved distinction at the bench or bar of the West during the last twenty-five years have been professors or graduates of the Union College of Law of the Northwestern University.

The School of Pharmacy occupies a part of the building of the medical school. It was organized in 1886 as the Illinois College of Pharmacy, but soon became the Northwestern University School of Pharmacy. It was designed for the systematic and thorough training of druggists. Its course includes thirty hours of instruction each week, on a plan which insures a great saving of time and expense in the work to be done.

The Dental School, lately consolidated with the American College of Dental Surgery, is located at the corner of Franklin and Madison streets, in Chicago. It is one of the most thorough schools of dentistry in the United States, being provided with every convenience that experience has shown to be necessary, or that can facilitate the work.

The Woman's Medical School is another of the famous colleges connected with this university. It is located at 333 to 339 South Lincoln Street, Chicago. This was founded in 1870 as the Woman's Hospital Medical College, but, in 1892, became a part of the university. It has obtained a wide and merited celebrity all over the world, drawing its students from every state in the Union, as well as from every civilized country in the world.

LAKE FOREST UNIVERSITY.

This is another of the distinctively, Chicago institutions, but which is located in one of the suburbs, as far as its headquarters goes. It was started as a Chicago enterprise by men whose interests and business was here; but they had also become interested in Lake Forest as a beautiful and growing suburb, and so, very naturally, thought to help forward its prospects by making it the seat of a great educational institution. The charter was obtained in 1857; but it was not formally organized until 1876. Its principal departments are undergraduate and philosophical, located at Lake Forest, and scientific, located in Chicago, the scientific comprising the Rush Medical College, Chicago College of Dental Surgery and the Chicago College of Law.

The Chicago College of Law was organized in January, 1888, as the Chicago Evening School of Law. The following year it was reorganized as the Chicago College of Law, and soon after became the Law Department of the Lake Forest University.

It is the personnel of the faculty that makes up the greatness of an institution of learning, and the faculty of this college was selected with that end in view. Such eminent jurists as Hon. Joseph M. Bailey, LL. D., justice of the Supreme Court of Illinois, was the first preceptor, and continued as dean down to the time of his death in 1895. In the fall of 1888 the Hon. Thomas A. Moran became associated with Judge Bailey in the work of the college, and it is largely through the combined efforts and zeal of the two that the institution has been raised to the front rank of legal educational institutions of the country.

THE VENETIAN BUILDING, 34-36 WASHINGTON STREET, BETWEEN STATE STREET AND WABASH AVENUE.

In 1890, a third year, or post-graduate course, was organized, leading to the degree of Bachelor of Laws. Judge Moran, who is practically at the head of this course, has a national reputation as a judge and a lawyer. His long experience on the bench and at the bar make him pre-eminent as an instructor in this course. Up to June, 1895, the college had graduated 766 persons from its two years' course, and 290 from its post-graduate course. It is contemplated to add still another course to the post-graduate, leading to the degree of Master of Laws. The business matters of the college are generally intrusted to Secretary Elmer E. Barrett, LL. B., who has occupied his position from the first organization.

Lake Forest is situated on a beautiful bluff overlooking Lake Michigan, twenty-eight miles north of Chicago. It is the highest elevation between Chicago and Milwaukee. It was originally laid out as a park, and is almost wholly given up to residences and the university buildings. The sale of intoxicating drinks is prohibited by the terms of its charter. The Chicago & Northwestern Railroad gives quick and easy communication with Chicago at all times. The institution is under the dominant influence of the Presbyterian Church, although the teaching is not sectarian. It has a generous endowment, which is receiving constant additions from time to time.

The undergraduate department comprises the following schools:

The Lake Forest College, offering three courses of study, each of four years, viz.: Classical, Latin, and Scientific. All studies are prescribed during the first two years, after which a considerable range of elective studies are allowed.

Ferry Hall Seminary, which prepares young women for college, has additional courses leading to degrees of Bachelor of Letters and Bachelor of Music.

Lake Forest Academy is the preparatory school for boys, but has special courses for those who do not contemplate taking a college course.

Rush Medical College is one of the oldest and most honored of Chicago's medical schools, and forms the medical department of the university. It is situated on the corner of Wood and Harrison streets, opposite the Cook County Hospital. It was located on the North-side before the great fire, where it was completely destroyed along with its extensive museum.

A LILY POND, LINCOLN PARK.

When the city was rebuilt it chose as its home its present site on account of its proximity to the County Hospital and the facilities which the hospital affords for clinical and hospital practice. The enormous popularity it has enjoyed has rendered necessary frequent additions until it is one of the largest and best equipped medical institutions in America.

Chicago College of Dental Surgery was founded in 1883. It was formed by a company of dental practitioners in response to a manifest need for an institution for the thorough training of dentists in the science of their profession. It attained to a wide popularity as a separate institution, and, in 1889, united with Lake Forest University as the dental department of that institution.

The course of instruction of the college embraces physiology, histology, oral surgery, materia medica, therapeutics, anatomy, operative and prosthetic dentistry, chemistry, dental pathology, and dental technics. The course in operative dentistry is given in formed classes, under special instructors, in order to give students an intimate knowledge of the tissues and parts upon which they operate, the physical qualities of the materials used and the use of instru-

scale of expenditure which the authorities of the university felt it requisite to maintain. The consequence was that it was constantly cramped for means and fell into embarrassments, which culminated in 1886 in its dissolution. In May, 1889, the American Baptist Educational Society determined to make another effort to found in Chicago a seat of learning under the controlling influence of that denomination. As a beginning it obtained a gift of $600,000 from John D. Rockefeller, conditioned that enough more should be obtained to raise the endowment fund to $1,000,000. The assistance of the denomination was enlisted generally, and the amount was raised. Marshall Field also contributed a fine tract of land as a site, covering about twenty-five acres. Up to the beginning of 1896 the contributions and subscriptions to the institution have amounted to $11,500,000. Mr. Rockefeller has

RUSH MEDICAL COLLEGE, 751 WEST HARRISON STREET.

ments. Truman W. Brophy, M. D., D. D. S., LL. D., one of the foremost men in the profession in this country, is dean of the faculty.

The University of Illinois School of Pharmacy, formerly the Chicago College of Pharmacy, at 465-467 State Street, is the pharmaceutical school of the same university. It offers rare facilities for a business training to young men and women in the profession of pharmacy.

THE UNIVERSITY OF CHICAGO.

Among the earliest institutions for higher education was the Chicago University, under the dominant influence of the Baptists. It had received various small endowments from prominent members of that denomination, principally from the Hon. Stephen A. Douglas, but they were not sufficient to maintain it on the

made several subsequent donations, amounting in all to $7,426,000. The university opened its doors to students October 1, 1892, and the first year enrolled upward of 800 students. The second year this was increased to 1,200, the third to 1,500, and the fourth to 2,000. Building has progressed rapidly, already sixteen are completed and others are in process of erection. Over $1,600,000 has already been expended in construction in Chicago. The Yerkes Observatory, one of its branches, located at Lake Geneva, Wisconsin, a favorite resort of the wealthy people of Chicago, was built at a cost of $400,000 for land, buildings and instruments. This is an addition to the amounts expended as above. Prof. W. R. Harper, formerly Semitic professor of languages at Yale, was chosen president of the University in September, 1890, since which time he has been its guiding spirit. Already a number of the independent unattached institutions of learning of various kinds have united with the University of Chicago, and the tendency seems to be somewhat general for them to unite under the direction of some one of these great institutions.

Outside of the universities there is a large number of medical schools, colleges of various kinds, institutes covering special fields of training, and seminaries, which are each doing a valuable and necessary work, which the present universities do not undertake.

The Chicago Homoeopathic Medical College is an outgrowth from the Hahnemann. It is located, along with so many of the medical colleges, in the immediate vicinity of the Cook County Hospital, at the corner of Wood and York streets, Chicago. It is a commodious structure, built expressly for the purposes for which it is used, and is provided with every modern appliance required for such an institution.

cago, is located at 813 W. Harrison Street. It is one of the youngest of the great medical schools of the city, but one of the strongest and most popular. The main building was constructed in 1881, is six stories in height, and is provided with every modern convenience for the purposes intended. Special prominence is given, in its course, to laboratory work. Although it has no endowment and no connection with any powerful university, it has had a rapid and steady growth from its first inception. Its annual attendance averages about four hundred.

Then follow the Chicago Physio-Medical College, which teaches that irritation, pain, fever and inflammation are not disease, but physiological symptoms of disease. In consequence of these fundamental principles of medicine, it, in accordance with this principle, discards the use of all poisons as curative

COLLEGE OF PHYSICIANS AND SURGEONS, WEST HARRISON AND HONORE STREETS.

The faculty includes many of the most prominent homoeopathic physicians in the country.

The Post-Graduate Medical School was established about ten years ago by some of the foremost physicians of Chicago in order to supply a place where regular practitioners could come from time to time and obtain the results of the advances in medical science. It has been a success from the start. More than fourteen hundred physicians from every State in the Union, from Mexico and from Canada, have availed themselves of the facilities offered. It is located at the corner of Dearborn and Twenty-fourth streets, in the center of a medical district embracing the Woman's Hospital, Michael Reese Hospital, Mercy Hospital, St. Luke's Hospital and the Chicago Hospital.

The College of Physicians and Surgeons, of Chi-

agents, and uses none but unquestionably harmless agents in the cure of disease, thus aiding nature in the cure of disease by efficient and harmless agents.

The Dunham Medical College is the latest addition to the list of homoeopathic medical colleges in Chicago. It has a beautiful new building, built for its own purposes, on Wood Street, opposite the County Hospital. Its equipment is remarkably complete and well adapted to the work, and it has a large faculty of some of the most progressive physicians in Chicago.

The Chicago Policlinic, a post-graduate medical school, is located at 174 to 176 Chicago avenue. It occupies a fine, six story building, built for its own use. This is its eleventh season. It numbers among its faculty of thirty-seven many of the foremost physicians in America, in addition to which it maintains a large corps of lecturers, instructors and assist-

EDUCATIONAL.

ants. It extends a cordial welcome to physicians visiting Chicago to inspect its equipment and attend its clinics.

The Illinois Training School for Nurses, situated near the County Hospital, is doing a most valuable work in training nurses for an intelligent exercise of their profession. It is the largest and most important institution of the kind in Chicago.

The Marion-Sims Training School for Nurses is another but smaller school of the same kind. It is located at 518 West Adams Street in connection with a sanitarium of the same name. This furnishes a practical training in the duties of the nurse, and is doing an excellent work.

The Chicago Veterinary College is for the training of veterinary surgeons in the use of modern methods of medical treatment of dumb animals.

are already under contemplation. There are at present about 1,000 pupils in regular attendance, under the instruction of fifty-four teachers, so that, while Chicago can boast of many great things, it has the largest art school in America. The collection of painting, sculpture, and other objects is such as to place the Art Institute among the four leading galleries in this country. A part of the exhibits are owned by the institute and a part are loaned to it, the total value of the collection being upward of $2,000,000, about one-half of which are the property of the institute. If the ratio of visitors to the institute continues throughout the year, as in the past, it will exceed 600,000 persons, being larger than any other museum in America. The galleries are open to the public free on Wednesdays and Saturdays between the hours of 9 a. m. to 5 p. m., and on Sundays from

ARMOUR INSTITUTE, ARMOUR AVENUE AND THIRTY-THIRD STREET.

In addition to these there is a long list of theological schools, colleges and seminaries, offering every variety of theological belief, from which people can choose to their liking, embracing Methodist, Baptist, Congregational, Presbyterian, Catholic and Episcopal.

The Art Institute was organized in 1879. It began by occupying rented quarters until its magnificent home was finished. The Art Institute building is on Michigan avenue, facing Adams street. It was built in 1892-93 at a cost for the structure alone of more than $650,000, which, together with the ground, is valued at upward of $2,000,000. Spacious as the building is, it is already inadequate to house the great collections of pictures, statuary, etc., which have been accumulated. And then, the quarters of the rapidly growing art school are filled to overflowing by pupils from every part of the country. Enlargements

1 to 5 p. m. On other days an admission fee of 25 cents is charged, the hours being the same as on other week days.

There are several other notable art collections in Chicago, such as that of the Illinois Art Association, at 154 Ashland Boulevard, open only to members and invited guests, and the Vincennes Gallery of Fine Arts, at 3841 Vincennes Avenue, which contains many valuable works of art, which is open at all times without admission fee. But there is nothing at all approaching the Art Institute.

The Chicago Academy of Sciences, founded in 1857, is another of these unattached institutions which is doing a valuable work of its own. It includes in its membership many of the most learned men in Chicago, specialists in their lines. It has a library of over 7,000 volumes, and a museum of its own.

This museum contains over 50,000 species, mostly of the fauna and flora of the United States, and is said to rank fifth among the valuable collections of the world. It has recently erected a fine building at the Center Street entrance of Lincoln Park, which furnishes a home to the society. The means for its construction were contributed by the late Mathew Laflin, one of Chicago's wealthy capitalists and early settlers. It is known as the Mathew Laflin Memorial Hall. The academy now has a membership of about four hundred and fifty, to which accessions are constantly being made.

Then comes the Chicago Historical Society, organized April 24, 1856, which is intended to collect and preserve whatever of value exists as to the early history of Chicago and Illinois. Its home is on Dearborn Avenue, and it is supported by contributions from some of the wealthy men of Chicago, who are proud of their State and city.

The Chicago Astronomical Society dates back to 1862. It is closely allied, if not actually connected with, the Northwestern University. When the old Chicago University was dissolved it became the possessor of the celebrated Dearborn Observatory telescope, the largest in the West. This it removed to Evanston, where it is now in the use of the university.

The Chicago Athenaeum is another of those unattached institutions. It was organized in October, 1871, immediately after the great fire. Its purpose is to promote mutual self-help in the work of education and for social intercourse. It was established in a building at the corner of Wabash Avenue and Twenty-second Street, where classes were organized and work carried on. As the burned over portion of the city began again to be covered with buildings, and business again centered down town, it was found necessary to remove to more accessible quarters. The Athenaeum went with the rest. It obtained good accommodations, employed competent instructors and pushed its work with vigor. Since that time it has grown to great proportions. It now occupies the entire building 18-26 Van Buren Street, employs a corps of twenty special teachers and gives instruction in

NEWBERRY LIBRARY, CLARK AND OAK STREETS.

five foreign languages, Greek, Latin, French, German and Spanish. Special attention is given to music, drawing, elocution, English literature, short-hand and gymnastics. The charges for tuition are merely nominal.

The Armour Institute of Technology.—This is an institution founded upon a magnificent endowment by Philip D. Armour. It embraces a technical college, a scientific academy, a department of domestic arts, a department of commerce, a department of music and a department of kindergartens. The curriculum embraces English literature, steam, mechanical and electrical engineering, chemistry, architecture, mathematics, modern languages, physics, drawing, metallurgy, wood-working, machine work, forging, decoration, painting, gymnastics, and a multitude of

LIBRARIES.

other practical matters necessary to the ambitious young man or woman. Manual training is introduced as a means of instruction in the technical departments.

Besides the equipment of the several scientific departments, the Institute has a fine gymnasium, a technical museum and a large library, which is a distinctive feature in the life and thought of the community.

which the City Council has appropriated nearly $2,000,000, will be ready for occupancy about May, 1897. Messrs. Shepley, Rutan and Coolidge are the designers of the architectural monument, which in its practical arrangement and the beauty of its interior decoration will place it in the front rank among the great library buildings of the world.

The number of volumes now in the library is nearly 220,000, and the collection is growing at the rate of

UNITY UNITARIAN CHURCH.

The Chicago Public Library has occupied, since 1886, the rooms on the top floor of the city hall. So rapid has been the growth of the library that those quarters are entirely inadequate to meet the demands made upon it by the 55,000 readers who draw books from the library for home use, and the thousands who frequent the reference and reading rooms. There has been erected on Dearborn Park, on Michigan Avenue, between Randolph and Washington streets, a magnificent new home for the library. This building, for

10,000 volumes a year. The total circulation of books and periodicals in all departments in 1895 was 2,485,052, of which nearly one-half were drawn from the library for home use. The annual expense of operating the library is $140,000. For the convenience of persons living at a distance from the main library the Board of Directors maintains thirty-two delivery stations, where books may be exchanged free of charge. In addition there are also in operation six branch reading rooms, each of which is equipped with a well-

98 UNRIVALED CHICAGO.

selected reference library and a selection of the best newspapers and periodicals. The public library and all its branches are open to the public every day in the year from 9 a. m. to 10 p. m. The librarian is Frederick H. Hild.

The Newberry Library.—Mr. Walter L. Newberry, one of the pioneers of Chicago, who attained to great wealth through sagacious investments in its early days, died November 6, 1868, leaving by his will one-half of his estate for the founding of a great library to bear his name. More than one million of dollars was thus realized, which, by careful investment, has been considerably increased, so that the fund now amounts to about $2,500,000. A magnificent library building has lately been erected, costing $500,000, facing Washington Park, between Clark Street and Dearborn Avenue. The library is being constantly added to, so that, on January 1, 1896, it embraced over 140,000 volumes.

In addition to these general collections of books, special libraries are numerous throughout the city.

The Law Institute is one of the most complete and valuable law libraries in America. It is intended strictly for the benefit of the bench and bar. It occupies commodious apartments on the top floor of the county building, in close proximity to the courts.

Medical Libraries.—Extensive and valuable libraries exist in connection with all the medical colleges and designed for the special use of their own faculties and students, but which can always be reached by members of the profession and others interested.

CHURCHES.

Of course, Chicago is well furnished with churches, where the religiously inclined can obtain amusement without going to the naughty theaters. Generally the aristocratic ones maintain famous preachers and elaborate choirs. And they are very fairly patronized. It is impossible to go into any elaborate description of particular organizations, but a person can find in Chicago every variety of religion, and almost every grade of ability in advocating it, that may be desired, from the aristocratic ones on the boulevards to the gospel missions on Van Buren and on Halsted streets. And if none of these should suit a discriminating taste, there remains the Salvation Army with its numerous gatherings on the street corners and its street parades.

FOURTH BAPTIST CHURCH, ASHLAND BOULEVARD AND WEST MONROE STREET

BIOGRAPHICAL SKETCHES.

PHYSICIANS.

LEWIS LINN M'ARTHUR, M. D.

Dr. Lewis Linn McArthur was born in Boston, January 23, 1858, his father being an officer in the army. He attended primary school in Chicago Academy, at Lake Forest, Illinois, and spent a year at Allen's Academy, in Chicago, in preparation for college. He then entered Santa Clara College, but left in the junior year on account of weakness of his eyes. He began the study of medicine under Dr. Walker Hay,

LEWIS LINN M'ARTHUR, M. D.

in 1876, afterward continuing under Dr. John E. Owens. In 1877, he entered Rush Medical, and graduated in 1880, having been assistant to Dr. Haines, Demonstrator of Chemistry, during the whole time.

Dr. McArthur was made interne in Cook County Hospital in 1880, after a competitive examination, taking first place. He spent one year abroad in study, at Heidelberg and Vienna, especially in the field of surgery, obstetrics, nose and throat, and of toxicology.

On his return he was placed in charge of the spring course of chemical lectures at Rush, during Prof. Haines' absence, after which he lectured for three years in the Chicago College of Dental Surgery as Professor of Chemistry.

Dr. McArthur occupies a place on the staff of the Michael Reese Hospital, St. Luke's Hospital, and the Chicago Orphan Asylum. He is a member of many of the leading medical societies and stands high in the profession.

ARTHUR DEAN BEVAN, M. D.

Dr. Arthur Dean Bevan was born in Chicago, in 1861. He was prepared for college in the Chicago High School. He entered the scientific department at Yale; but, at the beginning of his junior year, he left the college to begin his medical studies at Rush, where he graduated with high honors in the class of '83.

Passing the examinations he entered the United

ARTHUR DEAN BEVAN, M. D.

States Marine Hospital Service, in which he remained until 1888. While stationed in Portland, Oregon, he was appointed Professor of Anatomy in the medical department of the State University. In 1888, he was appointed to the chair of anatomy at Rush; and, in 1890, surgeon to the Presbyterian Hospital, Chicago. Two years later he spent a term in the University of Leipzig, and did some special work in Vienna and Berlin.

In 1895, he was appointed surgeon to St. Luke's and also St. Elizabeth Hospitals, and Professor of Surgery in the Woman's Medical School. In 1896, he was married to Miss Anna L. Barbee.

Dr. Bevan is a member of many medical societies, and Vice President of the Chicago Medical.

He has won distinction both as a teacher of anatomy and as an operating surgeon, and is one of the most prominent among the younger surgeons of the West.

WILLIAM T. BELFIELD, M. D.

Dr. William T. Belfield was born at St. Louis, Missouri, in 1856. He is a graduate of the Chicago grammar, the high school, and the Michigan University. Since his graduation he taught Latin and mathematics in the Chicago High School for four years. He then took a regular course at the Rush Medical College, graduating in 1878, after which he served a term as resident physician at the Cook County Hospital. In order to perfect his equipment for his life work, he then went abroad and spent two years in the great medical schools and hospitals of Vienna, Paris and London. On his return he was made professor of bacteriology and lecturer on surgery in Rush Medical College, professor of genito-urinary diseases in the Chicago Policlinic, and professor of surgery in the Chicago College of Dental Surgery. He has been five years surgeon of the Cook County Hospital; was lecturer for the Cartwright fund, New York, in 1883; and was President of the Chicago Medical Society in 1887. He is a member of the American Association of Genito-Urinary Surgery, and of the Athletic, the Marquette, and the Literary Clubs. He is also author of a volume in World's Standard Library, "The Diseases of the Urinary and Male Sexual Organs," of the section of the "System of Genito-Urinary Diseases." He has acquired an almost world-wide reputation in this special branch of medicine and surgery.

WILLIAM T. BELFIELD, M. D.

JOHN ERASMUS HARPER, A. M., M. D.

Dr. John E. Harper, one of the most eminent eye and ear specialists in America, was born in Trigg County, Kentucky, in 1851. His parents soon moved to Evansville, Indiana, where he was brought up. He read medicine under Dr. George B. Walker, of Evansville, and then took a full course in the medical department of the University of New York. At graduation he received first prize for best examination in diseases of the eye and ear. He then took a post-graduate course in the hospitals of London, Paris, and Vienna. On his return, he was made a professor in the medical college of Evansville; but he resigned in 1882, to accept a professorship of diseases of the eye and ear in the College of Physicians and Surgeons, of Chicago. His conspicuous ability contributed largely to the success of this school. For nine years he was surgeon-in-chief to the eye and ear department of the West Side Free Dispensary, and five years visiting surgeon to the eye and ear department of the Illinois Eye and Ear Infirmary. He has also filled the same position in numerous private institutions. He is a member of many of the medical societies, especially those relating to his specialty. He was also editor of the Western Medical Reporter for fifteen years.

SANGER BROWN, M. D.

Dr. Sanger Brown was born at Bloomfield, Ontario, February 16, 1852. He lived on a farm until he was twenty-one years old. He then attended the Albert College University at Bellville, Ont., where he matriculated in arts and civil engineering. He pursued his studies in civil engineering until 1877, when he took up the study of medicine at the Bellevue Hospital Medical College, New York City. After graduation in 1880, he became assistant physician on the medical staff of the New York City Insane Asylum, at Ward's Island. After remaining there fifteen months he was appointed assistant physician at the State Hospital for the Insane, at Danvers, Mass., which he resigned after eight months to accept a similar one at Bloomingdale Asylum, where he remained four years. In both positions he was eminently successful.

Dr. Brown was married in 1885 to Miss Belle Christie, of Chicago.

In the fall of 1886 he went to London and began a series of original investigations in the laboratory of University College with Prof. Schäfer, on the brains of monkeys, for the purpose of locating the centers of the various special senses. The results were embodied in a paper presented to the Royal Society of London, and published in the philosophical transactions. (Vol. 179 (1888), B., pp. 303-327. Returning from Europe he settled in Chicago in 1889, where he has since remained in the practice of his profession.

In 1890 he was appointed professor of nervous and mental diseases in the Post Graduate Medical School of Chicago, and in 1891 professor of medical jurispru-

SANGER BROWN, M. D.

dence and hygiene in Rush Medical College, both of which positions he still holds. He is attending physician in the neurological departments of the St. Elizabeth and St. Luke's hospitals; a member of most of the local, state and national medical societies, and an active member of the Neurological Society of London.

SETH SCOTT BISHOP, M. D., LL. D.

Dr. Seth Scott Bishop was born in Fond du Lac, Wis., February 7, 1852. He took a three years' course at Beloit College, after attending the preliminary and regular courses in the medical department of the University of New York, in the fall and winter of 1871-2. Subsequently he studied under Dr. S. S. Bowers, of Fond du Lac, and entered the Chicago Medical College. Here he graduated in 1876 and established himself in practice at Fond du Lac. In the fall of 1879 he removed to Chicago.

Dr. Bishop has devoted himself in recent years mainly to one special branch of practice, in which he has carried forward a series of original researches. His contributions to medical literature, on those subjects, have attracted wide attention from the profession and made a demand for a more extended and formal presentation of the results of his studies. In response to that demand, Dr. Bishop has in course of publication a work on "Diseases of the Ear, Nose and Throat," which is to be used as a text book in the medical colleges.

Dr. Bishop has been a member of the staff of the South Side Free Dispensary and the West Side Free Dispensary; is surgeon to the Illinois Masonic Orphan's Home, and the Illinois Charitable Eye and Ear Infirmary, and consulting surgeon to the Silver Cross Hospital at Joliet. He is professor of otology in the Post Graduate Medical School and Hospital of Chicago, and professor of diseases of the nose, throat and ear of the Illinois Medical College. He is a member of a great number of medical and other societies. The training Dr. Bishop received during youth,

SETH SCOTT BISHOP, M. D.

while serving his time in the printing office of a country newspaper, has naturally inclined him to cultivate journalistic work, in which he has been engaged for a number of years. He is one of the editors of the "Laryngascope," a journal devoted to diseases of the nose, throat and ear, and writes extensively for other journals in this and other countries.

THE GREATEST MEDICAL CENTER.

Nowhere else in this city or in the world is to be found, within so small a compass, so many first-class institutions for the practice and teaching of medicine. A glance at the accompanying engraving will give the reader a comprehensive view of this district. Clustered around the Cook County Hospital (No. 1), which of itself is probably second in importance to none in America, and which occupies the entire square bounded by Harrison, Polk, Wood and Lincoln streets, will be found Rush Medical College (No. 9), with its magnificent laboratory building (No. 11), the College of Physicians and Surgeons (Nos. 2 and 4), the Illinois Training School for Nurses (No. 6), Congress Hall (No. 5), Presbyterian Hospital (No. 8), the Chicago College of Dental Surgery (No. 10), the Chicago Homeopathic Medical College (No. 12), the Woman's College (No. 13), and the Dunham Medical College, at the corner of York and Wood streets, just beyond the view shown in the cut.

In addition to these purely medical institutions are the West Division High School (No. 3) and the Marquette school buildings (No. 7), which altogether makes the most remarkable group to be found anywhere in the world.

Visitors to Chicago who wish to reach this center direct from the depots can do so as follows, viz.:

From the Chicago & Northwestern depot, cross Wells street bridge from the depot, walk south to Madison street and take the Ogden avenue trailer attached to Madison street cars. Get off at Wood street.

BIOGRAPHICAL SKETCHES.

From Union depot, take Ogden avenue traller, attached to Madison street car at the corner of Madison and Canal street.
From the Wisconsin Central depot, take Harrison street car direct to County Hospital.
From the Rock Island and Michigan Southern depot take Van Buren street cars at the door. Get off at Wood street.
From Polk street depot, walk north on Dearborn street to Van Buren and take Van Buren street cars. Get off at Wood street.
From Illinois Central depot, take Wabash avenue car at 12th street north to Van Buren, walk two blocks west to Dearborn and take Van Buren street car to Wood street.
Early in 1897 the Elevated Union Loop will be completed in the downtown district, from Fifth avenue to Wabash, on which trains will run from all the elevated roads in the city. Passengers can then transfer from any of them or take the Garfield Park line of the Metropolitan Elevated, at any point on the loop, and get off at Ogden station, only a few steps away from this great medical center.

The Post-Graduate Medical School formerly occupied the building marked 2 in the accompanying cut; but it outgrew its accommodations and was compelled to remove to the south division of the city, where it built one of the most extensive colleges in America. The old building now serves as a hospital for the College of Physicians and Surgeons.

W. FRANKLIN COLEMAN, M. D., M. R. C. S.

Dr. W. Franklin Coleman was born in Brockville, Canada. He began the study of medicine at McGill College, Montreal, where, at the completion of his third year, an attack of typhoid induced him to relinquish medicine. Two years later his medical studies were resumed at Queen's College, Kingston, Canada, and after two years graduated with honors. For several years the young doctor practiced in his native village of Lyn. Desiring to perfect himself in one special branch of his profession, Dr. Coleman turned his attention to the department of eye and ear. He spent a year in England at Moorfield's Eye Hospital and the London Hospital, at the close of which he took the degree of M. R. C. S. England. Returning to Canada, he settled in Toronto, forming a partnership with Dr. Rosebrugh, an oculist and aurist of established reputation. He soon after was appointed surgeon to the Toronto Eye and Ear Infirmary, which position he held for seven years. With a view of acquiring further knowledge in his specialty, Dr. Coleman went abroad, spending a year in the clinics of Vienna and Heidelberg, under the guidance of Jaeger, Politzer and O'Becker. Upon his return to Canada he selected St. Johns, N. B., as his field for special practice; and here another seven years' service won him a Rachael and goodly wages. But the oculist's ambition outstripped the confines of this quiet Canadian city; and having, in addition to a large private practice, gained a rich experience from his position as sole oculist and aurist to the Provincial Hospital, he again turned westward and settled in Chicago, where, in a few years, he has earned a good practice and wide reputation. Finding here no school for graduates in medicine, Dr. Coleman, after a year of persevering labor, succeeded in organizing the Chicago Policlinic. The management of this institution proving unsatisfactory to himself and some of his colleagues, they established the Post Graduate Medical School of Chicago. Dr. Coleman is a member of the Chicago Opthalmological

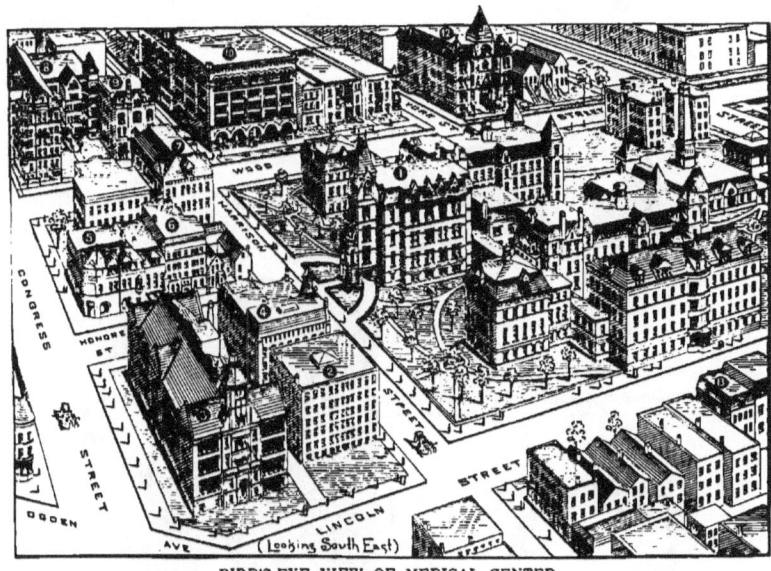

BIRD'S-EYE VIEW OF MEDICAL CENTER.

Society, of the Chicago Medical Society, of the Illinois State Medical Society and of the American Medical Association. He is oculist and aurist to the Chicago Charity Hospital, president and oculist to the Post Graduate Hospital, director and professor of ophthal-

W. FRANKLIN COLEMAN, M. D.

mology in the Post Graduate Medical School of Chicago; also examiner of pension claims for eye and ear applicants.

HENRY T. BYFORD, M. D.

Dr. Henry T. Byford was born in 1853, at Evans-

HENRY T. BYFORD, M. D.

ville, Ind. He was given exceptional advantages by his father, Dr. W. H. Byford, an eminent practitioner

in Chicago. At eleven, he was sent to school in Germany. Three years later he graduated at the high school in Berlin. After one term at the Chicago University, he began a course at Williston Seminary, graduating from the scientific department in 1870. He then entered the Chicago Medical College and graduated in 1873, valedictorian of his class, at the age of nineteen. Even while a student, he passed an examination and was appointed interne at Mercy Hospital. Since his graduation his progress in his profession has been rapid. He was one of the founders of the Post Graduate Medical School, holding the chair of gynaecology. He is professor of gynaecology in the College of Physicians and Surgeons; clinical professor of gynaecology in the Woman's Medical College; gynaecologist to St. Luke's Hospital, and surgeon to the Woman's Hospital. He is an active member of several medical societies.

In addition to his fame as a physician he has a wide renown as an inventor. Many of the now popular surgical operations were devised by him, and in addition to that he possesses a genius for mechanics which has enabled him to turn out a great number of mechanical appliances for use in his profession, of great practical utility.

Dr. Byford was married November 9, 1882, to Miss Lucy Larned, a woman of rare taste and accomplishments. They have four children, two girls and two boys.

JOSEPH ELLIOTT COLBURN, M. D.

Dr. Joseph Elliott Colburn was born in Massena, St. Lawrence County, N. Y., September 22, 1853.

After leaving school he began the study of medicine

JOSEPH E. COLBURN, M. D.

with Dr. Orrin McFadden, at Massena, and afterward entered the Medical College at Albany, in 1873. He graduated in 1877 and began practice as assistant to Dr. Fisher, at Colton, New York. At Dr. Fisher's death Dr. Colburn succeeded to his practice. In time this extended, and he was obliged to transfer his residence to Canton. Here he engaged in the special study of the eye and ear, prosecuting his researches in the New York Charity Hospital. In 1882 he came to Chicago on a visit, where he was offered a position as assistant surgeon of the eye department of the Illinois State Eye and Ear Infirmary, which he accepted, and thus became a resident of this city. In December of the same year Dr. Colburn was appointed ophthalmic surgeon to the Central Free Dispensary. In the spring of 1883 he was elected assistant medical director to the Northwestern Masonic Aid Association, and in 1886 he helped to organize the first Post Graduate Medical School, the Chicago Policlinic, of which he has been a lecturer since that time. In 1888 he was appointed surgeon of Cook County Hospital, and in 1890 went abroad for observation and study.

In 1893 Dr. Colburn's business became so large that he withdrew from the Northwestern Masonic Aid Association, and other outside connections, except the Chicago Policlinic. His contributions to the literature of the profession have been confined almost exclusively to the relation of functional nervous diseases to the eye, and the errors and maladjustment of the external muscles of the eye; also excentric poses of the head, due to cross-eyes and like mal-formations.

Dr. Colburn is married to Miss Lettie M. Ellis, of Colton, N. Y.

DR. CHARLES GILBERT DAVIS.

Both the father and mother of this eminent physician and surgeon were professors of the healing art, and the father, Dr. George W. Davis, was renowned in Kansas both for his courage and learning. The institutions of learning and practice through which Dr. Davis has passed are many, and include the Christian University of Ottumwa, Kan.; the Cincinnati Eclectic Medical Institute, the Virginia University, the Quarantine Hospital of St. Louis, the Missouri Medical College, and the International Hospital at Paris, France, where he passed six months under the eye of the

CHAS. G. DAVIS, M. D.

world-renowned surgeon, Dr. Péan. He has also attended the principal clinics of Europe. Dr. Davis founded the National Christian Temperance Hospital of Chicago, and is surgeon-in-chief of the Chicago Baptist Hospital. He has occupied his present offices for a quarter of a century, and lives on Prairie avenue, near Twenty-sixth street. He is still in the prime of life, is married, and is the father of two sons approaching manhood.

NATHAN SMITH DAVIS, JR., M. D.

Dr. Nathan Smith Davis, Jr., Chicago, Ill., son of Nathan S. and Anna M. (Parker) Davis, was born September 5, 1858, at Chicago, Ill. After receiving a preliminary education at private schools in Chicago, he attended Northwestern University, from which he received the degree of A. B. in 1880, and A. M. in 1883. He begun the study of medicine with his father, Dr.

N. S. DAVIS, JR., M. D.

Nathan S. Davis, in 1880; attended three courses of lectures at the Chicago Medical College, and graduated in 1883, when he began practice in Chicago, and has continued it since. In 1885 he took a post-graduate course in medicine at Heidelberg, Germany, and Vienna, Austria.

Dr. Davis was made associate professor of pathology in Northwestern University Medical College in 1884, and was transferred to the professorship of principles and practice of medicine and of clinical medicine, in the same school, in 1886. He became physician to Mercy Hospital in 1884. He was formerly secretary of the section of practice of medicine in the American Medical Association, member of the council of the section of pathology, Ninth International Medical Congress, and of the council of the section of practice, Pan-American Medical Congress; chairman of the section of practice, Illinois State Medical Society, 1893; trustee of Northwestern University; and member of the general board of management of the Young Men's Christian Association of Chicago. He is a member of the American Medical Association, American Academy of Medicine, Illinois State Medical Society, Chicago Medical Society, Chicago Medico-Legal Society, Chicago Academy of Sciences, Illinois State Microscopical Society, Chicago Literary Club, etc.

Dr. Davis is the author of numerous contributions to medical literature and of two books: "Consumption: How to Prevent It and How to Live with It," intended for physicians and consumptives; also a work on "Diseases of the Lungs, Heart and Kidneys."

He married, in 1884, at Madison, Wis., Miss Jessie B., daughter of the late Judge Hopkins. They have two children living, Nathan Smith Davis, third, and Ruth Davis; one child is deceased.

ALLEN CORSON COWPERTHWAIT, M. D., PH. D., LL. D

Allen Corson Cowperthwait was born May 3, 1848, at Philadelphia, Pa. His father was a dentist, a gentleman of liberal culture, a graduate of the University of Pennsylvania and noted as a mathematician, being author of a work on the calculus.

In his infancy his parents moved to Toulon, Ill., where he was brought up in a new and undeveloped country. He obtained, by way of schooling, whatever the common country schools could give, to which he added a course at the Toulon Seminary. He continued his studies, working in the meanwhile at the printer's trade and as book and insurance agent. "Parson Brownlow's Book," for which he was agent, was one of his successes. It was a material assistance in enabling him to sustain himself in his studies. He spent four years at this kind of work, when he began the study of medicine, under Dr. Bacmeister, of Toulon. Afterward he studied under the celebrated Dr. Constantine Hering, of Philadelphia, graduating from the Hahnemann Medical College of Philadelphia on March 3, 1869. After receiving his diploma he located for practice at Galva, Henry County, Illinois. Here he remained for four years, until he removed to Nebraska City, Neb.

Dr. Cowperthwait was one of the pioneers in homoeopathy in Nebraska; and it was mainly by his efforts that the homoeopathic physicians of the state were organized into the Nebraska State Homoeopathic Medical Association. It has since become a very flourishing organization. He also contributed extensively to the literature of medicine, soon becoming a recognized authority on many subjects. In 1876 his first complete medical work was published, "Insanity in Its Medico-Legal Relations," and in the same year he lectured before the faculty and students of the Central University of Iowa, so effectually that the institution conferred upon him the degree of doctor of philosophy. In 1877 he was elected to the chair of mental and nervous diseases in the Hahnemann Medical College of Philadelphia; but about the same time he was tendered the position of dean and professor of materia medica in the newly organized homoeopathic medical department of the State University of Iowa, which he accepted. This position he held for fifteen years, until he removed to Chicago in 1892.

Dr. Cowperthwait is the author of several valuable medical works, all of which have met with a large demand. In 1880 the first edition of his "Materia Medica" appeared, and it has since passed through seven editions, being the most extensively used as a text book of any on that subject published. In 1888 his "Gynaecology" was published and was well received by the profession. In 1885 Shurtleff College, at Alton, Ill., conferred upon him the degree of doctor of laws in recognition of his great literary attainments, and in 1887 he was elected a fellow of the Society of Science, Literature and Arts, of London, England.

Dr. Cowperthwait has been six times tendered a chair in the University of Michigan, and in 1884 he accepted the chair of materia medica and therapeutics in the Homoeopathic Medical College of that institution and became dean of the faculty, still retaining his connection with the University of Iowa, but at the end of one year he found that the demands were too heavy for his endurance and he resigned his Michigan appointment. In 1892 Dr. Cowperthwait removed to Chicago and was at once elected professor of materia medica and therapeutics in the Chicago Homoeopathic College, which place he still holds. Since coming to Chicago he has been honored with many hospital appointments. He is also prominent in all the medical societies to which he belongs. He has held official positions in nearly all of them. He is an active and influential member of the Independent Order of Odd Fellows, having filled every subordinate position in the lodge. He has been a member of the grand lodges of Illinois, Iowa and Nebraska, and has occupied the highest offices in the grand encampment.

The doctor has always been prominent in the activities of the state and national medical societies

ALLEN C. COWPERTHWAIT, M. D.

and is an honorary member of several state associations. He has been president of the state societies of both Iowa and Nebraska. In 1875 he became a member of the American Institute of Homoeopathy, having attended every meeting since and been closely identified with its work. In 1884 he was chosen to the vice presidency and in 1887 was elected president of the latter body.

In religion Dr. Cowperthwait is a Baptist, having been closely identified with the work of that denomination since 1866. Politically he is a Republican. He was married in 1870 to Miss Ida E. Irving, of Oscaloosa, Iowa. One son and a daughter have been the fruit of this union.

Professionally Dr. Cowperthwait has made his greatest reputation as a specialist in the successful treatment with medicines of the various diseases peculiar to women and without the use of the knife, except in purely surgical cases, he being unalterably opposed to the present popular method of operating upon all cases presented for treatment.

JAMES HENRY ETHERIDGE, M. D.

Dr. James Henry Etheridge, who for twenty - five years has occupied a leading place, not only in the practice of medicine, but in teaching it, was born in Johnsville, N. Y., March 20, 1844. His father, Dr. Francis B. Etheridge, was a physician and surgeon for forty-seven years. His mother was Fanny Easton, of Connecticut. His ancestry on his father's side, for five generations and on his mother's for seven, were English. His father served as surgeon of one of the Minnesota volunteer regiments during the war. He died at Hastings, Minn., in 1871.

Dr. James H. Etheridge, the subject of this sketch, early received just as complete a training as the common schools of New York furnished. He had prepared himself, and fitted himself to enter the junior class at Harvard, at the time of the breaking out of the war; but that put an end to his aspirations in that direction. He determined to devote his life to medicine, and in this he had the assistance of his father, with whom he took a four year course of reading and then entered the University of Michigan, where he took a one year course of medicine with his father; attended one course of medicine at the medical department of the University of Michigan and a two years' course at the Rush Medical College, at Chicago. Afterward, from 1869 to 1870, inclusive, he spent in Europe in study at the famous hospitals of the principal cities.

In 1871 Dr. Etheridge returned and began the practice of medicine in Chicago. He was, almost at once, elected as lecturer on materia medica and therapeutics in his Alma Mater, the Rush Medical College, which he held for two years, after which he was regularly elected to a professorship, occupying successively the chairs of materia medica, therapeutics, medical jurisprudence, gynaecology and obstetrics and gynaecology. He is one of the gynaecologists of the Presbyterian Hospital and of the Central Free Dispensary; also of the Chicago Polyclinic Hospital. He has occupied a position on the staff of the Woman's Hospital of the State of Illinois; and for many years was connected with the St. Joseph's and St. Luke's Hospitals. He is an occasional contributor to the medical journals, and a member of the Chicago Medical Society, the Chicago Medico-Legal Society, the Gynaecological Society (of which he was president in 1890), the Illinois Society, the International Medical Congress of Obstetricians and Gynaecologists and of the Pan-American Medical Congress.

JAMES H. ETHERIDGE, M. D.

He was president of the Chicago Medical Society in 1887 and of the Chicago Gynaecological Society in 1889.

Dr. Etheridge has been a conspicuous figure in the medical world of Chicago for many years. He stands in the very front rank of the practitioners of his day, a broad, liberal minded and progressive man; and with more than ordinary ability in his profession.

Dr. Etheridge was married June 20, 1870, to Harriett Elizabeth Powers, of Evanston, a daughter of Herman G. Powers, of the same place, who was long identified with the banking and commercial interests of Chicago. They have two daughters. Dr. Etheridge is a Presbyterian in religion and a republican in politics; but in local matters he cuts loose from party ties and votes for the best men regardless of politics.

In personal appearance, Dr. Etheridge is tall and commanding in appearance. He is more than average weight, genial, courteous and refined, popular alike with all who come to know him. He easily wins casual acquaintances and holds those who know him well.

JOHN E. GILMAN, M. D.

Dr. John E. Gilman, one of Chicago's most illustrious physicians, comes of a long line of ancestry of far more than ordinary ability and attainments. In 1638, John Gilman, an Englishman and a Puritan, came to America and settled at Exeter, New Hampshire. He was active in colonial affairs; and, in 1680, was one of the royal commissioners at the time of the separation of New Hampshire from Massachusetts. Other members of his family have been successively treasurer and governor of New Hampshire and leaders in the revolutionary war. Then we find them serving on the staff of George Washington, as members of the Continental Congress, in the house of representatives and in the United States senate. Later also we find them in the constitutional convention which framed the Constitution of the United States, at Philadelphia, followed by a long list of authors, doctors, teachers, divines and men famous in the field of science, among them Daniel Coit Gilman, the first president of Johns Hopkins University.

Such was Dr. Gilman's ancestry, no prouder which can be found in America. His father was an eminent practitioner who early sought to instill his own enthusiasm for his profession, into his son. From a boy he trained him to it, so that he looked forward to it as his life's work.

At the time of the great fire, Dr. Gilman had finished his education at Hahnemann Medical College in Chicago; and made for himself a considerable fame, when that fell calamity swept down upon the city. Without waiting to count the cost—without stopping to consider the laborious exertions which it entailed, or questioning whether or not he would ever be paid for his services—he at once offered those services to the city in the case of the sick and destitute sufferers by that calamity. Many a day, for twenty hours out of the twenty-four, he stood to his self-imposed task, ministering to the destitute and suffering. He was made secretary of the Relief and Aid Society, and, in that capacity, served with untiring devotion until the emergency was passed.

Dr. Gilman was born at Harmar, a suburb of Marietta, Ohio, July 24, 1841. As has already been stated, his father was an eminent practitioner. During his boyhood, John E. used to accompany his father on his visits; assist him in his surgical operations, and in many ways attend to the wants of patients. The father died when John was only seventeen years old; but a bent had been given to the young man's inclinations; and he neglected no opportunity to add to the fund of knowledge which he had been acquiring. He placed himself under the tutelage of his elder brother, at Marietta, O., for one year, after which he studied under Dr. George Hartwell, of Toledo. He finished his medical education at Hahnemann Medical College, of Chicago. Since that time he has been in active practice in this city.

JOHN E. GILMAN, M. D.

Dr. Gilman's generous conduct at the time of the great fire has already been partially told. The world does not permit services like that to go unrewarded, and honors have flowed thick and fast for Dr. Gilman. His private practice increased until it came to be one of the most considerable in the city. Then there came a demand for his services in the training of new candidates for the profession. In 1884 Dr. Gilman was appointed to the chair of physiology, sanitary science and hygiene in Hahnemann; and in 1892 he was elected to that of materia medica and therapeutics, which he continues to hold. He is equally gifted as a teacher and lecturer to what he is as a practitioner. He is a frequent contributor to the literature of the profession; and in all his writings he is clear, logical and forceful. Nor are his writings confined to medicine. They cover a wide range of subjects. He is an art critic of recognized merit; and has been identified with the promotion of art in Chicago for many years. He took part in building up the Crosby Opera House Art Gallery; and, for a long time, assisted in editing the Chicago Art Journal.

Dr. Gilman was married in 1860 to Miss Mary D. Johnson, also of old Puritan stock. They have one son, a physician of great promise.

Thus Dr. Gilman has fulfilled an ideal career as a physician, one full of helpfulness and sympathy for his fellow men and one in which his broad and comprehensive mind has found ample expression without pain or bitterness to others. He has sought, by lending a helping hand to reduce the sum total of human suffering, rather than to add to it by the oppression of others, and in doing so he has won the esteem both of the profession and the world.

ALBERT GOLDSPOHN, M. D.

Dr. Albert Goldspohn was born in Dane County, Wisconsin, September 23, 1851. He was always a student, preferring to spend his time in study and work than in the frivolities of his associates. After

ALBERT GOLDSPOHN, M. D.

passing through the graded schools he served an apprenticeship in a drug store for the study of drugs. Here he conceived a fondness for the study of medicine; and, after two years, entered the Northwestern College, at Naperville, where he graduated as Bachelor of Science, in 1875. He now entered Rush Medical College and graduated in 1878; and then, as a finish to his professional education, he served eighteen months as Interne in the Cook County Hospital, followed by a post graduate course of two years in the great European universities of Heidelberg, Wurzburg, Strasburg, Halle and Berlin, giving special study to surgery and gynecology. In 1887, he returned to Chicago and entered upon private practice. He became attending gynecologist at the German Hospital and professor of gynecology in the Post Graduate Medical School and Hospital of Chicago.

Dr. Goldspohn is a member of a number of local, national and international medical societies. He is a frequent contributor to the literature of his profession.

Dr. Goldspohn married Miss Victoria E. Escher for his first wife, who died in June, 1885. He is now married to Miss Cornelia E. Walz, of Stuttgart, Germany.

LEMUEL CONAUT GROSVENOR, M. D.

Dr. Lemuel Conaut Grosvenor is the eldest son of Deacon Silas N. and Mary A. (Conaut) Grosvenor. He was born at Paxton, Massachusetts, in 1833. His father was a leading business man of that place. From his early boyhood, Lemuel had a strong inclination to medicine, as a profession; but it was not until he began to prosecute his higher studies that he finally determined upon it.

Before he was thirteen years of age he attended the Williston Seminary, at East Hampton, Mass., but removed with his parents to Worcester, in 1844, where he entered the High School of that city, remaining four years. Here he took an active part in all the social and literary movements among the students. He cultivated a taste for public speaking and joined actively in their debates. All this had an important bearing upon his subsequent career. When he was seventeen years old his parents removed to Sauk County, Wisconsin. His first winter in Wisconsin he spent teaching school at West Point, Columbia County, where he made a great success. It was an ordinary country school where the teacher was required to "board round." For this winter's work he received $60 in gold, which seemed to him a fortune. He determined to spend it in perfecting his education. With his father's consent, he set out to do this and make his way in the world. With his little personal belongings he walked 100 miles to Milwaukee, and journeyed thence to his old home at Worcester, Mass. Here he re-entered the High School; taking post graduate studies, especially mathematics; supporting himself by work and supplementing that by teaching an evening school. He afterward taught at Scituate, Rutland and South Hingham. After two years he was made head master of the old Mather School in Dorchester, the oldest free school in America. Here he remained seven years, during three of which he was secretary of the Massachusetts Teachers' Association. He was offered a chair in the Brooklyn Polytechnic School; but he had formed other plans. He declined it to go west. He entered the Cleveland Medical College, from which he graduated in 1864, with the degree of M. D., establishing himself at Peoria, Illinois. He then returned east and married Miss Ellen M. Prouty, of Dorchester, a woman of rare beauty and personal attainments. She died in 1874.

From Peoria, Dr. Grosvenor removed to Galesburg, and there, in a remarkably short time, built up an extensive practice among the wealthy families; but he found that his sphere of usefulness was too prescribed, and that his real field of labor was in Chicago, which offered unlimited scope for development. Accordingly he removed here in 1870, the year before the great fire. When that fell disaster overtook the city he was the only physician in that portion of the North Side whose house was not burned. Dr. Grosvenor, like many other noble hearted physicians, volunteered his services, without thought of remuneration, to ministering to the wants of the sick and destitute by that catastrophe. Night and day he toiled to relieve suffering and care for the needy. So conspicuous was his work and so beneficent, that he won the gratitude of thousands and the esteem of the public in general. He was given the confidence of the people from the start. He also attracted the attention of the profession, which gladly recognized his superior abilities and crowned him with honors. When the new Homoeopathic College was completed, a new chair of sanitary science was created for him, the first of the kind in any college. He brought to it the same zeal and intelligent devotion that had marked his whole professional career; and through his efforts, he has made it one of the most important branches of medical science. Today, there is not a medical college without its chair of sanitary science. His lectures on his special subjects have won him worldwide renown. His improvements in the dress of infants have been adopted in almost every civilized country in the world. He has especially distinguished himself in obstetrics, having been appointed to the chair of clinical obstetrics in his college.

Dr. Grosvenor is a member of the Chicago Academy of Physicians and Surgeons; and was three times elected its president. He was three years president of the American Paedological Society and member of the American Institute of Homoeopathy. He is a member of the Lincoln Park Congregational Church; and for several years, was president of its board of trustees. He was a charter member of the Congregational Club. In politics, he is a Republican.

One distinguishing characteristic of Dr. Grosvenor's career is, that he had not finished his education when he left school. He had only learned how to educate himself. He has been acquiring his education ever since. He is notably one of those men who grow riper in knowledge, experience and personal character as they grow older. Such men never stop growing. They are always renewing their youth. One of Dr. Grosvenor's delights is to inspire young men and young women to right living, such as will develop their physical, mental and moral persons in harmonious relationships. His lectures to girls, on "How to be Beautiful," and those to boys, practically along the same line, are models of elegance and wisdom.

Three years after the death of his first wife, Dr. Grosvenor was again married; this time to Miss Naomi Bassett, of Taunton, Mass.

LEMUEL CONANT GROSVENOR, M. D.

SAMUEL PARKER HEDGES, M. D.

Dr. Samuel Parker Hedges was born July 23, 1841, in Sinclairsville, N. Y. He entered the office of his uncle, Dr. W. S. Hedges, of Jamestown, to study medicine, when President Lincoln issued a call for additional soldiers to carry on the war. He laid aside his books and enlisted as a private in the 112th New York Volunteer Infantry July 23, 1862, his twenty-first birthday. From private to sergeant and orderly-sergeant were quick promotions. He commanded his company in the battle of the Deserted House, where he won a second lieutenant's commission. Soon after he was made aide-de-camp on the staff of Brigadier-General R. S. Foster, and later, first lieutenant and adjutant of his regiment.

On May 16th, 1864, he was captured by the confederates. He was sent successively to Libby Prison, Macon, Ga., Savannah and to Charleston, S. C., where he was exposed to the fire of the Union batteries. At last, after it became impossible for the Confederates any longer to furnish even the wretched fare which they had done, Lieutenant Hedges, along with 1,400 other Union officers, was offered a parole if they would bind themselves not to bear arms against the Confederacy. Not a man accepted, and the whole were turned loose near Wilmington, N. C. On his return to his company, he was promoted to captain.

At the close of the war, Mr. Hedges entered the Homoeopathic Medical College at Cleveland, O. In 1866-7 he attended the Hahnemann Medical College, Chicago, and took his degree in 1867. In 1869 to 1874 he filled the chair of General and Descriptive Anatomy at the Hahnemann Medical College, Chicago. In 1887 and 1890 he was made Chairman of the Bureau of Gynaecology in the American Institute of Homoeopathy. He was secretary and president of the Cook County Homoeopathic Medical Society; has been president of the Illinois State Homoeopathic Medical Society and an active member of many others in the same field.

He was elected Professor of Theory and Practice of Medicine in the Chicago Homoeopathic Medical College, but his health would not permit him to lecture.

SAMUEL PARKER HEDGES, M. D.

He is a member of the Grand Army of the Republic; also a member of the Loyal Legion, Illinois Commandery.

JAMES NEVENS HYDE, M. D.

Dr. James Nevens Hyde was born in Norwich, Connecticut. He graduated at Yale in the class of '61,

JAMES N. HYDE, M. D.

receiving the degree of A. B., and later A. M., from the same university. His medical education began at the College of Physicians and Surgeons of New York, but was interrupted on his acceptance during the civil war of a position as assistant surgeon in the United States Navy, from which he was promoted, after examination, to past assistant surgeon. This office he resigned in order to complete his education at the medical department of the University of Pennsylvania, where he received his degree of M. D. In 1869 he received M. D. eundum from Rush.

Dr. Hyde has successfully occupied the position of professor of skin and venereal diseases at Rush. He is dermatologist at the Presbyterian and Michael Reese Hospitals; also consulting dermatologist at the Woman's and Children's Hospital. He is a member of several Greek letter college societies, and the following medical societies: The British Medical Association, the American Medical Association, American Dermatological Association, American Association of Genito-Urinary Surgeons, the Congress of American Physicians and Surgeons, the Chicago Medical Society and also the Practitioners' Club.

Among his many writings may be mentioned three editions of "A Treatise on Diseases of the Skin," and chapters on syphilis and skin diseases in the leading books on these subjects.

E. FLETCHER INGALS, M. D.

Dr. E. Fletcher Ingals was born in Lee Center, Ill., September 29, 1848. He attended the State Normal Institution and the Rock River Seminary, at Mt. Morris, Ill. He graduated at Rush Medical College in 1871, and became connected with its spring faculty, a position which he held until he was elected to the chair of Laryngology and Diseases of the Chest. He holds the chair of Diseases of the Throat and Chest in the Woman's Medical School, and is professor of

E. FLETCHER INGALS, M. D.

Laryngology and Rhinology in the Chicago Policlinic. He is attending physician for Diseases of the Throat at the Presbyterian Hospital; Laryngologist to St. Joseph's Hospital; Consulting Physician for Diseases of the Throat and Chest at the Central Free Dispensary; consulting Laryngologist for the Home for Destitute and Crippled Children; and consulting physician for the Washingtonian Home. Dr. Ingals has given special attention to diseases of the chest, throat and nose for twenty years, and is an author of many articles on these diseases and of a text book extensively used in the colleges, which has passed through its third edition.

He has been president of the American Laryngological Association, first vice president of American Climatological Association, president of the Section of Laryngology and Otology of the American Medical Association, president of the Section of Laryngology of the Pan-American Congress, president of the Illinois State Medical Society and president of the American Medical College Association.

and patience required of the physician and surgeon in combating these conditions.

"This hospital contains upwards of two hundred and fifty beds, a large number of which are free, being endowed in perpetuity by the individual gifts of wealthy people, or having annual endowments which are continued by Presbyterian churches, classes, or by individuals.

"The hospital building is of modern construction, is fitted with all worthy sanitary requirements. It is a model in the matter of service and management.

"Its private rooms are particularly cheerful and in

PRESBYTERIAN HOSPITAL.

PRESBYTERIAN HOSPITAL.

(Entrance on Congress Street.)

Congress, Wood, Harrison, Hermitage Ave.

"The Presbyterian Hospital has in but a few years, under very liberal endowments, and owing to intelligent management, grown to occupy a distinctly leading position among the medical charities of this great community. Immediately joining, as it does, the largest medical school of the west, it is looked to as the home of clinical teaching for an army of student minds; and great lessons in clinical medicine and surgery are traced from amphitheater to hospital ward, and back again, unfolding in the thousands of cases treated and watched each year the manifold intricacies of disease processes and the skill, ingenuity

demand; its nursing staff is drawn from the most competent sources, and there is a constancy in its medical staff, its internes, and its servant force. * * (El Chicago Clinical Review, January, 1897.)

SAMUEL J. JONES, A. M., M. D., LL. D.

Dr. Samuel J. Jones was born at Bainbridge, Pa., March 22, 1836. To exceptional school advantages in his youth he added diligent application, so that he graduated at twenty-one from Dickinson College, with the degree of A. B. Three years later his alma mater conferred upon him the additional degree of A. M., and in 1884 that of LL. D.

He began the study of medicine under his father, and, a year later, entered the medical department of the University of Pennsylvania, from which he graduated in 1860. After a competitive examination he was appointed assistant-surgeon in the United States Navy. His first active service was on the steam frigate "Minnesota," the flag-ship of the Atlantic blockading squadron. Until 1868, when he resigned to engage in private practice, Dr. Jones remained in the service, taking part in the various naval operations during the war and performing hospital duty

battle field of Shiloh, where he personally performed many operations. He is still as enthusiastic in his love of his profession as ever.

In politics Dr. Isham is a Republican, but has nev-

SAMUEL J. JONES, M. D.

RALPH N. ISHAM, M. D.

during that time and after the war. He was promoted to the rank of surgeon in 1863. After leaving the service he went abroad for professional study, and after his return engaged in practice and then settled in Chicago. There are few physicians who have had more extensive hospital connections or who have been more honored by the medical profession with official positions than Dr. Jones. He has frequently been chosen to represent the profession in various medical congresses held at home and abroad within the last twenty-five years. He has for twenty-six years been professor of ophthalmology and otology in Chicago Medical College.

He has been for thirty years a member of the Chicago Academy of Sciences, has served as vice-president of the Academy, and is now president of its Board of Trustees. He was for a number of years editor of the Chicago Medical Journal and Examiner.

RALPH NELSON ISHAM, M. D.

Dr. Ralph N. Isham was born in Manheim, New York, March 16, 1831. He studied medicine with Prof. John T. Metcalfe and Prof. W. H. Van Buren, in New York City. He graduated from the University of New York, served in Bellevue Hospital, and removed to Chicago in 1855. He was appointed surgeon of the U. S. Marine Hospital, at Chicago, by President Lincoln, in 1862. He was one of the founders of the Chicago Medical College, and was its first professor of surgical anatomy and operative surgery, which continued until 1880. He was the first in the west to teach anatomy as applied to the art of surgery. He still retains a chair in the same institution.

During the war, Dr. Isham was active in the organization of military hospitals and in the work of the sanitary commission. His corps was the first on the

er sought office. In religion he is a Presbyterian, a friend of the late Prof. Swing, and one of the principal supporters of his church.

Dr. Isham was married in 1856 to Miss Katherine Snow. They have two sons and two daughters, all living.

MILTON JAY, M. D.

Dr. Milton Jay was born near Dayton, Ohio, May 10, 1833. He enjoyed about the same educational advantages in his early youth that other farmer boys did, attending school in the winter and working on the farm in the summer. He early attended the Farmers' Institute at La Fayette, Ind., and afterward took a course at Earlham College, Richmond, Ind. He then took a four years' medical course at the Eclectic Medical College at Cincinnati, and at the Jefferson Medical College at Philadelphia, graduating in February, 1859. He then practiced surgery and medicine in Marion, Ind., for eleven years. In 1870 Dr. Jay, along with others, organized the Bennett Medical College of Chicago. For twenty years he was Dean and principal manager, as well as professor of surgery of that college. To his popularity as a lecturer on surgery, and his acknowledged skill as an operator, are due much of the success of that institution during the time of his administration. Since withdrawing from the active work in the college he has devoted himself to his large and lucrative practice of surgery. Dr. Jay is a member of Cook County Medical Society, Illinois State Medical Society, American Medical Association and National Association of Railroad Surgeons. He is chief surgeon of Chicago & Eastern Illinois Railroad, and has various hospital connections.

OSCAR A. KING, M. D.

Dr. Oscar A. King was born at Peru, Ind., February 22, 1851, one in a family of eleven children. Until he was fifteen years old he lived and worked on the farm. He graduated at the High School at Peru, after which he devoted himself to teaching for several years, at the same time prosecuting university studies. In 1873 he began the study of medicine under

Lake Geneva, for the treatment of nervous diseases, which has attained wide celebrity.

JAMES B. AND GEORGE WILBUR M'FATRICK, M. D.'S.

This is an instance where two brothers in the same profession, and practicing the same specialty in it, are united in the same firm.

JAMES B. M'FATRICK, M. D.

Dr. James B. McFatrick, M. S., M. D., was born in Lena, Illinois, April 4, 1862. He is a graduate of the Upper Iowa University, where he received the degree

OSCAR A. KING, M. D.

Prof. Henry Palmer, Surgeon General of Wisconsin, and afterward under Prof. Louis A. Sayer, graduating from Bellevue Hospital Medical College of New York in 1878. Soon after he was chosen first assistant physician to the Wisconsin State Hospital for the Insane, at Madison. Two years were spent abroad in hospital work in Vienna, under world-renowned masters. On his return, in 1882, Dr. King was elected professor of diseases of the mind and nervous system, College of Physicians and Surgeons of Chicago. In 1890 he was changed to the chair of clinical medicine. Dr. King is the founder of the Oakwood Springs Sanitarium, at

GEO. W. M'FATRICK, M. D.

of Master of Sciences. He began the study of medicine at Hahnemann Medical College, Chicago, in 1879, and graduated in 1885. He spent two years in Cook County Hospital, took a degree from the Bennett College of Eclectic Medicine and Surgery, and immediately entered its faculty. In 1886 he was appointed to the chair of Minor Surgery. Two years after he was given the chair of the Eye and Ear, a position he has retained ever since. In 1893 he was appointed a member of the State Board of Health. Dr. McFatrick's private practice has grown to such great proportions that he is now compelled to give his time wholly to it, except that of his college professorship and his position as surgeon to several insurance companies. Dr. McFatrick is a thirty-third degree Mason and deeply devoted to the good of the order. He has for many years been prominent in all Masonic affairs.

George Wilbur McFatrick, M. D., was born at Lena, Illinois, October 27, 1870. He graduated at Bennett Medical College in the class of '92, and thereafter served for eighteen months as house physician and surgeon at the Cook County Hospital. He is professor of diseases of the nose and throat, and clinical eye and ear surgery in Bennett Medical College; attending surgeon and oculist and aurist to Cook County Hospital and Willie Hipp Hospital. He also is an enthusiastic thirty-second degree Mason and member of the Mystic Shrine.

These two brothers McFatrick have jointly devoted themselves to the surgical treatment of diseases of the eye, ear, nose and throat and to correcting the errors of refraction. They have brought to their aid every appliance that science has made available for the prosecution of their work. Every appliance which science has made available is here used in the prosecution of their practice. They have recently organized and control the Northern Illinois College of Opthalmology and Otology, obtaining therefor a charter from the State of Illinois. In this school are taught surgery and diseases of the eye and ear.

CHARLES E. MANIERRE, M. D.

Dr. Charles E. Manierre was born in Chicago February 26, 1860, a descendant of one of the old New

CHAS. E. MANIERRE, M. D.

England families. His parents settled in Chicago in 1835 and lived here until their death. The family has been prominent all through the early history of the city.

Charles E. was educated in the public schools of the city until 1876, when he entered Cornell University from which he graduated in 1880. He then entered the Chicago Medical College; graduated in 1882, and immediately began practice. He has been connected with the Chicago Policlinic since it was first established; has been one of the instructors for about seven years, and for three has been professor of obstetrics in the institution. Dr. Manierre has built up a fine practice, devoted mainly to obstetrics and diseases of women. He was married in 1882 to Miss Elva Hitz. Their beautiful home is graced by two children.

FRANKLIN H. MARTIN, M. D.

Dr. Franklin H. Martin, secretary of the Post Graduate Medical School, was born at Oconomowoc, Wis., in 1857. He is a pupil of Dr. W. C. Spalding of Watertown. He took a three years' course at the Northwestern University Medical School, graduating in 1880. He became resident physician and surgeon at

FRANKLIN H. MARTIN, M. D.

Mercy Hospital for 1880-1, after which he entered upon a private practice. He has since drifted into gynecology and abdominal surgery as a specialty, while experimenting with apostoli electrical treatment for fibroid tumors of the uterus. In 1886 he was elected professor of gynecology in the Chicago Policlinic, and in 1887 surgeon of the Woman's Hospital of Chicago. In 1889, together with a number of other eminent physicians, he founded the Post Graduate Medical School, of which he became secretary. He has been an extensive writer on his specialty. One volume on "Electricity in Gynecology and Obstetrics" ran through two editions in a few months. In 1894 he was made chairman of the section of gynecology in the American Medical Association, and was also elected the same year as president of the Chicago Gynecological Society. His wife is a daughter of Dr. J. H. Hollister, one of Chicago's oldest and most eminent physicians.

LISTON HOMER MONTGOMERY, A. M., M. D.

Dr. L. H. Montgomery was born in McCutcheonville, Ohio, August 21, 1848. His early education was received at the common schools and at Mount Gilead High School; later he was a pupil at Heidelberg College, Tiffin, Ohio. Early in 1864, though but fifteen

116 UNRIVALED CHICAGO.

years of age, he enlisted and engaged in active service until the close of the civil war. After his discharge he taught school during the winters. Always having a taste for medical subjects he followed his bent and entered the Chicago Medical College in 1869, and graduated with honors in 1871, whereupon he was immediately appointed senior resident physician at Mercy Hospital. This was the beginning of a medical career which has been crowned with success. Such honors as that of being appointed delegate to the British Medical Association have been heaped upon him by his confreres. Dr. Montgomery uses his few leisure hours by writing contributions to the leading American and foreign medical journals.

REUBEN LUDLAM, M. D.

Dr. Reuben Ludlam stands pre-eminent among the homeopathic physicians of Chicago. There are none more honored and respected and none who have obtained a wider fame in their profession. Dr. Ludlam was born in Camden, New Jersey, October 7, 1831. His father was Dr. Jacob W. Ludlam, an eminent physician, who died in Evanston, Ill., in 1858. Reuben, while still a child, accompanied his father on his professional visits, even then taking the liveliest interest in the different cases. He graduated from the old academy at Bridgeton, New Jersey, with the highest honors of his class. At sixteen, under the supervision of his father, he began a systematic course of medicine at the University of Pennsylvania, where he received his degree of M. D. in 1852. After graduation he came to Chicago. At the time the doctrines of Hahnemann were causing universal agitation among physicians. Dr. Ludlam was one of those who became impressed with their truth. He cast aside the dogmas in which he was trained and placed himself under the banner of progressive homeopathy. He was active in forming the Hahnemann Medical College, and was elected to the chair of physiology, pathology and clinical medicine. Four years later

R. LUDLAM, M. D.

he was transferred to the chair of obstetrics and diseases of women and children; and thence to the professorship of medical and surgical diseases of women, becoming dean of the faculty. In May, 1891, he became president of the college and hospital.

In 1869 Dr. Ludlam became president of the American Institute of Homeopathy, presided at its meeting at Boston, and delivered the annual oration. He was also made president of the Chicago Academy of Medicine, the Illinois Homeopathic Medical Society and the Western Institute of Homeopathy. In 1871, after the great fire, he became a member of the medical department of the Relief and Aid Society. On the organization of the State Board of Health, in 1877, Dr. Ludlam was appointed a member. He served until December, 1892.

Dr. Ludlam has been a voluminous writer. For six years he was editorially connected with the North American Journal of Homeopathy of New York, and for nine years with the United States Medical and Surgical Journal of Chicago. For seventeen years he edited The Clinique, a monthly abstract of the work of the Clinical Society and of the Hahnemann Hospital. Dr. Ludlam's great work, "Clinical and Didactic Lectures on the Diseases of Women," published in 1871, is now in its seventh edition. It is used as a text book in all homeopathic colleges, and accepted as authority in this country and in Europe. Dr. Ludlam also translated from the French a very valuable work, "Lectures on Clinical Medicine," by Dr. Jousset, of Paris. He is the author of "A Course of Clinical Lectures on Diphtheria," the first strictly medical work ever published in Chicago.

Dr. Ludlam has been twice married; his first wife, Anna M. Porter, of Greenwich, N. J., died three years after marriage. By his second wife, Harriet G. Parvin, he has one son, Reuben Ludlam, Jr., also a physician of great promise.

THE HAHNEMANN HOSPITAL.

The new Hahnemann Hospital, which was first

opened in 1870, has recently rebuilt its hospital building on Groveland avenue, and it is a model in all its details. It was built at a cost of $100,000. It embodies every feature that has been found desirable in such structures. Perfect sanitation, the latest improvements in heating, electric lights, and improved service in every department make it as near perfect as modern science is capable of. It is seven stories and basement in height; has a capacity for 225 beds, and has a specially furnished operating room on each floor, thoroughly asceptic and supplied with every known convenience.

Overlooking Lake Michigan, on the Groveland avenue front, are suites of private apartments, elegantly and tastefully furnished, intended as suitable quarters where acute diseases can be properly treated, and where quiet for sick and convalescent patients can be secured.

The Post-Graduate Medical School and Hospital of Chicago was founded in 1888, occupying two floors in a building at 31 Washington street. Since that time it has made three moves, each one of which became necessary by reason of the rapidly increasing demands upon its resources by its own growth. Its present building, at 2400 Dearborn street, was finished for occupancy September 1st, 1896. Since its establishment, every state in the Union or in British America, as well as Mexico, Russia and even the Hawaiian Islands, have contributed students to its classes. Its faculty comprises the following:

General Medicine—Profs. H. W. Gentles, Chas. W. Purdy, M. H. Lackersteen, J. L. Van Valkenburg.

Surgery—Profs. L. L. McArthur, Alex Hugh Ferguson, Carl Beck, F. C. Schaefer, A. D. Bevan, W. P. Verity, J. B. Murphy, D. A. K. Steele.

Orthopedic Surgery—Prof. Frederic S. Coolidge.
Gynecology—Profs. H. T. Byford, H. P. Newman, Albert Goldspohn, Marie J. Mergler, Franklin H. Martin, Emil Ries, L. E. Frankenthal.
Stomach and Intestines—Prof. Fenton B. Turck.

Obstetrics—Profs. C. E. Paddock, A. McDiarmid, Eye—Profs. W. F. Coleman, Boerne Bettman, Casey A. Wood, Francis Dickinson, Chas. P. Pinckard.
Ear—Profs. Noval H. Pierce, Seth Scott Bishop, J. O. Ducker.
Nose and Throat—Profs. T. Melville Hardie, F. D. Owsley, George Morganthau.
Nervous Diseases—Profs. Daniel R. Brower, Sanger Brown, Sydney Kuh, Richard Dewey, W. Xavier Sudduth.
Genito-Urinary—Prof. D. J. Hayes.
Gynecology and Diseases of Rectum—Prof. Joseph B. Bacon.
Diseases of Children—Rosa Engelmann, J. C. Cook.
Pathology—Prof. Edwin Klebs.
Skin and Venereal Diseases—Profs. W. L. Baum, L. B. Baldwin.
Anatomy—Carl Wagner.
Urinalysis—Prof. Arthur R. Elliott.
Electro Physics—C. S. Neiswanger, M. D.

TRUMAN W. MILLER, M. D.

Dr. Truman W. Miller was born in Seneca County, New York, March 2, 1840. He is a graduate of Hobart College, Geneva, New York, and received his medical education at the College of Physicians and

TRUMAN W. MILLER, M. D.

Surgeons of New York City. In 1862 he was appointed a Medical Cadet, U. S. A., was promoted to A. A. Surgeon in 1863, and in the same year received his degree of M. D. from the Geneva Medical College. He served in the Army of the Potomac until after the battle of the Wilderness, when he was transferred to Chicago and assigned to duty as post and examining surgeon, where he remained until the close of the war. After this he held the position of examining surgeon in the recruiting service for four years, and for four years assistant surgeon U. S. Marine Hospital service. In 1877 he was promoted to surgeon, which position he held until his resignation in 1886. For six years he was surgeon of the First Regiment, I. N. G.

Dr. Miller has been president and professor of general and genito-urinary surgery of the Chicago Polyclinic since its organization in 1886; is consulting surgeon of St. Joseph and Alexian Brothers Hospitals; surgeon of Maurice Porter Memorial Hospital; surgeon in chief to many of the leading lines of railroads, and medical referee and consulting surgeon of several life and accident insurance companies. He is also a member of all the leading medical societies, general and local, and of many prominent social clubs. He has always taken an active interest in military matters, and is a member and one of the founders of the Military Surgeons' Association of the United States, and is an old member of the Grand Army of the Republic.

HENRY PARKER NEWMAN, M. D.

Dr. Henry Parker Newman, son of James and Abby (Everett) Newman, grandson of James Madison Newman, was born December 2, 1853, at Washington, N. H. After a preparatory education obtained at the New London (N. H.) Literary and Scientific Institution, he began to read medicine, 1874,

HENRY P. NEWMAN, M. D.

under Dr. George Cook, of Concord, N. H.; attended lectures at Dartmouth Medical College, which institution has since honored him with the degree of A. M., and at the Detroit College of Medicine, and was graduated from the latter in March, 1878. While a senior student he was house physician at St. Luke's Hospital, Detroit. He then spent two years in study in Germany in the universities of Strasburg, Leipsig, and Bonn. Returning to the United States he settled permanently in Chicago.

Dr. Newman is corresponding fellow of the Detroit Gynecological Society; member and chairman of the committee on membership of the Chicago Medical Society; fellow and secretary of the Chicago Gynecological Society; fellow of the American Gynecological Society; member and treasurer of the American Medical Association; member of the Illinois State Medical Society; of the Illinois State Microscopical Society, and of the International Medical Congress, having been a delegate to the tenth congress in Berlin, 1890. Dr. Newman is also president of the Laboratory of Experimental Research, Chicago, since 1889, a director and treasurer of the College of Physicians and Surgeons, Chicago, since 1893; a director and formerly president of the Post-Graduate Medical School,

Chicago, and professor of diseases of women in the same since 1888; professor of obstetrics and clinical gynecology, College of Physicians and Surgeons, of which institution he has been an active promoter since its organization in 1881; surgeon in the department of diseases of women in the Post-Graduate, St. Elizabeth and Chicago hospitals; and gynecologist-in-chief to the West Side Free Dispensary. Dr. Newman is also a member of the Society of the Sons of New Hampshire; examiner-in-chief and medical referee, Department of the Northwest, of the Berkshire Life Insurance Company; elder in the Third Presbyterian Church, Chicago, and member of Detroit Lodge No. 1, F. and A. M.

Dr. Newman has been editor of the department of obstetrics and gynecology of the North American Practitioner since 1893, in which journal appeared, in 1889, a "History of Obstetrics," from his pen. He is also the author of papers on "Shock and Nervous Influences in Parturition," Chicago Medical Journal and Examiner, 1885; "The Remote Results of Shortening the Round Ligaments for Uterine Displacements by a New and Original Method of Operation," American Journal of Obstetrics, Vol. XXIV.; "Prolapse of the Female Pelvic Organs," the Journal of the American Medical Association; "Curettage, Trachelorrhaphy, and Ventro-fixation"; "The Sequelae of Abortions;" "Six Years' Experience in Shortening the Round Ligaments for Uterine Displacements"; "A Plea for More Thorough Training in General Medicine and Obstetrics on the Part of the Gynecologist," etc. His original researches include abdominal, pelvic and plastic gynecological and obstetrical surgery, and he has devised surgical methods for shortening the round ligaments for uterine displacements. In colpoperineorrhaphy, a new method for operating for hernial conditions of the rectum, bladder and uterus; and in new instruments he has originated uterine dilators, combined dressing forceps and dilators, also instruments for tamponade of the uterus.

Married, in 1882, Miss Fanny Louise, daughter of Lothrop S. Hodges, Esq., of Chicago. Their children are Helen Everett and Willard Hodges, living, and Eugene Bush and Isabel Fairbanks, deceased.

JOHN EDWIN OWENS, M. D.

Dr. John E. Owens, a man of profound learning and of high professional attainments, was born at Charlestown, Md., October 16, 1836. He is a son of a Maryland planter, of Welch extraction, and of one of the old and influential families of the South. John completed his scholastic education under the renowned Edward Arnold, LL. D., at Mount Washington, Md., followed by his medical course, at first, under Dr. Justice Dunnott at Elkton, and afterward at Jefferson Medical College of Philadelphia, from which he graduated in 1862. He also took a post-graduate course in surgical anatomy and operative surgery under Dr. D. Hayes Agnew of Philadelphia. His thorough equipment for the work of his profession secured prompt recognition. He was elected resident physician at Blockley Hospital, Philadelphia, where he remained thirteen months. Early in 1863 Dr. Owens tendered his services to the Union Army, and was assigned to duty in the Military Hospital at Chicago. He is senior surgeon of St. Luke's Hospital. Dr. Owens has been prominently connected with Chicago medical colleges since 1867. For four years he was lecturer on surgical diseases of the urinary organs in Rush, and for nine years more he lectured on the principles and practice of surgery in the same institution in the spring course. He subsequently became professor of orthopedic surgery in the same institution, and in 1877 was made professor of "principles and practice of surgery" in the Woman's Medical College. In 1882 he joined the Chicago Medical College, occupying the chair of "operative surgery and surgical anatomy." In 1891 he was transferred to the chair of "principles and practice of surgery and clinical surgery."

Dr. Owens is a member of all the important medical societies, local and general, and for twenty-two

JOHN E. OWENS, M. D

years has been superintending surgeon of the Illinois Central Railway, and is also chief surgeon to the Chicago and Northwestern Railway. He was also medical director of the World's Fair. He was married December 30, 1869, to Miss Alethia S. Jamar. They have one daughter as the fruit of this union.

DR. J. W. STREETER.

John Williams Streeter was born on September 14, 1841, at Austinburg, in northeastern Ohio. He was six years of age when his father removed to western New York, and became pastor of a church in Henrietta, five miles from Rochester. Here he went to school and completed an academic education, when his father removed to Westville, Ohio, and accepted a professorship in Otterbein University. He wished to give his son a collegiate education, and was anxious that he should prepare himself for the study of medicine. As his means were limited John felt the necessity of striking out for himself, which he did, sometimes working on a farm and sometimes teaching. At the breaking out of the war young Streeter enlisted in the 1st Michigan Light Artillery, and went into active service. He was engaged in Kentucky, Tennessee, Alabama and Georgia, finally being mustered out in September, 1865, at the end of the war, as a first lieutenant.

On his muster out he began the study of medicine with Dr. Morse, of Union City, Mich., and in the fall of that year he went to Ann Arbor, where he attended his first course of medical lectures. He afterward read, for a time, under Dr. D. C. Powers, of Coldwater, Mich., who had been the surgeon of his battery during the war, and still later with Dr. Goodwin, an ex-naval surgeon, of Toledo, Ohio. He devoted three years to the study of medicine, and then came to Chicago and graduated from Hahnemann Medical College in 1868. Then accepting a position as physician in charge of the Hahnemann Medical College dispensary, he devoted himself for two years almost entire-

JOHN W. STREETER, M. D.

ly to a "charity practice." As he had practically exhausted his financial resources in obtaining his edu-

But finally his professional skill brought him the very best class of patronage. He made fast friends of the patients who came to him for treatment, and he has since swelled his income to more than that of the average railroad president.

He was one of the founders of the Chicago Homoeopathic College in 1877, and was assigned to the chair of "medical diseases of women and children." Two years later this was changed to "medical and surgical diseases of women." Dr. Streeter has given special attention to complicated diseases of women, and is recognized as one of the most successful gynecologists in the country. He has been for several years connected with the Cook County Hospital and the new hospital of the Chicago Homoeopathic College. He has also one of the largest private hospitals in the United States, the Streeter Hospital, which was established in 1888. From small beginnings it has grown to be one of the finest and best appointed private hospitals in the world. It is situated on Calumet avenue, is massive in construction, practically fire proof and perfectly adapted for its use. Every room has a southern exposure. The building is heated by hot water, lighted by electricity, furnished with a hydraulic elevator, ventilated by a system of electric fans, and is in every respect as complete as skill, experience and money can make it. There is a training school for nurses connected with the hospital. Prof. Streeter is in personal charge, performing all operations.

Dr. Streeter was united in marriage in 1869 to Miss Mary Clark, a daughter of Israel W. Clark, of Union City, Mich. Three children, one son and two daughters, complete the family circle.

HEMAN SPALDING, M. D.

Dr. Heman Spalding was born at West Creek, Indiana, September 10, 1852. He attended the Male and

THE STREETER HOSPITAL.

cation, these two years, which brought him scarcely enough paying practice to meet the outlay for office rent, constituted the most trying period of his life.

HEMAN SPALDING, M. D.

Female College at Valparaiso, after which he entered Asbury University (now De Pauw), where he took a three years' classical course. After this he engaged in teaching for several years, a part of the time as principal of the Grant Park school. He began the study of medicine under Dr. N. S. Davis, of Chicago, and at the Chicago Medical College, now the Northwestern University Medical School, and graduated in 1881. Dr. Spalding has been in constant practice since graduation. In 1890, without solicitation on his part or the part of his friends, he was appointed as medical inspector in the Department of Health by Dr. Wickersham, then Commissioner of Health. As such, he had charge of the work of suppressing contagious diseases on the south side in Chicago during the epidemic of small-pox of 1893-94-95. He continued to hold this position under five different administrations.

Dr. Spalding is a member of the American Medical Association, the Chicago Medical Society, the Physicians' Club, the Beta Theta Pi fraternity, and the Masonic order. He was married to Miss Evelyn Little, of Olathe, Kansas, December 24, 1889.

WILLIAM XAVIER SUDDUTH, M. D.

Doctor Sudduth was born January 18, 1853, at Springfield, Ill. He prepared for college at the Illinois State Normal, graduated Ph. B. from the Illinois Wesleyan University, Bloomington, Ill., and received therefrom the degree of A. M. in 1889. He began to read medicine in 1879 under Dr. James B. Taylor; attended lectures at the College of Physicians and Surgeons, New York, and the Medico-Chirurgical College, Philadelphia, receiving the degree of M. D. from the latter in 1885, and began practice in Philadelphia the same year.

From 1884-'90, Dr. Sudduth was Director of the Physiological and Pathological laboratory of the Medico-Chirurgical College of Philadelphia, and lecturer on clinical microscopy and genito-urinary diseases, with several leaves of absence during the time for Post-Graduate study abroad and lecture courses in the universities of Iowa and California. In 1890 he was elected professor of pathology and oral surgery in the medical department of the University of Minnesota, and filled the chair acceptably for five years, resigning in 1895 to engage in special practice.

Dr. Sudduth's literary efforts cover a wide range. He was for seven years, 1887-'94, on the staff of senior Editors of the Annual of the Universal Medical Sciences, Philadelphia. His contributions to medical and other literature on the subjects of heredity, narcotism and inebriety have been numerous. Having devoted considerable attention to psychology in its relation to medicine, he is considered an authority on the subject. His practice is limited to the treatment of the morbid psychological conditions that appear in mental and nervous diseases, vicious bodily habits, alcohol, morphine and other forms of inebriety.

Dr. Sudduth is Professor of Morbid Psychology and Psycho-Therapeutics and Director of the Psycho-Physical laboratory of the Post-Graduate Medical School and Hospital of Chicago.

He is an active member of a large number of medical and scientific societies, both in this country and Europe; taking special interest in all matters relating to morbid psychology and psychical research.

WILLIAM MARION STEARNS, M. D.

Dr. William M. Stearns, one of the foremost physicians in the city, was born at Dale, New York, June 20, 1856. His parents removed during his infancy to Will County, Illinois, where he received his early training in the common and high schools. He fitted himself for teaching, which he followed several years. At twenty-one he entered the Chicago Homoeopathic Medical College, graduating in 1880. He was then offered a position as house physician and surgeon of the state penitentiary at Joliet, which he accepted and held for three years. In 1883 he went to Europe for two years' post-graduate study in the great German and Austrian hospitals, devoting himself to his

WM. M. STEARNS, M. D.

chosen specialty, the diseases of the ear, nose and throat. On his return he was appointed assistant to the professor of otology and ophthalmology in the Chicago Homoeopathic Medical College; and in 1890 was elected professor of rhinology and laryngology in the same institution. In these specialties Dr. Stearns has taken high rank in his profession, his great abilities being fully recognized by the profession at large. In 1887 Dr. Stearns married Miss Fannie A. Foote, the daughter of Dr. Foote, a well-known dentist of Belvidere, Illinois.

EDWIN HARTLEY PRATT, A. M., M. D., LL. D.

Dr. Edwin Hartley Pratt is one of those strong, forceful characters which stamp their personalities upon the age in which they live. He was born at Towanda, Pennsylvania, November 6, 1849. His independence of character began to assert itself at an early age. While taking his preparatory course at Wheaton College, Illinois, the college authorities learned that he had been active in the organization of a Good Templar lodge, when they demanded that he sever his connection with it. This he refused to do, preferring to leave the school rather than submit to an arbitrary interference with his personal liberty. He then entered the Chicago University, graduating in 1871. In the meantime he had decided upon medicine as a profession, and so entered Hahnemann Medical College, graduating in 1873 with degree of M. D., being valedictorian of his class.

Upon graduation, his record having been so high, he was placed upon the staff of Hahnemann as a teacher and as assistant to the professor of anatomy. The regular professor being absent so much of the time, almost the whole of the duties fell upon him. Here he acquitted himself so well that, at the following term, he was tendered the chair of anatomy, with a fair salary, which he accepted. In the spring of 1876 Dr. Pratt resigned from the faculty along with nine others, out of thirteen professors, and assisted in the organization of the Chicago Homoeopathic College. He was given the chair of anatomy in the new institution. This he held until 1883, when he was transferred to the chair of surgery, which he still fills.

While Dr. Pratt's success as an instructor has been conspicuous, it is in the field of original research that are found his greatest achievements. It was while handling the complicated and obscure cases in his college clinics that he discovered the effect of certain surgical operations upon particular chronic diseases. From his observations he was enabled to draw certain deductions, which received a most unexpected and complete verification. After one of his lectures, sixteen members of his class presented themselves for treatment. The result was a marvelous success. Thenceforth orificial surgery became fully established in the curriculum of the college. A chair of orificial surgery was created, which was filled by Dr. Pratt. Dr. Pratt has been highly honored by his medical brethren at home and abroad for his important discoveries. He has been made an honorary member of the Missouri, Ohio, and Kentucky Medical Societies and the Southern Association of Physicians. He is an active member of the Illinois State Medical Association, the Chicago Academy of Medicine and the American Institute of Homoeopathy. He was also honored with the degree of LL. D. by his alma mater. It was he who established the beautiful and now famous Lincoln Park Sanitarium, where the principles of orificial surgery have been put to extensive and varied tests, which have demonstrated their great value. Here patients have come for treatment and physicians for instruction. A new monthly magazine has been established, The Journal of Orificial Surgery, of which Dr. Pratt is the editor-in-chief.

Dr. Pratt has since organized the Pratt Sanitarium, where the same high grade is continued as in the other. All the most complicated forms of chronic diseases are treated; and here physicians come from far and near to learn to apply the same skill shown by Dr. Pratt.

Dr. Pratt was married June 26, 1877, to Miss Isa N. Bailey, of Jersey Heights, New Jersey. Their marriage has been blessed with two children. One daughter, Isabel, died when eighteen months old; and a son, Edwin Bailey Pratt, was killed in a street car accident when eight and a half years old.

EDWIN H. PRATT, M. D.

THE CHICAGO COLLEGE OF DENTAL SURGERY.

(Lake Forest University.)

This institution was first organized in the summer of 1883, with a faculty of only three professors and eighteen matriculates. It was not until five years later that the lot was purchased upon which its present magnificent home has since been erected. Five more passed before the first section of its building

BIOGRAPHICAL SKETCHES.

was constructed; and now, during the season of 1896, it has its completed structure occupied by a faculty of 87 instructors and 503 matriculates. The new building was dedicated December 4, 1896. Dr. Truman W. Brophy, the dean of the faculty, in his address at the dedication, briefly sketched the history of the college and the causes which have contributed to its success. He said that "this was the first institution of its kind in this country to introduce and use for the benefit of its students a complete apparatus for the cultivation of bacteria, thus demonstrating

PRACTITIONERS' COURSE.

The practitioners' course begins April 1st and continues until July 1st. This course consists of practical and didactic work in all branches of dentistry.

In the department of prosthetic dentistry is taught the latest and most approved methods in plate, crown and bridge work, continuous gum, porcelain and metal work. Dr. A. O. Hunt is in constant attendance in this department.

The clinical staff of the infirmary is on duty

CHICAGO COLLEGE OF DENTAL SURGERY.

the active agents that cause caries of the teeth and methods for effecting their destruction. It was also the first to organize freshmen students into classes for practical work in dental technology, both operative and prosthetic. In addition to these innovations in teaching, clinics were organized in the college and conducted for the benefit of the senior students by skillful and successful practitioners."

The college building is now 120 feet front on Wood street by 85 feet on Harrison and is six stories high. It was designed after a careful examination of all the best dental schools in the United States. Every feature of special value in any of them has been incorporated; so that, in construction and arrangement, it comes as near perfection as the present knowledge of the art admits. In addition to this, no pains or expense has been spared in its equipment; so that the Chicago College of Dental Surgery is in the front rank of like institutions in America.

during the course; and clinics demonstrating the most approved methods of operation and the therapeutical actions of all the latest drugs are conducted daily. Superior advantages are offered to those who feel the need of advanced or special training in the branches of practical and scientific dentistry.

The regular surgical clinic is conducted every Tuesday at 2:30 p. m. in the surgical clinic room.

A complete course in practical oral surgery, embracing the discussion and presentation of surgical diseases, are given. The clinic, which is very large and replete with interesting cases, presents material for a variety of operations which are performed in the presence of the class. Each member of the class who attends four weeks' instruction, beginning at any time during the course, receives the practitioner's certificate. Letters of inquiry should be addressed to
Dr. Truman W. Brophy, Dean,
126 State Street, Chicago.

DENTISTS.

TRUMAN W. BROPHY, M. D., D. D. S., LL. D.

Dr. Truman W. Brophy, educated both as a physician and a dentist, undoubtedly stands at the head of the dental profession in Chicago. He is dean of the Chicago College of Dental Surgery, and was one of its founders. He was born in Will County, Illinois, April 12, 1848. He took a preparatory course at the Elgin Academy, and entered upon his professional studies in 1866. He took a course at the Philadelphia College of Dental Surgery, graduating in 1872. Then, after obtaining what experience he could by a tour of the

T. W. BROPHY, M. D., D. D. S., LL. D.

medical colleges and hospitals of the East, be returned to Chicago and began his practice. But he found cases requiring a more extended knowledge of medicine and surgery than was taught in the dental colleges, and so, in 1878, he began a regular course of study at Rush Medical College. He graduated in 1880 as president of his class with the degree of M. D., and was at once elected to the chair of dental pathology and surgery in that college. He has since taken rank at the head of his profession. Dr. Brophy stands high in all the professional societies, local and general, and also among the numerous social clubs, of which he is a member. He married Miss Emma J. Mason, of Chicago, in 1873.

JAMES E. LOW, D. D. S.

Dr. James E. Low was born in Otsego County, New York, in 1837. He is a son of Ronald and Susan (Howard) Low. His inclination and ambition always were to obtain for himself an education that would fit him for a professional career in life. With this end in view, his indomitable will power, which has been a leading characteristic through life, removed all obstacles. After gaining a reputation of being an expert as a dental surgeon in the East, Dr. Low came to Chicago in 1865, where he began the practice of dentistry; and, in a short time, established a remunerative and distinctive business. But the object of this sketch is more especially to speak of the many innovations he has made in dental practice from time to time. Being of an inventive turn of mind and of tireless industry, he has been constantly bringing new and valuable methods and ideas into practical use. Bridge and crown work, which was one of the first of his inventions, gave him a world-wide reputation. His great work for the benefit of mankind

JAMES E. LOW, D. D. S.

has given him a place in dental science which will never be forgotten; and he may well be placed in the front rank as one of the benefactors of mankind. He is always popular with his students and patrons, as well as his many assistants. His broad spirit and great energy have enabled him to bring his view before the people; and to-day he has the satisfaction of seeing them extensively incorporated into the practice of the profession.

His office, which is located in the First National Bank Building, 164 Dearborn street, where it has been since the completion of the building, is well patronized by a class of appreciative customers, who knowingly seek his valuable services.

www.ingramcontent.com/pod-product-compliance
Lightning Source LLC
Chambersburg PA
CBHW021938160426
43195CB00011B/1139